FAIR GAME?

FAIR GAME?

The Use of Standardized Admissions Tests in Higher Education

Rebecca Zwick

ROUTLEDGEFALMER
New York and London

Published in 2002 by
RoutledgeFalmer
29 West 35th Street
New York, NY 10001

Published in Great Britain by
RoutledgeFalmer
11 New Fetter Lane
London EC4P 4EE

RoutledgeFalmer is an imprint of the Taylor & Francis Group.

Printed on acid-free, 250-year-life paper.
Manufactured in the United States of America.
Design and typography: Jack Donner

10   9   8   7   6   5   4   3   2   1

Library of Congress Cataloging-in-Publication Data

Zwick, Rebecca.
    Fair game? : the use of standardized admissions tests in higher education
    / by Rebecca Zwick
        p. cm.
    Includes bibliographical references.
    ISBN 0-415-92559-2 — ISBN 0-415-92560-6 (pbk.)
        1. Universities and colleges—United States—Entrance examinations.
        2. Universities and colleges—United States—Admission. I. Title.

    LB2353.2 .Z95 2002
    378.1'617—dc21
                                            2001048564

CONTENTS

PREFACE

At about three or four o'clock in the morning of the examination day . . . a cannon shot sounded with a deafening roar. That was the signal for the students . . . to rise and prepare themselves . . . [L]ater, there was a second shot, at which the candidates left their quarters to go to the examination hall. With each one carrying in a basket everything needed for the examination—an inkstone as flat and light as possible, a first-class ink stick, brushes, lunch, water, and the like—they assembled before the gates. . . . Soon, at the third sounding of the cannon, the great doors were opened . . . and the candidates . . . surged in a crowd into the hall.

—From a description of nineteenth-century testing
in *China's Examination Hell* by Ichisada Miyazaki

Standardized tests have been around since 200 B.C., according to some historians, but after 2,000 years their ability to evoke strong reactions remains undiminished. This is especially true of standardized admissions examinations, which have been controversial since their debut in the United States 100 years ago.

Admissions tests have long been viewed as a major barrier to higher education for people of color. "The SAT is very effective at eliminating academically promising minority (and low-income) students . . . , " says a 1998 report from the National Center for Fair and Open Testing.[1] "If the College Board were truly public-spirited, it would abolish the SAT immediately," says another commentary.[2] And a recent opinion piece noted that "[a] persistent institutional faith in cognitive tests such as the GRE and LSAT . . . has . . . worsened the problems of widening access to graduate and professional education."[3]

Obviously, some politicians and educators are listening. Texas recently passed a bill limiting the use of standardized tests in graduate and professional school admissions, and several other states, as well as the U.S. Congress, have considered legislation to restrict or ban standardized tests. Public universities in Texas, California, and Florida now fill a portion of their freshman slots with students selected on the basis of their high school class rank, with no consideration of their test scores. And the president of the University of California announced in 2001 that he'd like to abandon the SAT completely, contending that reliance on test scores is "not compatible with the American view on how merit should be defined and opportunities distributed."[4]

But that's only one side of the public dialogue. According to a recent commentary by two Washington attorneys, test scores are "the single most reliable predictor of academic success for students from all racial, ethnic, social, and economic backgrounds. . . . The SAT was introduced . . . to help colleges . . . identify bright students . . . who might otherwise be overlooked because of their poor economic and educational backgrounds."[5] And in their widely praised book, *The Shape of the River*, former college presidents William G. Bowen and Derek Bok assert that, "far from being biased *against* minority students, standardized admissions tests consistently predict higher levels of academic performance than most blacks actually achieve."[6]

Standardized admissions tests—the SAT in particular—continue to play a prominent role in many arenas, despite the controversy. Newspapers present admissions test results as evidence of educational achievement trends, colleges publicize their SAT averages as evidence of their selectivity, real estate brokers offer the local high school's test results as an index of neighborhood quality, and the National Collegiate Athletic Association uses admissions test scores to decide which freshmen get to play on sports teams. Standardized admissions tests can also have an extraordinary impact on the prospective test-takers themselves; according to a cover story in the *New York Times Magazine*, the SAT serves as "an almost mystical barometer for self worth" for American high school students. [7]

Admissions tests, it seems, have come to occupy a central role in the national psyche. On one hand, they're portrayed as an evil that should be purged from our society; on the other, they're viewed as a trustworthy measure of the academic standing of students, schools, and communities— perhaps even the quality of American education. But despite the onslaught of publicity about standardized admissions tests, few people outside the rarefied world of psychometrics—the statistical analysis of test scores— know much about the procedures used to develop, score, and evaluate these tests. The purpose of *Fair Game* is to demystify the world of standardized admissions testing and to present a commonsense view of the important testing policy issues that we face today. Tests—like any method of allocating scarce resources—will always be the subject of public scrutiny, and that is as it should be. All too often, though, discussions of testing rely more on politics or emotion than on fact. This book was written with the aim of equipping the contestants in the inevitable public debates with some solid information about testing.

Fair Game focuses on the primary standardized tests used today in admissions decisions in colleges, graduate schools, and professional schools:

for college entrance, the SAT and ACT (now regarded as test names in their own right, rather than as acronyms); and for admission to graduate and professional school, the Graduate Record Examinations (GRE), Medical College Admission Test (MCAT), Law School Admission Test (LSAT), and Graduate Management Admission Test (GMAT). Much more research and media attention have been devoted to the SAT—often viewed as the quintessential standardized test—than to any of these other tests, and the amount of discussion in this book is correspondingly greater.

Tests that are not discussed in any detail here include the PSAT/NMSQT (formerly the Preliminary Scholastic Aptitude Test), which serves as a practice SAT for high school sophomores and juniors and is used in awarding National Merit Scholarships, the PLAN assessment (formerly the P-ACT+), which is billed as a "pre-ACT" test and is typically administered to high school sophomores, and the Test of English as a Foreign Language, which is required of foreign students who attend U.S. colleges or graduate schools. Supplementary admissions tests that focus on particular areas of study— the SAT II: Subject Tests and the GRE Subject Tests—are discussed only briefly.

Among the questions that *Fair Game* tackles are these:

- How much do tests count in admissions decisions today?

- What analyses do testing companies use to judge the quality of tests?

- Can a test be fair if average scores are higher for some racial groups than others, or higher for men than women?

- What is a computerized adaptive test? Are computerized tests fair?

- What impact do coaching schools have on the fairness and usefulness of tests?

- How do testing companies identify and stop test cheaters?

- Why is it misleading to use SAT results to measure the nation's educational achievement?

- Would eliminating standardized admissions tests increase ethnic diversity on our campuses?

- How can standardized tests and admissions procedures be improved in the future?

What's the ultimate message of *Fair Game*? Testing is not the great boon to society that the first president of Educational Testing Service (ETS) thought it to be when he proclaimed the "urgent need for a census of human abilities ... [to] provide a basis for realistic planning on a nationwide scale, in peace or war."[8] Nor is it the dangerously addictive drug, the crooked yardstick, the racist scourge to which its opponents allude. Like age, weight, cholesterol level, or any other measurement, test scores are incomplete and imperfect—they fail to tell us the whole story about the assessed individuals, and they are subject to error. Test scores can be used in ways that are reasonable or misleading, can be invoked to support policies that are wise or foolhardy, and can serve as both gateway and gatekeeper. In short, tests are intrinsically neither good nor evil. When evaluated in a balanced and thoughtful way, standardized test scores can provide information that is useful in admissions decisions. I hope that *Fair Game* will help to replace polemics and incendiary rhetoric with a more even handed, common sense attitude toward standardized tests.

A Note about Racial and Ethnic Designations

In referring to racial and ethnic groups in this book, I have maintained the group labels used in the original sources of data. Sources differ widely in their treatment of racial and ethnic designations, not only in terms of labels, but also in terms of how each group should be defined, and how refined the classification should be. It was therefore not possible to achieve a unified presentation while also preserving the integrity of the original material.

In addition, I have not drawn a sharp distinction between the terms "race" and "ethnicity," though this distinction is considered important by some scholars. In general, I use the term "ethnic groups" as shorthand for "groups defined on the basis of race and ethnic background."

ACKNOWLEDGMENTS

It is impossible to catalog the contributions of my research assistant, Pam Freitas, to *Fair Game*. Pam sought out obscure books and articles in cyberspace and on dusty library shelves, checked dozens of facts, provided insightful comments on the manuscript, which she read cover-to-cover (twice), compiled endless lists of references, and created the index. And she did all this with an amazing calm and grace. I offer her my deepest thanks.

I am indebted to the University of California, Santa Barbara for providing the supportive environment that made the book possible. I am thankful as well to Nancy Petersen of ACT, Inc. for her thorough and perceptive review of the manuscript and to my other key testing program contacts, who reviewed portions of Chapter 1 and generously shared materials: Ellen Julian (MCAT), Anne Ninneman (SAT), Kathy O'Neill (GRE), and Lynda Reese (LSAT). I also greatly appreciate the contributions of the colleagues who took the time to provide detailed comments on individual chapters: Henry Braun, Brent Bridgeman, Nancy Burton, Neil Dorans, Carol Dwyer, Cynthia Hudley, Patricia McAllister, Bill Mehrens, Don Powers, and Mark Reckase.

I would like to thank Jeffrey Sklar for his work in producing graphics for the book; Amy Darlington, Tracy Smith, Lorraine Carmosino, and Tim Corlis for their invaluable assistance with ETS archive materials, photographs, and permissions; and the countless people who helped by sending materials, answering questions, or providing other forms of support, including Richard Backer, Luz Bay, Hunter Breland, Robert Brennan, Pamela Burnett, Walter Haney, Mary Hegarty, H. D. Hoover, Ernie Kimmel, Judy Koenig, Dan Koretz, Judy Kowarsky, Ida Lawrence, Louis Roussos, Amy Schmidt, Linda Shapiro, Martha Stocking, Dorothy Thayer, Steven Velasco, Cathy Wendler, Warren Willingham, and Rob Woolfolk.

I am most grateful to my able editor, Joe Miranda, for his invaluable guidance throughout the publication enterprise, and to the other individuals who participated in the editing process, Floyd Rogers, Ben McCanna, Jeanne Shu, and the untiring Paul Foster Johnson, editorial assistant *par excellence*. Finally, I would like to thank Heidi Freund, who first encouraged me to pursue this project.

CHAPTER 1

Today's Standardized Admissions Tests

How Did They Come to Be?

If you wanted a job with the Chinese Imperial Civil Service any time after 200 B.C., you had to take a test.[1] In fact, you had to undergo an elaborate selection process with several rounds of examinations that could take years. These tests covered a lot of territory—not only history, philosophy, and literature, but also calligraphy, poetry, and painting. Because a civil service post could assure both income and prestige, families often invested in years of special tutoring for promising test candidates. In just a single round of testing, these men might spend several exhausting days working until dark in a silent and forbidding examination hall. After the tests were completed, the ordeal still wasn't over. The names of successful candidates were posted in public, leading to dishonor for those unfortunates who were not listed. For some men, efforts to pass the tests extended over a decade or more. In their later attempts, they shaved their beards and gave phony ages, hoping to pass themselves off as youths.

Standardized testing had its beginnings in these Chinese civil service assessments. University admissions tests have a much shorter history, although there is some disagreement about the time and location of the first such test. Admissions testing may have had its debut in eighteenth-century France. The idea of admitting students to universities based on test scores, rather than privilege, was certainly compatible with the principles of equality that characterized the French Enlightenment. One historical account describes the Enlightenment philosophy this way: "[B]efore God, each individual is one among equals, no matter what his background or social class. If . . . [European class-consciousness] inhibited natural man's potential for creative self-expression, government should actively intervene. . . ."[2] Another account of the history of testing alludes to an earlier French admissions test—a Sorbonne entrance examination that was required in the thirteenth century.[3] And a 1998 College Board publication titled "Why Hispanic Students Need to Take the SAT" says that "the idea of testing students for college admission has Hispanic roots. It was in Madrid in 1575 that a scholar ... proposed that the king establish an examination board to determine university admission."[4] Most historians agree that admissions testing had been instituted in Germany and England by the mid-1800s. It's interesting that in most countries, the use of tests to get *out* of universities preceded the use of tests to get *in*. In the early part of the nineteenth century, when Oxford and Cambridge established stricter examination procedures for graduation, it was still the case that anyone who had the money could get into these prestigious universities.

Standardized admissions testing first took root in the United States during the early part of the twentieth century. In 1900, only about 2 percent of 17-year-olds—more than three-quarters of them men—went on to receive a college degree.[5] Those applying to college at the turn of the century were faced with a bewildering array of admissions criteria. Course requirements and entrance examinations differed widely across schools. In an attempt to impose order on this chaos, the leaders of 12 top Northeastern universities formed the College Entrance Examination Board in 1900. The College Board created a set of examinations that were administered by the member institutions and then shipped back to the Board for painstaking hand scoring. Initially, the Board developed essay tests in nine subject areas, including English, history, Greek and Latin; it later developed an exam that contained mostly multiple-choice questions—the Scholastic Aptitude Test. This precursor to today's SAT was first administered in 1926 to about 8,000 candidates.

The first SAT consisted of questions similar to those included in the Army Alpha tests, which had been developed by a team of psychologists for use in selecting and assigning military recruits in World War I. These Army tests, in turn, were directly descended from IQ tests, which had made their first U.S. appearance in the early 1900s. (It's clear, though, that the Alpha test questions were revised with the military in mind. A sample arithmetic problem: "A certain division contains 5,000 artillery, 15,000 infantry, and 1,000 cavalry. If each branch is expanded proportionately until there are in all 23,100 men, how many will be added to the artillery?")[6] The relationship between the Army Alpha and the SAT is just one example of the interplay between the educational testing world and the U.S. military, which today boasts the world's largest testing program.[7] The needs of the military fueled the growth of standardized testing in the United States in several ways. In World War II, as in World War I, tests played a role in screening individuals for military service and assigning them to jobs. During this period, the College Board and the Iowa Testing

Programs, which would later spawn the testing company ACT, Inc., helped the military develop personnel tests. Although the publicity about wartime testing was not always favorable, it produced a surge of interest by educational institutions.

World War II also fueled an expansion in the use of standardized testing by creating an urgent need for well-trained individuals who could be recruited into the military; this led to an increased emphasis on college study in the United States. And the passage of the GI Bill in 1944 sent thousands of returning veterans to college, boosting the popularity of the efficient multiple-choice SAT. Between 1940 and 1950, the number of college degrees granted more than doubled, to about 400,000.[8]

Between the wars, another development was to have a major impact on the testing enterprise—the automatic scoring of tests. Beginning in 1939, the monumental task of scoring the SAT, which had once required many hours of training and tedious clerical work, was done by a machine. This change transformed testing from an academic venture to a bona fide industry. The stage was now set for the birth of Educational Testing Service.

ETS, currently the largest U.S. testing organization, was founded in Princeton, New Jersey, in 1947 through the merger of the testing activities of the College Entrance Examination Board, the Carnegie Foundation for the Advancement of Teaching, and the American Council on Education. These companies had painstakingly negotiated the terms of their union over a period of ten years. (All three continue to exist as separate organizations.)

Although its original facilities were modest, with printing presses and collating machines nestled among water pipes and boilers, ETS was to be no mere test factory, according to Henry Chauncey, the first president. "[T]he new organization will make important contributions to American education," he said, "through developing . . . tests of the highest standards, by sponsoring distinguished research . . . and by providing effective advisory . . . services to schools and colleges."[9]

The 1949–50 ETS annual report gives an idea of the astonishing optimism about testing that prevailed at that time. The report, by Henry Chauncey, sounds stunningly naive from today's perspective: "[W]ith respect to knowledge of individuals, the possibilities of constructive use [of tests] are far greater than those of misuse. Educational and vocational guidance, personal and social adjustment most certainly should be greatly benefited. Life may have less mystery, but it will also have less disillusionment and disappointment."[10] According to the report, " . . . [T]he field of testing is exceedingly broad and the opportunities for ETS almost limitless."[11]

Henry Chauncey at work in 1947.
Photographed by Orren Jack Turner, Princeton, NJ. Reprinted by permission of Educational Testing Service.

Henry Chauncey (second from left) and General Lewis B. Hershey (far right) in a 1951 radio broadcast on "Youth and the Draft."
Photographed by Del Ankers, Washington, D.C. Reprinted by permission of Educational Testing Service.

After World War II, the military continued to have an influence on the development of the testing industry. ETS was awarded a contract in 1951 to develop the Selective Service College Qualification Test—the exam used to determine whether college students would be allowed to defer their military service. (This exam, consisting of 150 mathematical and verbal questions, was surely the ultimate in high-stakes testing.) With this lucrative contract in hand, ETS could make the transition from shaky newborn to well-established company.[12]

The Early Test Promoters:
Sinister Pseudo-Scientists or Egalitarian Do-Gooders?

As test critics like to point out, the beliefs held by some of the early proponents of standardized testing were nothing short of abhorrent. Consider Carl Brigham, an early College Board advisor for whom the library building at ETS's countryside headquarters south of Princeton is named. Although he later famously recanted, Brigham, who has been called "the father of the SAT," sounds like an almost absurd caricature of bigotry in his early writings. Based on his extensive analysis of test results collected solely from (male) Army recruits during World War I, Brigham published a number of conclusions. First, immigrants were less intelligent than native-born Americans, and each succeeding wave of immigrants was less intelligent than the last. (He explicitly rejected the explanation that newer immigrants scored lower because they were less familiar with English.) Second, Americans of Nordic heritage were superior in intelligence to those of Alpine or Mediterranean heritage. In particular, Brigham noted that his data "would rather tend to disprove the popular belief that the Jew is highly intelligent. . . . The able Jew is popularly recognized not only because of his ability, but because he is able and a Jew."[13] (This sounds a lot like Samuel Johnson's quip: "A woman's preaching is like a dog's walking on his hinder legs. It is not done well; but you are surprised to find it done at all.") And finally, American intelligence was expected to deteriorate rapidly if action was not taken to halt a particularly "sinister" form of immigration, "the importation of the negro."[14] Ironically, Brigham himself remarked that "it is difficult to keep racial hatreds and antipathies out of the most scholarly investigations in this field."[15]

A particularly vivid account of the racist tendencies of some progenitors of standardized testing appears in Stephen Jay Gould's *The Mismeasure of Man*. Although he concedes that testing may be acceptable for some "limited practical purposes," Gould largely views the testing of cognitive capabilities as a successor to craniometry—the attempt to relate skull and brain measurements to intelligence—and other scientifically flawed efforts to reinforce the existing social structure through "objective" study. These misguided endeavors, says Gould, are based on the "general proposition . . . that society follows nature, and that social rank reflects innate worth."[16] Gould offers a compelling criticism of two related beliefs that, he says, typify the viewpoint of supporters of intelligence tests (the ancestors of standardized admissions tests). The more fundamental of these is the assumption that test scores represent something real: "a single scalable thing in the head called general intelligence." Second is the belief that intelligence is determined genetically and therefore cannot be improved.[17]

As unpalatable as these views are to many, do they justify discarding the entire concept of standardized testing? Not necessarily. Here's what one eminent scientist had to say about Charles Darwin's attitudes on Blacks and women, which are undeniably offensive from a modern viewpoint: "How can we castigate someone for repeating a standard assumption of his age, however much we may legitimately deplore that attitude today? . . . I cannot excoriate individuals who acquiesced passively in a standard societal judgment." Ironically, this articulate argument against judging yesterday's leaders by today's standards was made by none other than Stephen Jay Gould.[18] But some test critics believe that today's SAT remains tainted by the views of its early promoters: " . . . [A]lthough much of the blatant racism of the early part of this century has been attenuated, the elitist values and assumptions embedded in the origins of the SAT persist," according to a University of California professor.[19] But before undertaking a wholesale rejection, it's important to consider that some early testing devotees had benign or even egalitarian motives, and that few in the testing profession today share the beliefs criticized by Gould.

According to a historical account of educational testing in a 1992 congressional report, "It was not just the hereditarians and eugenicists who were attracted to such concepts as 'intelligence' and the 'measurement' of mental ability; many of the early believers in the measurement of mental . . . processes were progressives, egalitarians, and communitarians committed to the betterment of all mankind."[20] As we saw earlier, the French also viewed the introduction of "objective" admissions tests in the 1700s as an egalitarian alternative to the status quo—a way to fight entrenched privilege. Some modern-day commentators see the SAT this way too. For example, according to Harvard professor Christopher Jencks, "[t]he SAT was developed . . . to help selective colleges identify 'diamonds in the rough'—talented students from mediocre high schools who performed poorly on traditional achievement tests because they had not studied the relevant subject matter."[21]

Even Gould singles out Alfred Binet, the French psychologist who is the father of the Stanford-Binet IQ test, as a test developer with an honorable motive—to improve the education of children. Although Binet "flirted with craniometry" in the late 1800s, he later focused on the identification of children who needed special instruction and argued against the "brutal pessimism" of the belief that intelligence cannot be increased through education.[22]

Another staunch supporter of equal opportunity was James Bryant Conant, the Harvard president who in the late 1930s promoted the idea that the leading U.S. testing agencies be merged into a single centralized company, and who eventually became the first chairman of the ETS board of trustees.[23] In a series of *Atlantic Monthly* articles in the early 1940s, Conant—whose name, like Brigham's, adorns an ETS building—cautioned against the development of a caste system in America and argued for a fluid society in which people's roles would be determined by their merit.[24] Conant continued to be an advocate of educational reform throughout his career. In a 1964 book, he deplored the continued existence of segregated schools and the "deep-seated pattern of racial discrimination ... in housing and in employment," and called for an educational policy that would "mitigate [the] evil influence" of racial prejudice.[25]

Even Brigham, after collecting several years' worth of data on immigrants, revised his opinions, not only on minority groups, but also on the entire testing enterprise. Seven years after his 1923 book, *A Study of American Intelligence*, he published an article on intelligence testing in immigrant groups. He described two problems that, he said, had led to misleading results in his earlier analyses. First, he had added together the scores on the eight components of the Army Alpha, which included such diverse tests as Arithmetical Reasoning, Practical Judgment, Analogies, and Disarranged Sentences. (The practice of combining scores was particularly problematic in Brigham's research since it obscured the role of language skills in the performance of foreign-born test-takers.) In some analyses, the combined Alpha score was added to the score on other tests, such as the Stanford-Binet IQ test. In his 1930 article, Brigham pronounced such analyses "akin to adding apples and oranges" and therefore meaningless. In a passage that is in some ways strikingly modern, Brigham also critiqued his earlier failure to understand the issue of native language: "For purposes of comparing individuals or groups, it is apparent that tests in the vernacular [i.e., American English] must be used only with individuals having equal opportunity to acquire the vernacular of the test. . . . Comparative studies of various national and racial groups may not be made with existing tests. . . . [O]ne of the most pretentious of these comparative racial studies—the writer's own—was without foundation."[26]

The sharp distinction between the bigotry of Carl Brigham's early writings and the egalitarian stance of James B. Conant is reflected in the dual perceptions of the role of testing that exist today: To some, standardized testing is a cruel and capricious gatekeeper that bars the road to advancement; to others, it's a golden gateway to opportunity.

What Admissions Tests Are Used in Higher Education Today?

Let's take a brief look at the SAT, GRE, MCAT, LSAT, GMAT, and ACT (described here in order of development). At the end of the chapter are tables summarizing basic information about these tests. Each table gives the content areas and types of questions included in the test, along with important events in the test's history.[27] The tables also include the most recent score results for key groups of test-takers, which we will explore in later chapters.

Today's SAT

The current version of the SAT (now officially called the SAT I: Reasoning Test) is claimed to measure "developed verbal and mathematical reasoning abilities related to successful performance in college." (Originally, "SAT" stood for "Scholastic Aptitude Test," which was later changed to "Scholastic Assessment Test." Now, "SAT" is no longer considered to be an acronym, but the actual name of the test.) All the verbal questions and most of the math questions are multiple-choice; each SAT also includes a few math questions that require "student-produced" answers—there are no response choices. When they register for the SAT, students can choose to complete the Student Descriptive Questionnaire, which asks about course background, interests, and plans. This information is then passed on to the colleges to which students send their scores.

The SAT program also includes the SAT II: Subject Tests (formerly the College Board Achievement Tests), which assess the candidates' knowledge in particular areas. Over twenty SAT II tests are available, including Writing (which contains an essay), World History, Mathematics, Biology, Chemistry, Physics, French, Spanish, Chinese, and Modern Hebrew.

The GRE, LSAT, and MCAT

The ETS calendar of testing programs for 1949–50 listed twenty-two distinct exams—quite an impressive array for a brand-new company. In addition to some tests that have now faded into obscurity—"Knights of Columbus" and "National College Home Economics Testing Program"— were the Graduate Record Examinations, the Medical College Admission Test, and the Law School Admission Test; three of today's principal admissions tests for graduate and professional school were already in existence fifty years ago.[28]

The Graduate Record Examinations program of the Carnegie Foundation for the Advancement of Teaching administered its first exam in 1937. The "Profile Tests" (as the fledgling GRE was called) consisted of assessments in eight areas, including literature and fine arts as well as math, science, and verbal skills. In 1948, the GRE program was transferred to the newly formed ETS. Today, the GRE is developed and administered by ETS under the direction of the Graduate Record Examinations Board, an independent sixteen-member committee that is affiliated with the Association of Graduate Schools and the Council of Graduate Schools. The exam is available in test centers around the world.

The GRE General Test, says the test bulletin, "measures verbal, quantitative, and analytical skills that have been acquired over a long period of time and are not related to any specific field of study." ("Analytical" scores were first provided in 1985.) In addition to the General Test, fourteen GRE Subject Tests (formerly called the Advanced Tests) measure achievement in particular areas, ranging from engineering and computer science to music and literature. In 1999, a new GRE test (separate from the General or Subject tests) was introduced—the Writing Assessment. This new test, which consists of two analytical writing tasks, was "developed in response to the interest expressed by the graduate community for a performance-based assessment of critical reasoning and analytical writing." The GRE program has announced that the Writing Assessment will replace the Analytical section as part of the General Test in October 2002.

The GRE was the first major admissions test to be administered as a *computerized adaptive test* (CAT). In chapter 3, we'll explore how CATs work; in chapter 7, we'll take a look at the test security problems that made the GRE's transition to CAT status somewhat bumpy.

The MCAT, sponsored by the Association of American Medical Colleges, began in 1946 as the Professional Aptitude Test. (An earlier medical school admission test, called the Scholastic Aptitude Test for

Medical School or the Moss Test, was used between 1930 and 1946.) ETS inherited the MCAT program (along with the GRE) from the Carnegie Foundation and continued to develop and administer the test until 1960. The MCAT contract then began a nomadic period, migrating first to The Psychological Corporation, then to ACT, Inc. In the 1990s, it returned briefly to ETS. Today, the test is administered by ACT, Inc. Another (undisclosed) contractor is responsible for test development and scoring. Sponsorship and overall responsibility for the test, however, have always resided with the AAMC, which now represents about 140 medical schools, 400 teaching hospitals, and various academic societies and medical professionals. (Lest the role of the AAMC be overlooked, the MCAT candidate booklet warns that "the AAMC owns all test results, including examinees' scores.")

As described in an MCAT bulletin, the test assesses skills and concepts "identified by physicians and medical educators as prerequisite for the practice of medicine" including "mastery of basic concepts in biology, chemistry . . . and physics; facility with scientific problem solving and critical thinking; and writing skills." The MCAT, which was overhauled in 1991, now consists of three multiple-choice sections— Verbal Reasoning, Physical Sciences, and Biological Sciences—as well as a writing sample composed of two essay questions.

The LSAT was conceived at a 1947 meeting between College Board staff and representatives of an association of nine law schools. This group of institutions, the precursor of the Law School Admission Council, wanted an SAT-like test that would be appropriate for use by law schools. In 1948, the first LSAT was administered by ETS, which had just assumed responsibility for the testing activities of the College Board. Since 1979, however, the LSAT has been developed by the LSAC itself, which today has nearly 200 member institutions in the United States and Canada. Portions of the work have been contracted out to other companies; the test is now developed and administered with the assistance of ACT, Inc. The test is "designed to measure skills that are considered essential for success in law school: the reading and comprehension of complex texts with accuracy and insight; the organization and management of information and the ability to draw reasonable inferences from it; the ability to reason critically; and the analysis and evaluation of the reasoning and argument of others," according to an information brochure. All questions are multiple-choice except a 30-minute writing sample, which is not graded, but is sent to the law schools to which the candidate applies.

The GMAT

In the late 1940s and early 1950s, the GRE was used to screen business school applicants. In 1953, however, representatives of nine graduate schools of business agreed that they needed an admissions test of their own. They commissioned a feasibility study by ETS, and a year later the first Admission Test for Graduate Study in Business—later renamed the Graduate Management Admission Test[29]—was administered. The sponsoring organization for the GMAT is the Graduate Management Admission Council, whose membership has grown from the original nine schools in 1953 to more than 100 schools of business and management today.

The 1954 business school test included four sections—Verbal, Quantitative, Best Arguments, and Quantitative Reading. Today's GMAT, according to its information bulletin, "measures general verbal, mathematical, and analytical writing skills that are developed over a long period of time.... The GMAT does not presuppose any specific knowledge of business ... [and] does not measure achievement in any particular subject area." Since 1997, the GMAT has been a CAT, like the GRE. (A record number of test-takers—about 85,000—flocked to the last paper-and-pencil administration.) The verbal and math items are multiple-choice; the writing skills section, added in 1994, requires the test-taker to key in responses to two questions, with half an hour allowed for each. The GMAT essay scoring procedures have made a big splash because computers, as well as humans, participate in the grading. We'll take a closer look at this novel approach in chapter 3.

The ACT

In 1959, ETS acquired a competitor in the college admissions test market. The American College Testing Program was begun in Iowa City "with no equipment and not even one full-time employee," according to the organization's own description.[30] (Today, the test is simply "ACT," and the company is "ACT, Inc." Like "SAT," "ACT" is no longer considered an acronym.) ACT, Inc. was founded by E. F. Lindquist, a University of Iowa statistician and a man of many talents. Lindquist was the director of the Iowa Testing Programs, which started the first major statewide testing program for high school students. As an expert in standardized testing, he served on ETS's first advisory committee on tests and measurements. Remarkably, he was also the inventor, with Phillip Rulon of Harvard, of the "Iowa scoring machine." Unveiled at a conference sponsored by rival ETS in 1953, this device was the first to use electronic scanning techniques (rather than simply a mechanical approach) to score test answer sheets.

The founding of ACT, Inc. was, in fact, closely tied to the development of this test scoring machine, "a marvel of blinking panels backed by a forest of cables that could ingest pulsations and emit a record of achievement from the brief encounter of small black marks on paper and the photocells in a reading head."[31] In 1953, Lindquist formed the not-for-profit Measurement Research Corporation, which was to continue the development of test processing systems and offer services to other testing programs. ACT, Inc., in turn, was a spin-off of the MRC and the Iowa Testing Programs.[32]

Why start a new college admissions testing program? In Iowa testing circles, the SAT was considered to be geared toward the elite institutions of the East, and its developers were viewed as sluggish and resistant to change. From the beginning, the ACT was somewhat different from the SAT in terms of underlying philosophy: While the SAT consisted only of verbal and mathematical sections, the ACT was more closely tied to instructional objectives. The original version of the ACT had four sections—English, Mathematics, Social Studies Reading, and Natural Sciences Reading. It's no coincidence that these subject areas were also included in the Iowa Tests of Educational Development, which had been used to assess Iowa high schoolers since 1942. In fact, because of scheduling constraints, the very first ACT was constructed from the same pool of test items that was being used to assemble new forms of the ITED. In its early years, the ACT was administered primarily in Midwestern states, but it is now used much more widely.

The content of the ACT is based on an analysis of what's taught in grades 7 through 12 in each of four areas—English, math, reading, and science reasoning. Educators are consulted to determine which of these skills they consider necessary for students in college courses. All questions are multiple-choice. The information bulletin notes that "test passages and questions used in the ACT Assessment are deliberately chosen to reflect the range of cultures in our population."

As well as being more strongly linked to instructional goals than the SAT, the ACT also places a greater emphasis on facilitating course placement and academic planning.[33] In keeping with this goal, the ACT registration booklet includes a survey about the student's educational and vocational accomplishments and plans, an interest inventory, and a questionnaire on high school courses and grades.

Admissions Testing in 2000 and Beyond

Testing companies and advocacy groups alike repeatedly warn schools to use test scores as only one of several factors in admissions. As we will see in chapter 2, most colleges, graduate schools, and professional schools evidently heed this warning and consider other criteria, particularly grades, along with test scores. It seems equally clear, though, that the use of standardized admissions testing is pervasive at the undergraduate and graduate levels, and is especially well entrenched at professional schools. Ninety percent of colleges and universities require either the ACT or SAT, the majority of Ph.D. programs either recommend or require the GRE General Test, and nearly all medical, law, and business schools use standardized admissions tests as a key factor in admissions decisions.

The overwhelming role of standardized tests in determining access to higher education inevitably—and appropriately—gives rise to questions about the fairness and validity of the tests and about the accountability of the test makers. But tackling these complex issues in any but the most superficial way requires a basic understanding about how tests are developed, scored, and used, and about how the tests themselves are assessed. All too often, the public debate about standardized tests is based on fuzzy and incomplete notions about these fundamental facts. The goal of the chapters that follow is to shed some light on this shadowy landscape.

SAT I: Reasoning Test

BASIC INFORMATION

This is the test we usually call "the SAT." Originally, "SAT" stood for "Scholastic Aptitude Test," which was later changed to "Scholastic Assessment Test." Now, "SAT" is no longer considered to be an acronym, but the actual name of the test. (The SAT program also includes the SAT II: Subject Tests, formerly the College Board Achievement Tests, which measure knowledge in particular subject areas.)

Purpose: To evaluate candidates for college admission

Organizations: Developed and administered by Educational Testing Service, Princeton, New Jersey, for the College Board, New York. Websites: www.ets. org, www.collegeboard.org, www.collegeboard.com

Main sections and item types: Mathematical (multiple-choice, except for ten "student-produced response" items for which no answer choices are offered; see "Significant events," below) and Verbal (multiple-choice). Students receive a math score and a verbal score. (When they register for the SAT, students can choose to complete the Student Descriptive Questionnaire, which asks about demographic background, course preparation, interests and plans.)

First administered: 1926

Approximate number of candidates tested per year: more than 2 million

Significant events:

1994—A major change in the SAT I was implemented. Some math items that are not multiple-choice were introduced; they require students to compute the answer rather than merely select the correct answer from several alternatives. Also, an earlier prohibition on the use of calculators was lifted. In addition, antonym items were eliminated from the verbal section, reading comprehension items were made more complex, and sentence completion items were introduced. (An early plan to include an essay section in the SAT I was dropped, but a writing test that includes an essay component was incorporated in the SAT II: Subject Tests.)

1995—The score scales for the Mathematical and Verbal sections (and for the SAT II: Subject Tests) were "recentered" so that a score of 500 would represent an average score for each section, as in the original SAT. Post-recentering scores are not comparable to pre-recentering scores without adjustment. (See chapter 3 for more on recentering.)

SAT I: Reasoning Test—SAMPLE ITEMS

(from *Taking the SAT I: Reasoning Test,* 1999–2000 edition, published by The College Board and ETS, 1999)

Verbal (Sentence completion item)

Despite Atlanta's large Black community, African American theater companies in that city are anything but _____ ; in fact, in 1993 there was only one, Jomandi Productions.

    (A) legion *[correct answer]*
    (B) advantageous
    (C) bourgeois
    (D) nondescript
    (E) wily

Mathematical (This is a student-produced response item; no response choices are offered. Calculator use is permitted on all math items.)

In a certain group of 1,000 students, 20 percent have reached the voting age of 18. If 60 percent of those 18 or older are registered to vote, how many students in the entire group are registered to vote?   *[correct answer: 120]*

SAT test questions reprinted by permission of the College Entrance Examination Board, the copyright owner. Permission to reprint SAT materials does not constitute review or endorsement by Educational Testing Service or the College Board of this publication as a whole or of any other questions or testing information it may contain.

SAT I: Reasoning Test—AVERAGE SCORES (College-Bound Seniors, 2001)*

Test Section	Male	Female	Total
Verbal	509	502	506
Mathematical	533	498	514
Number of Test-Takers	592,366	683,954	1,276,320

Test section	American Indian or Alaskan Native	Asian, Asian-American, or Pacific Islander	African-American or Black	Mexican or Mexican-American	Puerto Rican	Latin, South, or Central American, other Hispanic or Latino	White
Verbal	481	501	433	451	457	460	529
Mathematical	479	566	426	458	451	465	531
Number of Test-Takers	7,622	102,312	120,506	46,849	14,074	40,249	703,724

*SAT verbal and mathematical scores range from 200 to 800. In the above results for the total group, the standard deviation (average distance of a score from the average score) was 111 for verbal scores and 113 for math scores. Results are from *2001 College-Bound Seniors*, published by the College Board (2001).

ACT

BASIC INFORMATION

"ACT" formerly stood for "American College Testing"; now, the acronym itself is considered to be the name of the test.

Purpose: To evaluate candidates for college admission, to aid in course placement and academic planning

Organizations: Developed by ACT, Inc., Iowa City, IA. Website: www.act.org

Main sections and item types: English, Mathematics, Reading, and Science Reasoning. Students receive a score in each subject area, as well as a composite score. Seven subscores are also reported—two in English, three in Mathematics, and two in Reading. All test questions are multiple-choice. (In addition to its four main sections, the ACT includes questionnaires on high school courses and grades, educational and career aspirations, extracurricular activities, and educational needs, as well as an inventory of occupational interests.)

First administered: 1959

Approximate number of candidates tested per year: 1.7 million

Significant events:

1989—A new version of the ACT was introduced which incorporated major changes in the test content. The original ACT had sections called English Usage, Mathematics Usage, Social Studies Reading, and Natural Sciences Reading. The "enhanced" ACT assessment, released in 1989 and still in use, includes the sections described above. At the same time, the scoring of the test was changed (see chapter 3). Scores on the original ACT cannot be compared with scores on the enhanced ACT without adjustment.

ACT—SAMPLE ITEMS

(from *Preparing for the ACT Assessment 1999–2000*, published by ACT, Inc., 1999)

English (This item is part of a passage editing task.)

Currently, six billion bank notes <u>are now</u> printed annually.

F. NO CHANGE
G. are, at this time,
H. are   *[correct answer]*
J. are presently

Mathematics (Calculators are permitted.)

Anna wants to completely cover the rectangular ceiling of her room with soundproof tile so she can play her stereo as loudly as she wants. Her ceiling is 16 feet long and 10 feet wide. The tiles are 2-feet-by-2-feet squares. How many tiles does Anna need to cover her ceiling with one layer of soundproof tiles?

F. 20
G. 26
H. 40   *[correct answer]*
J. 52
K. 80

Reading (Only the relevant portion of the reading passage is given here.)

In the last couple of decades, Victorian houses have been enjoying a renaissance. Recent generations raised on the skim milk of modern architecture lately have acquired a taste for the butterfat and flamboyance of late 19th century design.

As it is used [above], the phrase "skim milk of modern architecture" apparently describes modern architecture's:

F. dependence on late-nineteenth-century design.
G. lack of financial support.
H. excess of detail.
J. austere and minimal style.   *[correct answer]*

Science Reasoning (Only the relevant portion of the passage is given here.)

A biologist observed that a specific wildflower species was found in a forest and not in the adjacent meadows. The forests and meadows both had the same soil types and had rabbits which eat many plants including the wildflowers. Seeds of the wildflower were observed in both habitats. To further investigate the growth of this wildflower, the biologist collected 10 seeds from each of 100 randomly selected plants of this species and thoroughly mixed them for planting in the spring.

(continued)

Experiment 1

One hundred sites, each approximately one meter square, were selected: 50 sites in the forest and 50 sites in the meadow. Half of each site was cleared of existing vegetation. The other half was left undisturbed. The same number of wildflower seeds was planted in each half. After 12 weeks the resulting wildflower plants were dried and weighed.

Which of the following factors was controlled by the biologist in Experiment 1?

    A. Plant mass
    B. Soil moisture
    C. Presence of rabbits
    D. Presence of neighboring plants *[correct answer]*

ACT test questions selected from Preparing for the ACT Assessment, 1999–2000. *Reprinted by permission of ACT.*

ACT—AVERAGE SCORES (High School Graduating Class of 2001)*

Test Section	Male	Female	Total
English	20.0	20.8	20.5
Mathematics	21.4	20.2	20.7
Reading	21.1	21.5	21.3
Science Reasoning	21.6	20.6	21.0
Composite	21.1	20.9	21.0
Number of Test-Takers	459,547	604,808	1,069,772

Test Section	African-American	American Indian	Caucasian	Mexican-American	Asian-American	Puerto Rican/Hispanic
English	16.2	17.8	21.3	17.5	20.7	18.6
Mathematics	16.8	18.4	21.3	18.7	23.1	19.4
Reading	16.9	19.2	22.2	18.6	21.1	19.7
Science Reasoning	17.2	19.3	21.8	18.8	21.5	19.5
Composite	16.9	18.8	21.8	18.5	21.7	19.4
Number of Test-Takers	112,924	11,386	763,377	42,414	36,267	17,302

*ACT English, Mathematics, Reading, Science Reasoning, and Composite scores range from 1 to 36. In the above results for the total group, the standard deviation (average distance of a score from the average score) was 4.7 for the Composite score and ranged from 4.6 to 6.0 for the four individual test sections. The total sample size exceeds the sample sizes given for men and women because some test-takers do not provide gender information. Results are from *2001 ACT National and State Scores: Selections from the 2001 National Score Report*, available at www.act.org.

Graduate Record Examinations General Test (GRE)

BASIC INFORMATION

The GRE General Test was formerly called the GRE Aptitude Test. (The GRE program also includes the GRE Subject Tests, formerly known as the Advanced Tests, and the GRE Writing Assessment.)

Purpose: To evaluate candidates for admission to graduate school

Organizations: Developed by Educational Testing Service, Princeton, New Jersey, for the Graduate Record Examinations Board. Website: www.gre.org

Main sections and item types: Verbal, Quantitative, and Analytical sections, all scored separately. All items on the General Test are multiple-choice.

First administered: 1937

Approximate number of candidates tested per year: 360,000

Significant events:

1985—The Analytical section became an official part of the General Test.

1993—The computerized adaptive test (CAT) version of the GRE was instituted.

1999—The paper-and-pencil GRE was discontinued (except limited administration to address access issues).

1999—The GRE Writing Assessment (which is separate from the General and Subject tests) was introduced. The GRE program has announced that in October 2002, the Writing Assessment will be incorporated into the GRE General Test, replacing the Analytical section.

GRE—SAMPLE ITEMS

(from *Preparing for the GRE General Test*, published by ETS, 1999)

Verbal Ability

The _____ science of seismology has grown just enough so that the first overly bold theories have been _____.

    (A) magnetic . . accepted

    (B) fledgling . . refuted *[correct answer]*

    (C) tentative . . analyzed

    (D) predictive . . protected

    (E) exploratory . . recalled

Quantitative Ability

In a certain year, Minnesota produced $2/3$ and Michigan produced $1/6$ of all the iron ore produced in the United States. If all the other states combined produced 18 million tons that year, how many million tons did Minnesota produce that year?

(A) 27   (B) 36   (C) 54   (D) 72   *[correct answer]*   (E) 162

Analytical Ability

The greatest chance for the existence of extraterrestrial life is on a planet beyond our solar system. This is because the Milky Way galaxy alone contains 100 billion other suns, many of which could be accompanied by planets similar enough to Earth to make them suitable abodes of life.

The argument above assumes which of the following?

(A) Living creatures on another planet would probably have the same appearance as those on Earth.

(B) Life cannot exist on other planets in our solar system.

(C) If the appropriate physical conditions exist, life is an inevitable consequence.

(D) More than one of the suns in the galaxy is accompanied by an Earth-like planet.

(E) It is likely that life on another planet would require conditions similar to those on Earth.   *[correct answer]*

GRE test questions selected from Preparing for the GRE General Test, 1999. *Reprinted by permission of Educational Testing Service, the copyright owner. Permission to reprint GRE materials does not constitute review or endorsement by Educational Testing Service of this publication as a whole or of any other testing information it may contain.*

GRE—AVERAGE SCORES (1999–2000 Test-Takers)*

Test Section	Male	Female	Total
Verbal	470	461	465
Quantitative	634	537	578
Analytical	576	551	562
Number of Test-Takers	144,129	195,202	339,331

Test Section	American Indian	Asian/ Pacific	Black/ African	Mexican- American	Puerto Rican	Other Hispanic	White
Verbal	453	480	392	428	402	437	490
Quantitative	485	610	419	479	475	487	547
Analytical	513	571	427	488	465	491	572
Number of Test-Takers	1,466	10,821	21,208	5,352	2,451	5,548	183,419

*GRE Verbal, Quantitative, and Analytical scores range from 200 to 800. In the above results for the total group, the standard deviation (average distance of a score from the average score) was 116 for the Verbal score, 147 for the Quantitative score, and 141 for the Analytical score. Ethnic group results are based on United States citizens only. Results are from *Sex, Race, Ethnicity, and Performance on the GRE General Test 2001–2002*, published for the Graduate Record Examinations Board by ETS (2001).

Medical College Admission Test (MCAT)

BASIC INFORMATION

Originally called the Professional Aptitude Test.

Purpose: To evaluate candidates for admission to medical school

Organizations: Today, the test is administered by ACT, Inc. for the Association of American Medical Colleges. Another (undisclosed) contractor is responsible for test development and scoring. Website: www.aamc.org

Main sections and item types: Verbal Reasoning, Physical Sciences, Biological Sciences (all multiple-choice), and a Writing Sample consisting of two essay questions. All four sections are scored separately.

First administered: 1946

Approximate number of candidates tested per year: 55,000

Significant events:

1991—A major revision of content and scoring was implemented, and the Writing Sample was added to the test.

MCAT—SAMPLE ITEMS

(from the *MCAT 1999 Announcement*, published by the Association of American Medical Colleges, 1999)

Verbal Reasoning (Only the relevant portion of the passage is given here.)
A naturalist, of course, must have style these days if he hopes to be read by any but the specialists. Interest in Nature is declining, to say the least. Bedichek knew this and lamented it; Dobie and Webb knew it too, and they too lamented it. Indeed, the note of lamentation for Nature Despoiled is sounded so many times in the twenty-nine volumes [written by the three] that it comes near achieving the opposite of its intended effect. After a time one begins to wonder if man's divorce from nature is really as bad and as belittling as they make it out to be.

The "intended effect" mentioned in line [6] most likely refers to:

A. the despoilment of nature.

B. divorce from nature.

C. concern for nature.   *[correct answer]*

D. the enjoyment of books.

Physical Sciences

Light moving through a medium encounters a second medium that has a smaller index of refraction. If the angle of incidence is greater than the critical angle, what happens to the light after it reaches the interface?

    A. It is totally reflected.   *[correct answer]*

    B. It is totally absorbed.

    C. It is totally transmitted.

    D. It is partly transmitted and partly absorbed.

Writing Sample (30 minutes allowed)

Consider this statement:

No matter how oppressive a government, violent revolution is never justified.

Write a unified essay in which you perform the following tasks. Explain what you think the above statement means. Describe a specific situation in which violent revolution might be justified. Discuss what you think determines whether or not violent revolution is justified.

Biological Sciences

The quaternary ammonium ion $(CH_3CH_2)_4N^+$ undergoes elimination when treated with a strong base, forming ethane and triethylamine. However, the ion $CH_3CH_2N_3^+$ does not undergo elimination under similar conditions. This difference in reactivity is primarily a result of the fact that:

    A. $CH_3CH_2N_3^+$ will protonate the base.   *[correct answer]*

    B. $CH_3CH_2N_3^+$ is resonance stabilized, but $(CH_3CH_2)_4N^+$ is not.

    C. $(CH_3CH_2)_4N^+$ will protonate the base.

    D. $(CH_3CH_2)_4N^+$ is resonance stabilized, but $CH_3CH_2N_3^+$ is not.

MCAT test questions selected from the MCAT 1999 Announcement. *Reprinted by permission of the Association of American Medical Colleges.*

MCAT—AVERAGE SCORES (April and August 2000 administrations)*

Test Section	Male	Female	Total
Verbal Reasoning	7.8	7.7	7.8
Physical Sciences	8.7	7.7	8.2
Biological Sciences	8.7	8.0	8.3
Writing Sample	0	0	0
Number of Test-Takers	26,140	28,655	54,808

Test Section	White	Black	Mexican/American/ Chicano	Puerto Rican Commonwealth	Asian	Other Hispanic
Verbal Reasoning	8.3	6.0	6.9	4.6	7.6	7.2
Physical Sciences	8.4	6.3	7.1	5.4	8.9	7.5
Biological Sciences	8.6	6.3	7.3	5.3	8.8	7.8
Writing Sample	0	N	0	K	0	0
Number of Test-Takers	31,495	5,116	1,222	951	11,351	1,282

*MCAT Verbal Reasoning, Physical Sciences, and Biological Sciences scores range from 1 to 15. The Writing Sample is scored on an alphabetic scale ranging from J (lowest) to T (highest). In the above results for the total group, the standard deviation (average distance of a score from the average score) was 2.4 for the three numerical scores. In the upper table, the total sample size exceeds the sample sizes given for men and women because some test-takers do not provide gender information. In the lower table, results for ethnic groups with fewer than 500 members were not included here. Results were provided by an AAMC assistant vice president, Ellen Julian, March 2001.

Law School Admission Test (LSAT)

BASIC INFORMATION

Purpose: To evaluate candidates for admission to law school

Organizations: Developed and administered by the Law School Admission Council with the assistance of ACT, Inc. Website: www.LSAC.org

Main sections and item types: Four sections serve as the basis for a single score: one Reading Comprehension, one Analytical Reasoning, and two Logical Reasoning sections (all multiple-choice). A 30-minute writing sample is also included; it is not scored but is sent to the law schools to which the candidate applies.

First administered: 1948

Approximate number of candidates tested per year: 100,000

Significant events:

1982—A writing sample was added to the LSAT. (Other writing assessments had been included in earlier versions of the LSAT.)

1991—The LSAT score scale was changed to the current 120–180 scale.

1995—LSAC embarked on a research program to help decide whether the LSAT should become a computerized adaptive test.

LSAT—SAMPLE ITEMS

(from *LSAT & LSDAS Registration Information Book 1999–2000*, published by Law School Admission Council, 1999)

Reading Comprehension (Only the relevant portion of the passage is given here.)

In *Invisible Man*, Ellison's protagonist, like Ellison in his early life, experiments with a variety of roles. As he assumes new roles, each a result of racial pressure, he realizes paradoxically that while his options should be decreasing, they are actually increasing. Most frightening to him is the prospect that there might be innumerable roles for him to play, that the perception of "infinite possibilities" would become the terrifying perception of chaos; he might, in other words, be without any permanent "form."

Which one of the following terms could best be substituted for the word "chaos" (line [5]) without changing the author's meaning?

  (A) racial pressure

  (B) literary incoherence

  (C) contradictory roles

  (D) limited identity

  (E) unstable identity   *[correct answer]*

Analytical Reasoning

From a group of seven people—J, K, L, M, N, P, and Q—exactly four will be selected to attend a diplomat's retirement diner. Selection conforms to the following conditions:

> Either J or K must be selected, but J and K cannot both be selected.
>
> Either N or P must be selected, but N and P cannot both be selected.
>
> N cannot be selected unless L is selected.
>
> Q cannot be selected unless K is selected.

If P is not selected to attend the retirement dinner, then exactly how many different groups of four are there each of which would be an acceptable selection?

(A) one

(B) two

(C) three   *[correct answer]*

(D) four

(E) five

Logical Reasoning

Electrons orbit around the nucleus of an atom in the same way that the Earth orbits around the Sun. It is well known that gravity is the major force that determines the orbit of the Earth. We may, therefore, expect that gravity is the main force that determines the orbit of an electron.

The argument above attempts to prove its case by

(A) applying well-known general laws to a specific case

(B) appealing to well-known specific cases to prove a general law about them

(C) testing its conclusion by a definite experiment

(D) appealing to an apparently similar case   *[correct answer]*

(E) stating its conclusion without giving any kind of reason to think it might be true

Writing Sample (30 minutes allowed)

The Citizens' Association of Winchester is deciding whether to renovate the town's original Park and Shop shopping center or to demolish and replace it. Write an argument favoring one plan over the other based on the following guidelines.

- The association wants to increase the variety of shops and services in the neighborhood by attracting new merchants to the area.

(continued)

- The association wants the building to remain a center of community-oriented activity for residents of the neighborhood.

One proposal calls for renovating the Park and Shop by adding two stories to the existing structure for additional shops and a restaurant. The original two-story structure surrounded by thirty parking spaces, currently houses twelve family-owned businesses, including a gift shop, a bakery, a hardware store, and a small clothing boutique. The building also houses the offices of a doctor, an attorney, and a dental group. It is architecturally undistinguished, but it blends well with the neighborhood, and every Saturday morning, a section of the parking lot is used for a flea market where people from the neighborhood come to buy crafts and fresh produce. The current shop-owners are not likely to be able to afford the rent if the center is demolished and a new building is constructed.

The other proposal is to demolish the existing Park and Shop and replace it with a six-story building that features a dramatic forty-foot atrium and an underground parking garage. The top two floors of the new structure will be used for offices, the ground floor will house a four-screen movie theater, and the remaining floors will be used for clothing and jewelry stores, exotic gift shops, and the like. Three "open air" restaurants, each with an ethnic theme, will surround the atrium on the first floor. The developer has agreed to provide a large room on the ground floor rent-free for ten years for community art work and projects.

LSAT test questions selected from the LSAT & LSDAS Registration Information Book, 1999–2000. *Reprinted by permission of the Law School Admission Council.*

LSAT—AVERAGE SCORES (1999–2000 Test-Takers)*

	Male	Female	Total
LSAT Score	150.8	149.3	150.0
Number of Test-Takers	42,778	44,074	86,887

	African-American	Native American	Asian-American	Caucasian	Hispanic	Mexican-American	Puerto Rican
LSAT Score	141.6	147.2	151.3	152.1	146.4	147.4	138.5
Number of Test-Takers	9,841	712	6,190	58,901	3,538	1,620	2,366

*LSAT scores range from 120 to 180. In the above results, the standard deviation (average distance of a score from the average score) within the test-taker groups is reported to range from 8.3 to 9.9. The total sample size exceeds the sample sizes given for men and women because some test-takers do not provide gender information. Results have been excluded for the Canadian Aboriginal group, which had only 57 members. Results are from "LSAT Performance with Regional, Gender, and Ethnic Breakdowns: 1993–1994 through 1999–2000 Testing Years," by Susan P. Dalessandro, Lisa C. Anthony, and Lynda M. Reese, Law School Admission Council Technical Report 00–01, 2001.

Graduate Management Admission Test (GMAT)

BASIC INFORMATION

The test was originally called the Admission Test for Graduate Study in Business. It was renamed the GMAT in 1976.

Purpose: To evaluate candidates for admission to graduate school in business and management

Organizations: Developed and administered by Educational Testing Service, Princeton, New Jersey, for the Graduate Management Admission Council. Website: www.gmac.com

Main sections and item types: Verbal (multiple-choice), Quantitative (multiple-choice), and Analytical Writing (essay). Separate scores are reported for each section; a total score that reflects performance on the Verbal and Quantitative sections (but is not the total of the Verbal and Quantitative scores) is also reported.

First administered: 1954

Approximate number of candidates tested per year: 200,000

Significant events:

1994—The Analytical Writing Assessment was added to the test.

1997—Administration of computerized adaptive GMAT began; last paper-and-pencil version of GMAT was given.

GMAT—SAMPLE ITEMS

(from the *GMAT Information Bulletin*, published by the Graduate Management Admission Council, 1999)

Verbal (Critical reasoning item)

Since 1975 there has been in the United States a dramatic decline in the incidence of traditional childhood diseases such as measles. This decline has been accompanied by an increased incidence of Peterson's disease, a hitherto rare viral infection, among children. Few adults, however, have been affected by the disease.

Which of the following, if true, would best help to explain the increased incidence of Peterson's disease among children?

(continued)

(A) Hereditary factors determine in part the degree to which a person is susceptible to the virus that causes Peterson's disease.

(B) The decrease in traditional childhood diseases and the accompanying increase in Peterson's disease have not been found in any other country.

(C) Children who contract measles develop an immunity to the virus that causes Peterson's disease. *[correct answer]*

(D) Persons who did not contract measles in childhood might contract measles in adulthood, in which case the consequences of disease would generally be more severe.

(E) Those who have contracted Peterson's disease are at increased risk of contracting chicken pox.

Quantitative (Problem solving item)

One-third of the rooms in the Chateau Hotel have a harbor view, and the rate for each of these is 1.2 times the rate for each of the remaining 180 rooms. If the rate for the rooms without a harbor view is d dollars per day, what is the hotel's maximum income, in dollars, from room rentals for one day?

(A) 204d (B) 234d (C) 240d (D) 270d (E) 288d *[correct answer]*

Analytical Writing Assessment
("Analysis of an Argument" item; 30 minutes allowed)

The following appeared as part of an article in a daily newspaper.

"The computerized onboard warning system that will be installed in commercial airliners will virtually solve the problem of midair plane collisions. One plane's warning system can receive signals from another's transponder—a radio set that signals a plane's course—in order to determine the likelihood of a collision and recommend evasive action."

Discuss how well reasoned you find this argument. In your discussion be sure to analyze the line of reasoning and the use of evidence in the argument. For example, you may need to consider what questionable assumptions underlie the thinking and what alternative explanations or counterexamples might weaken the conclusion. You can also discuss what sort of evidence would strengthen or refute the argument, what changes in the argument would make it more logically sound, and what, if anything, would help you better evaluate its conclusion.

GMAT—AVERAGE SCORES (1999–2000 Test-Takers)*

	Male	Female	Total
GMAT Total Score	543	505	528
Number of Test-Takers	115,808	73,290	190,264

	White (non-Hispanic)	Black/ African American	Asian/ Asian American	Mexican-American/ Chicano	Puerto Rican	Other Hispanic/ Latin American/ Latino	American Indian/ Alaskan Native/ Other Native American
GMAT Total Score	538	428	541	480	461	479	496
Number of Test-Takers	70,795	8,195	8,248	1,526	779	2,784	614

*GMAT total scores range from 200 to 800. In the above results, the standard deviation (average distance of a score from the average score) within the test-taker groups is reported to range from 90 to 110. The total sample size exceeds the sample sizes given for men and women because some test-takers do not provide gender information. Results are from *Profile of Graduate Management Admission Test Candidates*, published by the Graduate Management Admission Council (2000).

CHAPTER 2

The Big Picture

How Are Standardized Tests Used in Admissions Decisions?

"Like a drug addict who knows he should quit, America is hooked. We are a nation of standardized testing junkies."[1] That's according to a 1997 article in *Change* magazine. Another recent article says that the "Scholastic Assessment Test is the most influential test in American life— a key to the doors of the nation's best public and private colleges."[2] A paper commissioned by the National Research Council reports that the number of four-year colleges requiring either the SAT or ACT held steady at slightly over 90 percent between 1979 and 1992, and the number of students taking either of these tests increased from about half of those graduating from high school in 1979 to about two-thirds of the 1998 graduates.[3] Standardized admissions test scores crop up everywhere—not only in the assessment of the test candidates themselves but also in the evaluation of neighborhoods, high schools, colleges, and state education systems.

But neither standardized tests nor any other academic criteria need be part of the admissions decision—their usefulness depends entirely on the goal of our admissions policies. As Robert Klitgaard, a public policy professor at Harvard, pointed out in his thought-provoking 1985 book, *Choosing Elites*, "[t]he first question to ask about selective admissions is why it should be selective at all." We have mixed feelings about selectivity, Klitgaard says; the down side is that "[s]electivity has unpleasant connotations of elitism, unfairness, snobbishness, and uniformity." So, if we assume that it is not realistic for colleges to simply expand the number of available places to accommodate all applicants, how should we allocate the limited number of slots? If we wanted all applicants to have equal access to an education at the college of their choice, a "first come, first served" policy, or even a <u>lottery</u> should be acceptable procedures for selecting an entering class.[4] Although a lottery does provide equal access, most people find this solution unreasonable precisely *because* it is blind to all student characteristics. Here, the flip side of society's ambivalent attitude toward selectivity emerges: "[W]e laud excellence, recognize its scarcity and utility, and endorse admissions on the basis of merit rather than ascriptive characteristics." The lottery seems unfair because it does not reward academic excellence, unusual motivation, or hard work.

One argument for selectivity in college admissions is that it encourages high schools to provide a quality education. The same argument could be extended to the graduate and professional school admissions process. But most institutions are selective for a more immediate reason: They consider it desirable to admit candidates who are likely to be able to do the academic work required of them, and they use standardized admissions tests, along with other criteria, in an attempt to identify these candidates.

For most people, the words "standardized testing" conjure up an image of overwrought, sleep-deprived candidates filing into a classroom and using No. 2 pencils to "bubble in" the answers to an interminable series of multiple-choice questions. But as we will soon see, standardized admissions tests include essays and other questions that require candidates to write out their own responses. And as more and more exams switch to computer administration, bubble answer sheets are becoming far less common. *What makes a test "standardized" is that it's administered and scored under uniform conditions. This means that candidates are given either the same test or alternative versions of the test that have been designed to yield comparable scores.* With some special exceptions (like providing Braille test forms to blind candidates), testing programs arrange for all test-takers to receive the same instructions, to operate under the same testing conditions and time constraints, to have the same opportunities to ask questions, and to be assigned a score using the same procedures. A typical state driver's exam is a standardized test, with both a written section and a performance component—the road test. Though driver's tests are susceptible to some of the same criticisms that are made about admissions tests, their legitimacy is rarely questioned, perhaps because the danger of allowing an incompetent driver on the streets is considerably more compelling than the risk of sending an unpromising student to college.

Are Admissions Tests Really IQ Tests?

We've already seen that the SAT is the grandchild of the intelligence test (with the Army Alpha test of World War I serving as the intermediate generation). And the GRE, MCAT, LSAT, and GMAT, with their links to the College Board and ETS, are certainly cousins of the SAT. Are *all* these tests essentially IQ tests?[5] And what about the ACT, which has a different lineage? At a glance, it's not always easy to tell an "intelligence" test from an "achievement" test. Both, for example, may include algebra problems, questions based on reading passages, and assessments of vocabulary. And testing experts have not been particularly helpful in clarifying the niche that admissions tests are intended to fill. Consider the ever-changing name of the best-known admissions test, which evolved from "Scholastic Aptitude Test" to "Scholastic Assessment Test," only to be simplified, ultimately, to "SAT"—now deprived of its acronym status. Similar confusion reigns about the GRE. While a 1960 document from the ETS archives says that its purpose is "to offer standardized evaluation of student learning in college," a 1965 archival note says the GRE is intended "to assist in appraising intellectual qualities of individual candidates."

IQ tests carry a lot of baggage. They conjure up the idea of an inborn unchangeable characteristic that determines whether we will succeed in life. They're associated with the views of the eugenicists of the early twentieth century and are often considered racist. The simmering controversy about the relationship between admissions tests and IQ tests emerged again in 1999, following the publication of *The Big Test: The Secret History of the American Meritocracy*. At times, author Nicholas Lemann seemed to suggest that the SAT is an IQ test that has been disguised as a more benign type of test through a sophisticated conspiracy. As Henry Chauncey, the first president of ETS, remarked, Lemann "doesn't say precisely that it is an IQ test. . . . But he always goes back to talking about IQ tests, so readers get the impression that the SAT measures native ability, which of course, it doesn't."[6]

In many ways, the "IQ test versus achievement test" debate is a tempest in a teapot. As sociologist Christopher Jencks has noted, "Many people—including federal judges—think that both intelligence and aptitude are innate traits. . . . Yet almost all psychologists now agree that while an individual's score on an intelligence or aptitude test depends partly on his or her genetic makeup, it also reflects a multitude of environmental influences."[7] So while it's true, as Chauncey noted, that the SAT doesn't measure pure "native ability," neither do intelligence tests. Labeling tests as measuring "intelligence" or "achievement" is useful primarily as a way of conveying the focus of the test's content. Achievement tests and intelligence tests can be considered endpoints of a continuum, with exams that focus on specific course material lying closer to the "achievement test" pole, while those that are less reliant on mastery of particular content fall near the "intelligence test" end.

Where do our six admissions tests lie on the aptitude-achievement continuum? The content of the SAT (now officially called the SAT I: Reasoning Test; see chapter 1) is not tied to particular high school courses. Instead, the SAT is claimed to measure "developed verbal and mathematical reasoning abilities related to successful performance in college," although its content is influenced to some degree by trends in curriculum and instructional practices. The GRE General Test, GMAT, and LSAT are similar to the SAT: I in that they too focus on verbal, math, and reasoning skills rather than course content.[8]

On the other hand, the content of the ACT is based on an analysis of what's actually taught in grades 7 through 12 in each of four areas of "educational development"—English, math, reading, and science reasoning.[9] The MCAT, which was previously more of a general ability test, now includes an assessment of candidates' knowledge of material taught in undergraduate biology, chemistry, and physics courses. The ACT and MCAT, then, are more like achievement tests, while the rest of these exams might be characterized as tests of academic aptitude (though the phrase "developed abilities" is in vogue at the moment). But even though the ACT is not a mere clone of the SAT, scores on these two tests are highly correlated, meaning that they would order candidates in nearly the same way.[10] And although the ACT and the SAT are somewhat different in content, their sponsors present the same evidence for the tests' value: They are useful for predicting academic achievement in college. In fact, even though the types of test questions differ, the primary role of all admissions exams is essentially the same—to predict a candidate's academic performance—usually defined in terms of first-year grade-point average—in a future educational program.

How Are College Admissions Decisions Made Today?

In the imagination of the public, the recipe for making admissions decisions goes something like this: Using standardized test scores and possibly a dash of other measures of academic performance, create a giant rank-ordered list of candidates. Then adjust the list as needed to boost the rankings of individuals covered by affirmative action; star athletes; and children of big-time donors, prominent alumni, and friends of the university president. When the list is done, start at the top and admit as many as you have room for.

The procedures at certain large schools may, in fact, bear some resemblance to this picture. But viewed more broadly, the college admission process is more complex and less reliant on test scores than most people think. The sorting procedure actually starts with the applicant, who decides where to apply. This decision is likely to be based on a combination of academic factors (for example, the school has an outstanding reputation or a great program in music) and nonacademic ones (the school is close to—or possibly far from—the applicant's home). Today, this step often involves the use of web-based search facilities, which allow the prospective student to obtain lists of colleges that meet his criteria at the click of a mouse. If the candidate picks one of the "open-door" colleges that make up 11 percent of four-year institutions, all that's required is to complete an application and, in some cases, show proof of high school graduation. But suppose the applicant prefers not to attend an open-admissions school. Since about 65 percent of four-year institutions admit at least three-quarters of their applicants, chances of getting admitted somewhere are still quite good.[11]

College selectivity

How important are test scores in the admissions process? Although their role has reached mythic proportions in our collective imagination, the actual influence of standardized tests on admissions decisions may be far less, at least at the undergraduate level. A College Board survey found that only 46 percent of four-year colleges considered test scores to be a "very important" factor in admissions decisions; by comparison, 87 percent rated high school achievement as very important.[12] A recent investigation of the role of tests in admissions, conducted by the California Postsecondary Education Commission, also yielded some relevant results. This study of 1996 graduates of California public high schools showed that only 2.5 percent of the grads were declared ineligible to attend the University of California solely because they had inadequate test scores. About three-quarters of the grads were ineligible because of deficiencies in their course backgrounds.[13] (See chapter 5 for more detail.) Unfortunately, inadequacies in course background, which are remediable through changes in educational policies and instructional practices, tend to attract far less public attention than test scores.

Nonacademic Factors

"We should take care not to make intellect our god; it has, of course, powerful muscles, but no personality." So said Albert Einstein in 1950. Everyone agrees that academic performance shouldn't count for everything in admissions decisions, but controversy always arises about which other factors to consider and how much weight they should carry. To what degree should we take into account the broader contributions an applicant could make? For example, how important is it for the campus to maintain a diversity of talents, fields of study, and geographical backgrounds? How valuable are leadership qualities and commitment to community service?

And of course, there is the perennially inflammatory issue of race. Under what circumstances, if any, should racial preferences be allowed? Many argue against race-based affirmative action on the grounds that the admissions system should return to a presumed "natural state," in which decisions are based entirely on academic merit. But of course, a purely merit-based approach has never existed. In particular, exceptions have always been made for two categories of applicants: athletes and children of alumni or of wealthy potential donors. The actions of the regents of the University of California in 1998 provide a pointedly ironic illustration: Three years after the regents voted to prohibit UC from taking ethnicity and gender into account in the admissions process, they reaffirmed the right of the university to make exceptions to the established admissions criteria for the children of wealthy or influential parents.[14] And the 1996 Hopwood decision (discussed later in this chapter), which banned the use of race in admissions decisions in Texas, Louisiana, and Mississippi, explicitly stated that a university *was* allowed to "favor one applicant over another because of his ability to play the cello," or "make a downfield tackle," or even because of his "relationship to school alumni."[15]

Affirmative action to achieve gender equity in college admissions has also been in the news of late—not to promote the admission of women, but to increase the number of men. For several years, the University of Georgia, where women constitute a sizable majority, gave a preference to men in making admissions decisions about borderline candidates.[16] The practice was discontinued in 1999, after a White female applicant filed a lawsuit. Figures from 1997 showed that 55 percent of four-year-college students were women.[17] This gender imbalance has prompted some contentious discussions of whether preferences for men ought to be implemented on a nationwide basis. One presenter at the 2000 annual meeting of the National Association for College Admission Counseling called the question of affirmative action for men "the issue that dare not speak its name."[18]

Despite these deep-seated controversies about admissions, there are some areas of consensus. Few would argue about the desirability of admitting the kid from the projects who won the statewide science fair, the student who started his own computer consulting business in high school, or the violinist who made her Carnegie Hall debut at age ten. A frequent argument about the SAT and ACT is that they are of little help in identifying these talented applicants (who may have mediocre test scores), nor are they of any use in weighing diversity considerations against academic performance. This is indeed true, which is why colleges use many factors other than test scores in the admissions process. Most colleges have committed themselves to professional standards like the *Statement of Principles of Good Practice* of the National Association for College Admissions Counseling. The principles declare that minimum test scores should not be the sole criterion for admission, and that test scores should be used "in conjunction with other data such as school record, recommendations, and other relevant information. . . ."[19]

What nonacademic aspects of a candidate's qualifications are likely to be considered today? One high school counselor described the screening process this way: "[C]olleges . . . need to fill the positions that will make the college community run. As one director of admissions put it, 'If I need a quarterback, I'm going to get one.' Beyond quarterbacks, those people the admissions dean will want to find include legacies [children of alumni]; leaders for school publications, student government, and other areas of student life; children of influential families; musicians, athletes, public speakers, and others with special talents; and students from under-represented ethnic groups and geographical areas."[20]

In a 1997 "tell-all" book, Michele A. Hernández describes admission procedures at Ivy League schools, based on her experiences as assistant admissions director at Dartmouth (a position from which she resigned before publication). Hernández says that among the Ivies, one factor that's likely to work against an applicant is a privileged background: "Despite the fact that most people are convinced that wealth, fame, and position in society will be looked upon as positive factors in the Ivy League admissions process, this is simply not the case anymore . . . [C]oming across as a preppy, well-off kid will work against you. . . ."[21]

"The best thing you can do if you come from a privileged background," she adds later, "is to deemphasize it as best you can."[22] She even suggests that applying for financial aid could boost the likelihood of admission.[23] Hernández also discusses affirmative action, attesting that "[i]n the case of the minority applicant, there appears to be no hard-and-fast cutoff—in terms of class rank, test scores, or [academic index]—that automatically disqualifies him from consideration." Still, she acknowledges that, for every accepted minority applicant with below-average academic credentials, "there is an accepted White recruited athlete or accepted legacy with equally low scores and rank."[24]

In fact, in the 2000 presidential campaign, two contenders—both White and male—were described as affirmative action beneficiaries.

Princeton allegedly admitted Bill Bradley despite a mediocre verbal SAT score (485) because he could play basketball; George W. Bush reportedly got into Yale despite his less-than-stellar verbal score (566) because he was the son and grandson of prominent alumni.[25]

Processing of College Applications

Schools differ vastly in their procedures for considering applications, even within the same university system. Consider the 1999 admissions procedures at two of the University of California's nine campuses, San Diego and Berkeley.[26]

UC San Diego's admissions decisions are driven primarily by grades and test scores. A staff of about 25 in a room stuffed with more than 32,000 applications tackled the task of selecting the top 13,250, to yield an entering class of 3,300. The candidates' grades and test scores, along with information about courses they had taken, were combined into a single index by computer according to a prescribed formula. A list was then generated in which candidates were ranked by index score. Half of those admitted were chosen by simply accepting the top 6,625 on the list. Choosing the remaining admits involved consideration of nonacademic as well as academic factors. Readers spent about five minutes per folder determining whether the applicant had demonstrated unusual leadership qualities or an extraordinary ability to overcome hardship. Applicants also got points for being a potential first-generation college student, a member of a low-income family, or pupil at a disadvantaged school. These nonacademic factors were combined with the academic index into a single score, again using an established formula, and applicants were selected according to their rank on this combined score.

At UC Berkeley, 600 miles away, the monumental task of admissions involved selecting about 8,200 students out of the roughly 31,000 who applied. Nearly half of the applicants had a high school GPA of at least 4.0.[27] In an effort to consider the candidates' achievements in light of their educational opportunities and challenges, each admissions folder was reviewed and evaluated by at least two people out of a team of more than 50 readers.

Each reader assigned two scores to each folder—an academic score and a comprehensive score. The readers didn't use a predetermined formula to obtain the scores, but were given a list of factors to consider. The academic score, which ranged from 1 to 7, was based on courses taken, grades, test scores, academic awards or honors, and other "evidence of intellectual or creative achievement." The applicant's accomplishments were evaluated relative to the performance of other applicants in the same high school. The comprehensive score, which ranged from 1 to 5, was based on everything in the student's file, including academic achievement, demographic characteristics, "employment or community service; demonstrated leadership qualities and concern for others and for society; and likely contributions to the intellectual and cultural vitality of the campus."[28]

Half the freshman slots were filled on the basis of the academic score; the other half were filled using the comprehensive score. Berkeley's approach, which does not involve prescribed cutoffs for grades or test scores and does not assign weights to particular admissions criteria, is a substantial departure from the formulaic admissions procedures that are common at large public universities. This doesn't mean Berkeley's selection process is less rigorous than San Diego's, however. In 1999, San Diego admitted 85 percent of the applicants with high school GPAs of 4.0; Berkeley admitted only about half of those who achieved a 4.0.[29]

The ACT versus the SAT

"Which college-entrance test is *required* by more four-year private colleges? The ACT. Which test is *preferred* by more four-year public universities? The ACT." Yes, as these excerpts from the ACT, Inc. website illustrate, there *is* a bit of competition between the creators of the ACT and the makers of the SAT. Over 2 million kids take the SAT each year, compared with about 1.7 million for the ACT. But that's not the only way to assess the relative importance of the tests. For example, the ACT, Inc. website claims that there are 25 states in which at least 55 percent of the high school grads take the ACT and only 17 states in which at least 55 percent take "another college entrance exam."[30] Using somewhat different criteria, a 1995 article in the *Journal of College Admission* reported that the ACT is "dominant" in 21 states (primarily in the Midwest and South); the SAT is dominant in another 21 (mostly in the Northeast or West), plus the District of Columbia. Eight states are listed as "neutral."[31]

Although this has not always been true, the tests are now used almost interchangeably by the majority of institutions. What do colleges do when some applicants submit ACT scores and others submit SAT scores? ACT scores can be "translated" to the SAT scale (or vice versa), based on analyses of scores from candidates who took both tests. The linkage, however, is only an approximate one. Because the content of the tests is not identical, the association between SAT and ACT scores may not be the same for all types of test-takers. In particular, the relationship between the scores will depend on whether the test-takers have been exposed to the curricular content in the ACT. Nevertheless, to allow at least rough comparisons to be made, colleges and testing companies create tables of "concordance" between ACT and SAT scores (usually between the ACT composite and the sum of SAT verbal and math scores). The most recent large-scale effort to produce one of these concordance tables was undertaken jointly by researchers from ETS and ACT, Inc., using data from more than 100,0000 students who took the tests between 1994 and 1996.[32]

How Are Graduate and Professional School Admissions Tests Used?

On the graduate and professional school level, the admissions process is quite different from its undergraduate counterpart.[33] Graduate and professional school programs tend to be smaller, and admissions policies less formalized and less public. Decisions are typically in the hands of faculty, rather than admissions officers, and although a great deal of self-selection by applicants takes place, admission rates tend to be much lower than at undergraduate institutions.

Doctoral Admissions: The GRE

Admissions policies and rates vary widely over the hundreds of fields of doctoral study available in the United States. Decisions tend to be made by faculty at the department level, and procedures are typically very flexible. As a 1997 College Board report noted, "published statements about [doctoral] admissions provide ample latitude for almost any decision."[34]

A recent study of 48 leading graduate schools examined admissions rates in 1990 and 1991 for doctoral programs in biochemistry, economics, English, mathematics, and mechanical engineering. Counter to stereotype, English was the most selective of these five disciplines, accepting only 20 percent of its applicants in 1991, while math, with a 1991 admission rate of 47 percent, was the least choosy.[35] The study also found that the participating graduate programs gave "substantial preference in all fields to underrepresented minorities [African Americans, Hispanic Americans and Native Americans] over other U.S. citizens,"[36] indicating that affirmative action principles were being invoked. In all five fields, women were at least as likely to be admitted as men with similar credentials; in mechanical engineering, the evident preference for women was quite large.

Although there is wide variation across schools and fields of study, surveys have shown that the majority of grad programs require or recommend the GRE General Test, and use it in combination with undergraduate grades and other factors. Some schools require certain GRE Subject tests as well. The Miller Analogies Test, developed by The Psychological Corporation, is accepted by a small percentage of graduate programs as an alternative to the GRE.

Medical School Admissions: The MCAT

Getting into med school is tough! Figures from the Association of American Medical Colleges (AAMC) show that more than 60 percent of applicants were not accepted anywhere for the 1996–1997 academic year, though most applied to ten to twelve institutions.[37] The MCAT is required by nearly all American medical schools. College grades, the quality of the undergraduate institution, and letters of recommendation are also important factors in admissions decisions. Medical schools are unique in their heavy emphasis on personal interviews: A recent survey of accredited U.S. medical schools found that 98 percent of the responding institutions used interviews in the admissions process; in fact, the 92 responding schools conducted an average of about two interviews per applicant.[38] Overall, the interview was rated as the most crucial factor in selecting among candidates, followed by undergraduate GPA in science courses, letters of recommendation, MCAT scores, and undergraduate non-science GPA, in that order.

Another study, which considered medical school applicants from 1978 through 1992, found that Black, Native-American, Mexican-American, and Puerto Rican applicants were admitted at substantially higher rates than comparable students who were not members of underrepresented groups. Affirmative action, then, also plays a role in med school admissions. "The schools often offer admission to underrepresented minority students whose grades and MCAT scores are lower than they would find acceptable in other students," the study concluded.[39] The AAMC, which actively promotes affirmative action for African Americans, Mexican Americans, American Indians, and mainland Puerto Ricans, now offers workshops, called the Expanded Minority Admissions Exercise, to help schools evaluate applicants on the basis of noncognitive factors, such as leadership skills, determination, drive, social support, maturity, and coping ability. According to an AAMC official, the MCAT program is also considering the addition of measures of personality characteristics for use in the medical school admissions process.

Law School Admissions: The LSAT

It's no surprise that law schools, like medical schools, are highly selective. A recent survey showed that the most prestigious law schools received more than twenty applications for each slot; about 40 percent of schools received at least ten applications for each available place. Overall, though, nearly 60 percent of the applicants do eventually get admitted somewhere.[40] Test scores and undergraduate grades tend to be weighted heavily in law school admissions decisions; schools often use an index score that combines LSAT and undergraduate GPA. Every one of the nearly 200 American and Canadian law schools that belong to the Law School Admission Council (LSAC) requires the LSAT, and most other law schools do as well.

Another factor that law schools weight heavily in admissions decisions is racial and ethnic background. Since the hotly debated Hopwood decision involving the University of Texas Law School (discussed later in this chapter), the role of affirmative action in law school admissions has attracted a great deal of attention in professional journals and the popular press. Two academic studies of students who applied to LSAC member law schools in the early 1990s revealed that, in general, minority candidates were substantially more likely to be admitted than White candidates with similar LSAT scores and undergraduate grades.[41] The more favorable admission rates occurred for American Indian, Asian-American, Black, and Hispanic applicants. These findings demonstrated clearly that ignoring race and relying only on college GPA and LSAT scores would lead to a plunge in minority representation at law schools. California and Texas law schools don't need academic research to tell them about the difficulty of maintaining diversity in the absence of affirmative action: In 1997, the year after Californians approved an affirmative action ban, Boalt Hall, the law school of the University of California, Berkeley, enrolled exactly one Black student—a candidate who had been admitted previously but had deferred enrollment. In 1999, the University of Texas Law School enrolled nine Black students, compared with twenty-nine in the last pre-Hopwood entering class.

Business School Admissions: The GMAT

Test critics applauded in 1985 when Harvard Business School decided, in the words of *Forbes* magazine, that the GMAT "flunked out." But eleven years after abandoning the GMAT, Harvard reinstated it, saying that the test had improved. According to its website, the GMAT is used by more than 1,700 schools worldwide, with about 1,000 of these requiring test scores from each applicant. Undergraduate grades and math background are also important factors in business school admissions, and according to a brochure from the Graduate Management Admission Council, the "vast majority of schools specifically require applicants to have work or military experience."[42] Essays, letters of recommendation, and interviews may also be considered. Business schools don't usually require a specific undergraduate major and tend to attract a student body with diverse academic backgrounds. The more prestigious schools admit only 10 to 15 percent of applicants, while some part-time masters of business administration programs accept more than 60 percent of those who apply.

As in medical schools and law schools, affirmative action apparently plays a major role in business school admissions. A recent study by the Graduate Management Admission Council showed that the GMAT scores and undergraduate GPAs of Whites and Asian Americans who were *rejected* by their chosen MBA programs were, on the average, higher than those of Black and Hispanic applicants who were *accepted*. Asian Americans had the highest test scores, but the lowest acceptance rate, among the four ethnic groups that were studied. The authors concluded that these patterns were not fully explained by differences in the selectivity of schools to which individuals chose to apply. "Whether in an attempt to achieve racial diversity or to rectify past discriminatory practices," the researchers said, "graduate management schools appear to give preference to [African-American and Hispanic] applicants."[43]

Who's in Charge of Admissions Testing in the United States?

Foreign scholars who visit Educational Testing Service are often surprised that ETS is a private company, not a government agency. In Europe and Asia, standardized testing is ordinarily a government function. In China, for example, all students who want to go to college take a brutal government sponsored test that lasts three days; their scores, and not their high school grades, determine which, if any, colleges they are eligible to attend.[44]

In the United States, the situation is quite different. At the college level, two competing admissions tests, the SAT and the ACT, are available, each developed by an independent company. Institutions can choose to require one or the other, to accept either test, or to require neither of them. In the case of graduate school, business school, law school and medical school, there's essentially no competition—only one major standardized test is used for admission to each of these kinds of advanced training, but schools may choose not to require it. Again, the tests are developed by independent organizations whose practices are not directly regulated by government. So who's keeping an eye on the American testing industry? And who's watching out for inappropriate uses of admissions test scores?

According to a 1990 report by a national commission, "those who take and use many tests have less consumer protection than those who buy a toy, a toaster, or a plane ticket."[45] Periodically, there are calls for some kind of centralized official oversight of standardized testing. As early as 1925, Giles Ruch, himself an author of standardized tests, asserted that test buyers, like food buyers, are entitled to a list of "true ingredients printed on the outside of each package."[46] In 1990, Professor George Madaus of Boston College (who was also involved with the national commission report) wrote an essay titled, "Standardized Testing Needs a Consumer-Protection Agency." He argued that a regulatory organization, possibly modeled after the Food and Drug Administration (FDA), was needed to make sure exams meet professional standards, to monitor the use of tests, and to deal with individual complaints. A 1999 National Research Council report renewed the call for "new methods, practices and safeguards" for ensuring appropriate test use, possibly involving government regulation or an independent oversight body.[47]

We still don't have that FDA of standardized testing. Public oversight does exist, but it's not coordinated through a single organization. Instead, it is achieved through a mishmash of government actions, commissioned reports, academic research, and litigation, as well as monitoring by watchdog organizations, journalists, and the testing profession itself. Let's take a look at some of the pieces that make up this patchwork.

Professional Codes and Review Procedures

The testing profession has established principles for developing or selecting an appropriate test, judging the technical adequacy of a test, interpreting scores, ensuring fairness, and providing information to test-takers. The primary professional code is the *Standards for Educational and Psychological Testing* of the American Educational Research Association, the American Psychological Association, and the National Council on Measurement in Education, most recently revised in 1999. These groups are also among the coalition of professional organizations behind the *Code of Fair Testing Practices in Education* of the Joint Committee on Testing Practices, which applies to admissions testing, as well as other forms of educational assessment. The International Test Commission, an organization whose members are psychological associations, test commissions, and publishers (mostly from Europe and North America), has developed *The ITC Guidelines on Test Use,* a document that spells out requirements for the competent and ethical use of tests. And a relative newcomer to the stack of professional codes is the *Guidelines for Computerized–Adaptive Test Development and Use In Education,* published by the American Council on Education in 1995.

Another category of oversight mechanisms is the self-monitoring activities of testing organizations themselves. All reputable testing companies have formal technical and ethical standards. Implementation is typically monitored in part by external committees. Finally, tests are subject to review and criticism in professional books and journals, in the *Mental Measurements Yearbook,* a compendium of test reviews first published by the Buros Institute in 1938, and of course, in the popular press—often the source of the most blistering critiques of standardized testing.

Federal Government Involvement

Although the federal government has no centralized testing oversight agency, it nevertheless has a substantial impact on the study and regulation of standardized testing. One way the government exerts an influence is through the National Academy of Sciences, which was chartered by Congress over a hundred years ago. In 1993, the Academy established a Board on Testing and Assessment to provide scientific expertise about testing in education, the workplace, and the armed services. In 1999, the National Research Council, an arm of the NAS, published a report entitled *Myths and Trade-offs: The Role of Tests in Undergraduate Admissions,* which endorsed the use of testing as part of admissions screening, but warned against over reliance on test scores. In particular, the report said, "[I]nstitutions should avoid treating scores as more precise and accurate measures than they are and should not rely on them for fine distinctions between applicants."[48] Other government reports have addressed testing issues as well. In 1992, the Office of Technology Assessment of the U.S. Congress published *Testing in American Schools: Asking the Right Questions,* which also included some discussion of college admissions testing. And in the late 1970s, the Federal Trade Commission even launched an investigation of the test-coaching business (see chapter 7).

Office for Civil Rights Antidiscrimination Guidelines

Another product of federal involvement in testing issues is the "resource guide" on high-stakes testing published in 2000 by the Office for Civil

Rights (OCR) of the U.S. Department of Education, which deals with complaints about testing involving claims of discrimination. Initially, the document, intended to apply to any institution receiving federal funds, created turmoil in the testing world. The first publicly issued draft, entitled "Nondiscrimination in High-Stakes Testing: A Resource Guide," warned against the use of any educational test that "has a significant disparate impact on members of any particular race, national origin, or sex" unless it is "educationally necessary" and there is no satisfactory alternative that has less "impact."[49]

Although the guide was meant to apply to educational tests in general, its pronouncements about admissions testing drew the most attention. If the tendency of African-American, Latino, and Native American test-takers to score lower than Whites on standardized admissions tests was considered to be an instance of "disparate impact," then the apparent goal of the guide was to discourage test use. While the guide was hailed by some civil rights organizations as a tool for countering the ongoing siege on affirmative action by reducing the gatekeeping role of tests, university officials reacted with confusion and even panic. Although the OCR claimed that the guide merely affirmed existing law, college administrators protested that new standards were being imposed and expressed concern that their current admissions policies might violate the guidelines. Some educators predicted that enforcement of the OCR rules would lead to the admission of grossly unqualified students, and ultimately, to a surge in college dropout rates. A congressional subcommittee also criticized the guidelines, noting that they seemed to be at odds with the Clinton administration's professed goal of increasing accountability in America's schools.

From the perspective of testing professionals, the most fundamental problem with this draft version of the guide was that it appeared to pit legal requirements against psychometric concerns. According to the College Board, for example, the "Resource Guide clearly elevates any measure with lower disparate outcomes, irrespective of validity, cost, or burden to the educational institution, above any test having greater disparate outcomes.... If the primary objective of OCR is to reduce differences in outcomes between groups without weighting the impact of differences in validity and utility, educational institutions will be forced to employ minimally acceptable, but vastly less accurate (and more subjective) measures for the same high stakes decisions." The College Board also pointed out that the "Resource Guide holds tests to a much higher legal and professional standard than other measures (e.g., rank, ratings, samples of student work, grades) in terms of producing uniform results across groups."[50]

The final version of the guide, issued in late 2000, was considerably more temperate than the initial draft. For starters, it had a less inflammatory title, "The Use of Tests When Making High-Stakes Decisions for Students: A Resource Guide for Educators and Policymakers." The stark pronouncement that a test with disparate impact is discriminatory unless it is educationally necessary had been toned down, and, in a seeming nod to the College Board's concerns, the guide now stated that, in evaluating the effectiveness of a proposed alternative to a test, the "feasibility of [the] alternative, including costs and administrative burdens is a relevant consideration."[51] Most significantly, the revised guide included an entire chapter on psychometric standards, which drew extensively from the newly revised *Standards for Educational and Psychological Testing*. The guide now pointed to the connection between measurement standards and legal principles, noting that "[u]nderstanding professional test measurement standards can assist in efforts to use tests wisely and to comply with federal nondiscrimination laws."[52]

Given the sustained uproar about the guide, it is ironic that the document has evidently been quietly put aside by the Bush administration. According to the *New York Times*, the guide has been "shelved," and the OCR website now labels it dismissively as a "document from the previous administration."[53]

Testing and the Courts

"In recent years, courts have had a significant impact on the formulation of public policy issues associated with testing," said legal scholar Michael A. Rebell in 1989. [54] Rebell sees many advantages to court involvement in the regulation of testing: Courts can be useful in "clarifying basic principles and standards" that underlie testing policies, can serve as "highly efficient fact-finding vehicles" through the mechanism of cross-examination, can press for the implementation of lasting solutions to testing problems, and can convey an "aura of . . . legitimacy" that tends to produce compliance by the offending party.

Rebell mentions several "down sides" to court involvement too; in particular, judges may sometimes lack the psychometric expertise needed to fully understand the issues at hand, which may lead to poorly conceived rulings. A National Research Council report on testing described a 1977 case in which "a court sustained the use of fixed cutoff scores on the National Teacher Examination as the basis for certifying new teachers, even though the test developer, the Educational Testing Service [filed a brief claiming] that such use was improper."[55] Another disadvantage of litigation is that it can be phenomenally long and expensive. In one of his many calls for oversight, testing expert George Madaus gave the example of a legal challenge to an Alabama teacher certification test that cost taxpayers about $4 million.[56] Given the increasing litigiousness of American society, however, Rebell predicts that "judicial involvement in social reform issues, including testing, is likely to be a permanent part of the public policy landscape for the foreseeable future."[57]

Hopwood v. Texas and Other Admissions Lawsuits

In 1992, Cheryl Hopwood, a single White mother with a middling academic record, was rejected by the University of Texas School of Law. She and three other White applicants sued the university, claiming they were denied admission because preference was given to less qualified minority candidates. The plaintiffs won a narrow victory in the initial ruling; they received a dollar apiece and the right to reapply without any further application fees. A subsequent appeal led to a 1996 ruling by the U.S. Court of Appeals in the Fifth Circuit (which includes Texas, Louisiana, and Mississippi) that the University of Texas School of Law "may not use race as a factor in deciding which applicants to admit."[58] Later interpretations by the Texas attorney general asserted that the Hopwood ruling made it illegal to consider race or ethnicity in admissions, financial aid decisions, or recruitment programs at any publicly financed college or university in Texas unless the use of race was "narrowly tailored" to remedy recent discrimination by the institution in question. In 1997, after post-Hopwood minority enrollment plunged as expected, Texas implemented an alternative undergraduate admissions procedure requiring publicly financed colleges to admit, without considering test scores, any applicants with grade-point averages in the top 10 percent of their high school graduating classes (see chapter 5). And in 2001, Texas passed a law stating that standardized test scores may not be used as the sole criterion in graduate and professional school admissions and scholarship decisions.

The decision in the Hopwood case, which the U.S. Supreme Court has twice declined to hear, is especially significant because it contradicts the opinion issued in 1978 by Supreme Court Justice Lewis Powell in the landmark case, *Regents of the University of California v. Bakke*. That case resulted from a "reverse discrimination" lawsuit filed by a White applicant, Allan Bakke, who was denied admission to the medical school at the University of California, Davis. Although the court decided in favor of Bakke, the portion of the ruling that has proven to have the most far-reaching consequences was Powell's statement that schools *could* consider race in admissions decisions as a way to foster diversity, provided that race was not the only factor in the decision and was not a part of a quota system or a separate admissions "track" for minorities. *Hopwood*, on the other hand, says that race can't be used at all, which has led to concern and confusion among educators and government officials alike. Indeed, one victim of Hopwood was M. Michael Sharlot, dean of the University of Texas Law School, who announced his resignation in late 1999. The reason, he told the *Chronicle of Higher Education*, was his frustration in trying to cope with the constraints of the decision. "Having to struggle now under such enormous restrictions has been very disheartening," he said.[59]

Although admissions lawsuits charging discrimination against people of color continue to be filed occasionally, "reverse discrimination" lawsuits seem to be the order of the day. Recent legal challenges have forced the University of Michigan, the University of Georgia, and the University of Washington to defend their affirmative action admissions policies in the courts, with mixed success. Legal scholars expect that, within the next year or two, the U.S. Supreme Court will select for consideration a case involving affirmative action in admissions.

State Legislative Action on Admissions Testing

Students who take standardized admissions tests should understand the basis for their scores. This was the eminently reasonable principle behind "Truth in Testing" legislation passed by California and New York in the late 1970s. The California law, passed in 1978, originally required only that test sponsors file facsimile tests with the California Postsecondary Education Commission; it was later amended to require that test questions and answers for some SAT and ACT administrations be released to students. New York State's Standardized Testing Act of 1979 (often called the LaValle Law, after the state senator who introduced it) was much more sweeping. The new law "required full and immediate disclosure of postsecondary admission tests . . . this law require[d] that test agencies file copies of test questions and answers with the Commissioner of Education's office and that students be provided the opportunity to request copies of test questions, correct answer keys, scoring instructions, and their answer sheets."[60]

The passage of the New York law led to an interesting mixture of rebellion and compliance by testing companies. The Association of American Medical Colleges, sponsor of the MCAT, immediately filed a legal challenge, claiming that the law would force it to quickly exhaust the supply of usable MCAT questions. The AAMC succeeded in receiving an exemption from the law until the case was decided. In 1990, a federal court prohibited the State of New York from enforcing the test disclosure law against the AAMC, saying the law was in conflict with federal copyright law. Following that decision, ETS, the College Board, and the GRE Board, the Graduate Management Admission Council, and the Policy Council for the Test of English as a Foreign Language, all of which had initially decided not to fight the New York law, sought and received partial relief from it. In 1991, however, a federal appeals court overturned the 1990 decision, in favor of the AAMC, and in 1995, New York State withdrew the exemptions to the law which it had previously granted. The disclosure law was revived, and the legislation continued.

Between 1992 and 1996, the various testing companies negotiated agreements with the State of New York in which they consented to disclosure of some but not all test forms, and the statute was amended to reflect these modifications. Although the GMAC settled earlier, the remaining test disclosure lawsuits were not dismissed until 1999, twenty years after the LaValle Law was passed.[61]

Despite the many years of courtroom battles, however, the Truth in Testing Act has ultimately succeeded in changing testing practice. Disclosing a portion of admissions test questions, along with the answers, has become a nearly universal practice and has even been belatedly embraced by some testing company officials. When the New York law was extended in 1996 to cover computerized-adaptive tests (see chapter 3), ETS issued a press release bravely titled, "New York Students Win With Testing Bill."

Proposition 209 and Its Clones

In 1998, the freshman enrollment numbers for the University of California's most prestigious campuses showed a startling plunge in the representation of people of color. At UC Berkeley, African-American enrollment dropped by more than 60 percent from 1997 levels, and Latino enrollment dropped by nearly 50 percent. Educators had feared just such a drop since the passage of Proposition 209, a voter initiative that banned consideration of race, ethnicity, or gender in public education, employment and contracting. Proposition 209 signaled the end to affirmative action in admissions to California's public colleges and universities, beginning with the 1998 freshman class. Like the dean of the University of Texas Law School, Robert Laird, the UC Berkeley admissions director, left his post in 1999. Exhausted from the effort of coping with the Proposition 209 aftermath, he told the *Chronicle of Higher Education*, "I want to walk out rather than be carried out."[62]

Proposition 209 has not only had a sweeping effect within California; it has been propagating across the country as a result of the efforts of UC Regent Ward Connerly, father of Proposition 209. In 1998, the state of Washington passed Initiative 200, a ballot measure patterned after Proposition 209, and similar efforts were undertaken in other states. In 1998, a Proposition 209 clone was even introduced in the U.S. House of Representatives. The proposal, put forth by California Republican Frank Riggs, received surprisingly little national attention and was voted down, along with a similar measure by another California Republican.

The demise of affirmative action in California has led to legislative attempts to de-emphasize or abandon admissions tests in an effort to expand opportunities for Black and Latino students, who tend to score lower than White and Asian-American students. Anti-testing legislation was introduced in the California Senate in 1998 and 1999; so far, it has not become law. Proposition 209 also spurred the development of new admissions policies at the University of California. The "4% Plan," which went into effect in 2001 (see chapter 5), confers UC eligibility on the top 4 percent of graduates of every California high school who have completed the required college preparatory courses, regardless of their test scores. And UC regents have voted to expand this plan to include the top 12.5 percent of high school students, although the less qualified of these would need to complete two years of community college first.

In 2001, UC President Richard Atkinson unexpectedly announced that he wanted to eliminate the use of the SAT: I in University of California admissions, an idea that had been raised years earlier but had fizzled. Although he proposed continuing to use the SAT II: Subject Tests for admissions purposes in the short term, Atkinson said he hoped to eventually develop new curriculum-based tests to aid in selecting students. His proposal will take effect only if it is approved by UC faculty and by the Board of Regents.

Independent Centers and Organizations That Study Testing

Several university centers play a significant role in the oversight of testing. One is the National Board on Educational Testing and Public Policy (NBETPP), established in 1998 and housed at the Center for the Study of

Testing, Evaluation, and Educational Policy at Boston College. Its prede-cessor, the National Commission on Testing and Public Policy, created in 1987 with support from the Ford Foundation, was organized for a partic-ular purpose—to prepare a report on the role of standardized tests in the allocation of educational and employment opportunities in the United States. The Ford Foundation has now awarded a grant to the Boston College Center and the RAND Corporation to establish the NBETPP as a permanent body for monitoring testing in America. The NBETPP inves-tigates exams used for making promotion and graduation decisions and tests used to evaluate schools and school reform, as well as admissions testing. Its goal is to issue research-based reports "on testing topics and policy choices in a manner accessible to a wide range of people" and to disseminate testing information via press seminars and "PBS-type videos." Although these activities should help to fill the general public's need for well-researched testing information, the NBETPP does not plan to regulate or accredit testing programs or to respond to the questions and complaints of individual consumers.

Another university-based center devoted to testing research is the National Center for Research on Evaluation, Standards, and Student Testing. CRESST is based at the Center for the Study of Evaluation at the University of California, Los Angeles, and has associates at other institu-tions, including five universities, the RAND Corporation, and, yes, Educational Testing Service. About 40 percent of its $10 million annual budget comes from federal government grants and contracts. CRESST conducts research, publishes reports, and holds conferences on testing issues.

The National Center for Fair and Open Testing, nicknamed FairTest, is another very visible participant in the business of test oversight. FairTest describes itself as "a nonprofit, public education and advocacy organiza-tion working to eliminate the flaws and misuses of the more than 100 million standardized, multiple-choice tests administered annually in America." (Recently, the organization criticized as unfair the TV quiz show, "Who Wants to Be a Millionaire" on the grounds that "responding quickly to recall-based, multiple-choice items in a high-pressure setting is a skill in which men in general, and brash white men in particular, excel.")[63] The organization opened its doors in 1985 after receiving $75,000 in startup funds from the Golden Rule Insurance Company, which had just settled a major testing lawsuit against ETS (see chapter 5).[64] FairTest has also received money from the Ford Foundation, the Rockefeller Family Fund, and the Lilly Endowment. FairTest publishes reports such as *Fallout from the Testing Explosion* and *The SAT Coaching*

Coverup, as well as a quarterly newsletter. It also markets testing commentaries published by others, including *The Reign of ETS*, a scathing critique published in 1980 by Ralph Nader's organization, and the much more thorough and reasoned argument against SAT use, *The Case against the SAT*, by James Crouse and Dale Trusheim.

Life without the SAT

In a 1998 report with the catchy title, *Test Scores Do Not Equal Merit*, FairTest proclaimed that nearly 300 four-year colleges and universities "do not use the SAT or ACT to make admissions decisions about some or all" of their incoming freshmen. According to the report, "university officials have identified standardized admissions tests as significant barriers to entry for thousands of academically qualified minority, first-generation, low-income and female college students." An ACT representative, responding to an earlier edition of FairTest's list of colleges that make limited use of tests, called the FairTest findings "one of the most misleading surveys ever done"; a College Board spokesman also disputed the accuracy of the list.[65] But, although their number may be in dispute, it's certainly true that some colleges have elected to dispense with admissions test requirements. In 2000, Mount Holyoke became the latest "name" school to make the submission of test scores optional. What do the schools that have kicked the standardized testing habit say about the success of this policy?

The institutions that have de-emphasized admissions test scores fall roughly into two categories. In recent years, public university systems in Texas, California, Florida, and other states have instituted admissions policies in which college admissions depends on grades, rather than test scores (see chapter 5). The primary goal of these admissions plans has been to prevent campus "whiteouts" as a result of actual or anticipated assaults on affirmative action.

Other schools that have abandoned or de-emphasized admissions tests are small liberal arts colleges, some of which reduced their reliance on tests over a decade ago. Because these small schools have the luxury of closely examining each applicant folder and interviewing candidates, broad screening devices are not a necessity. And with the capability to conduct an intensive review of applications and the freedom to consider students' ethnic and racial backgrounds, these liberal arts colleges are more likely than large university systems to succeed in fostering diversity while toeing the line on academic quality.

One small liberal arts school that doesn't require admissions tests is

Bates, a highly regarded college in Maine, which made all admissions tests optional in 1990. Bates has accumulated an 18-inch-thick file of press clippings about its reduced emphasis on tests, according to its admissions director, and the publicity has helped to attract more students. Nevertheless, about three-quarters of Bates applicants choose to submit test scores, and submitters are accepted at a higher rate (about 35 percent) than nonsubmitters (about 20 percent).[66] It's intriguing that, at all three colleges profiled in FairTest's 1998 report, most applicants apparently choose to submit test scores even though they're not required to. In that case, how could these test-optional polices have much effect on the makeup of the entering classes? The answer, according to the report, is that minorities are deterred from applying by the mere existence of test requirements.

According to Bates College's own research, the test-optional policy has resulted in an increase in the enrollment of people of color, nonnative English speakers, and working-class Whites, and has not degraded the academic quality of the student body: The average college GPA for students who choose not to submit test scores as part of their applications is about the same as the average GPA for those who do submit scores. In a 1993 interview, William Hiss, then the dean of admissions at Bates, noted that Black and Latino applicants were less likely to submit test scores than Whites, and women were less likely to do so than men. Mainers, too were less likely to be submitters. Hiss attributed this to the fact that many in-state applicants came from "rural towns . . . where . . . the family doesn't sit around talking about Kant over the family dinner table."[67]

Hiss's position on standardized testing is actually quite moderate—the SAT can be useful, but there are exceptions:

> I don't quarrel with the notion that standardized testing can have some predictive validity for a large number of people. . . . [F]or the three quarters of the students who choose to submit standardized testing to Bates, the standardized testing does have a reasonable, if not massive, level of predictive validity. But the folks I'm interested in are the ones who choose not to submit testing and turn out to do fine. . . . [W]e have found . . . that when they say, 'I'm a better student than the testing would suggest,' they're right. . . . Those people are proving the testing wrong. . . ."[68]

Bates, which receives about 3,400 applications for an entering class of 400, takes a very close look at each applicant, including the student's high school grades, enrollment in Advanced Placement or honors courses, extracurricular activities, letters of recommendation, personal essay, and test scores if submitted. The school is also committed to conducting personal interviews of its candidates. Should other schools go the way of Bates? Says Hiss, "I have a hard time imagining how it would work at a very large state university that has perhaps an admissions staff no bigger than ours. . . . [I]t just cannot do this sort of careful sifting . . . that a small college does."[69]

Although most schools that stop requiring admissions tests probably do so in the spirit of being more flexible and fair, a much darker picture was painted by an article in the *New Republic* in 2000. When SATs are optional, the article pointed out, only the top students submit their scores, boosting the school's SAT average. Also, more students are likely to apply when no tests are required, reducing the acceptance rate and making the college look more selective, all of which leads to the "dirty little secret" that the *New Republic* claimed to have unearthed: Some colleges abandon the SAT solely for the purpose of making a better showing in *U.S. News & World Report*'s widely read college rankings.[70]

CHAPTER 3

Conventional and Computerized Admissions Tests

How Are They Developed and Scored?

Imagine taking an exam that tailors itself to the right level of difficulty for you. It doesn't waste your time on test items that are too easy, nor does it include items that are much too hard for you. The test requires fewer questions than a conventional test to measure your skill level because it excludes the too-easy and too-difficult items, neither of which provide much information about you. This is the key principle of adaptive testing, an idea for test administration that first emerged a century ago and finally came to full fruition, thanks to advances in computer technology. The GRE and GMAT are now computerized adaptive tests (CATs), as are several professional licensing tests, the main test used for screening U.S. military personnel, and the Test of English as a Foreign Language, taken by applicants to universities in English-speaking countries. Experimental CAT versions of the SAT and ACT already exist, and the sponsors of the LSAT and MCAT have been investigating the possibility of developing a CAT version. But unless you've taken a CAT yourself, you may not be familiar with this new breed of test.

What's a Computerized Adaptive Test?

In a typical CAT, the candidate is first given a test question of medium difficulty. If she answers incorrectly, she'll then receive an easier item, selected from a large pool of items; if she gives the right answer, she'll get a harder item. After the candidate responds to each question, the computer generates a revised estimate of her skills, based on her responses to all the items she's received so far. The computer then selects the item that is most appropriate to her performance level as the next item to be administered. In reality, the procedure is usually more complex than this description suggests because the CAT is programmed to maintain certain features of the test: Specific content areas must be covered, some items should be given together as a set, certain items should never appear together (for example, if one gives a clue to the other), and so on. Within these constraints, the questions will be targeted to the skill level of the test-taker. Before responding to the CAT, the candidate can typically take as much time as she wants to review a tutorial that explains how to use a computer mouse, how to scroll, and how to enter and confirm answers.

The idea of adaptive administration has been around, at least in embryonic form, since the development of the intelligence test published by Alfred Binet and Théophile Simon in 1905. The Binet scale (later, the Stanford-Binet) was conceptualized as a ladder of intellectual skills. Based on his previous research, Binet linked each test question with a particular age level. If about 50 percent of 9-year-old test-takers answered an item correctly, for example, it was an "age 9" item. In administering the early versions of the Binet scale, the psychologist was to begin with items about a year below the child's age level, or possibly at a lower level, if the child was thought to be "dull." When the child reached the point where he

College Board clerks record test results, circa 1935.
Reprinted by permission of Educational Testing Service and the College Board.

answered all items in a set incorrectly, the test was terminated, and his "mental age" was determined according to the most difficult question he answered correctly.[1]

A feature that today's adaptive tests have in common with Binet's intelligence scale is that candidates don't all get the same set of questions; in fact, they take tests that are intended to differ in difficulty. Obviously, then, it wouldn't be reasonable to score tests of this kind by simply counting the number of correct answers. What's necessary is to *calibrate* each item—estimate its difficulty—ahead of time, so that the difficulty of the questions can be taken into account when scoring the test. Binet calibrated his test items on the basis of previous experiments, and that's essentially how it's done today: Test questions that are to be included in the item pool for a CAT are calibrated by administering them to a group of individuals ahead of time and then performing statistical analyses to estimate their difficulty (along with other characteristics). We won't delve into the computational complexities of how this is done; what's important is that the calibration procedure assigns a difficulty level to each test question.

Hand scoring tests at ETS, 1950.
Reprinted by permission of Educational Testing Service.

Data processing for the National Merit Scholarship Program, 1955.
Photographed by R. H. Crawford, Candid Photos, Princeton, NJ. Reprinted by permission of Educational Testing Service.

Processing test data, 1955.
Reprinted by permission of Educational Testing Service.

ETS keypunch operations, 1957.
Photographed by IBM. Reprinted by permission of Educational Testing Service and IBM Corporate Archives.

The adaptive tests used by Binet in the early twentieth century were simple to administer without a computer. Because the test was administered to one child at a time, the psychologist could easily select questions of the appropriate difficulty. But what if you wanted to develop a "flexible" test, suitable for administration to a group, in which test-takers' performance on one section would determine what section they would be given next? Tailored tests of this kind were under investigation at ETS as early as the 1950s. (According to one of the main progenitors of adaptive tests, Frederic M. Lord, the term *tailored tests* was coined in 1951 by William W. Turnbull—later to become the second president of ETS.) Administering a tailored test, however, requires that the first section be scored before the second is administered. This approach proved to be too cumbersome for widespread application until the computer technology caught up with the psychometric theory.

The 1970s was a crucial decade in the development of CATs. The U.S. Defense Department began a research program that would eventually lead to the CAT version of the Armed Services Vocational Aptitude Battery (ASVAB), used in military personnel screening. Also, computer advances allowed researchers to conduct studies that involved the administration of CATs to live test-takers. (Most earlier research was based on theoretical analyses or computer simulations.)[2] By the late 1990s, the CAT versions of the ASVAB, the GMAT, and the GRE had all been implemented nationwide.

Advantages of CATs

From the test-taker's perspective, CATs have several benefits. Since the tests require fewer items than conventional tests for accurate measurement, they tend to be less draining for the candidate. The GRE CAT, for example, contains about half as many items as the paper-and-pencil GRE.) Scheduling is much more flexible—tests can be offered year-round instead of just a few times a year. The GRE and GMAT CATs can be taken as often as once a month. And unofficial score reports are available immediately (to be confirmed later on). Another benefit is that timing and instructions can be more easily standardized than in conventional tests. Computerized testing also allows the use of more innovative types of test questions, involving simulations of real-life situations, sophisticated graphics, and even audio components (see chapter 8), although these kinds of items have yet to be incorporated in computerized admissions tests. Giving the test on the computer also facilitates testing research by making it possible to record the amount of time spent on each item, as well as every keystroke made by the test-taker. Finally, computerized administration eliminates some kinds of test security problems—there are no test booklets to be lost or stolen, and copying from a seatmate won't work.[3]

Limitations of CATs

Along with their much-touted advantages, CATs have some drawbacks as well. One obvious disadvantage is that administration and scoring procedures are complex and hard to explain to the general public. Also, a very large number of items is needed in order for the CAT to work properly without unduly "exposing" items: Administering a test question very frequently increases the risk that it will be memorized and publicized (see chapter 7). The number of test questions in an item pool is commonly at least six times the number of items answered by any one test-taker and may even be fifteen or twenty times as large. To further protect the security of test questions, testing programs often maintain multiple pools of items, which are used on a rotating basis.[4] The cost of writing these test questions is one reason that CATs are tremendously expensive to develop. Inevitably, some of that cost is passed on to the test-taker. When the GRE "went CAT," the fee increased from $45 to $90.

Administration can be costly as well: To take advantage of the flexible scheduling that CATs allow, it's necessary for test centers to be staffed and available all year. And of course, where there are computers, there are computer problems, including hardware obsolescence and incompatibilities between hardware and software.

The most serious question about CATs is whether they are fair to test-takers of all backgrounds. Certainly, providing tests only via computer can be unfair under some circumstances. This became painfully obvious when the CAT versions of the Test of English as a Foreign Language, the GMAT, and the GRE replaced their paper-and-pencil counterparts in sub-Saharan Africa. A lack of computer familiarity among test-takers was just one of the problems that arose. Some countries didn't have reliable electrical service or adequate roads for getting to the new mobile test sites that had been established for computerized administration. Protests from test-takers and scholarly organizations mounted, and ETS ultimately announced that paper-and-pencil versions of the TOEFL and GRE would be reinstated in at least twenty countries. (The GMAT continues to be offered mainly by computer.)[5]

How about computerized testing that's done under more ordinary circumstances in the United States? According to one 1999 account, 30 percent of White Americans live in a household with a computer, compared to only 13 percent of African Americans, and more Whites than Blacks use computers at home, at work, or in public places such as libraries.[6] Not surprisingly, several studies have shown that ethnic minority students tend to be less familiar and less comfortable with computers than White students. Some research has revealed differences in computer familiarity between men and women as well, although in at least one study, women reported being less anxious about computer use than men, contrary to expectation.[7] In any case, anxiety level doesn't always have the expected effect on test performance or on preference for one administration mode another. Some studies have found that anxiety impaired performance on computerized tests, while others have concluded it did not.[8] And a study of an early version of the computerized GRE showed Asian Americans to be the most likely of all ethnic groups to have a computer at home, but also the most likely to prefer paper-and-pencil tests.[9]

Some studies have compared test-takers' performance on computerized and paper-and-pencil ("P&P") versions of the same test. A study in which about 4,000 test-takers were randomly assigned to CAT or P&P administrations of the GRE showed that average scores for Asian-American, Hispanic, and African-American test-takers were very similar across administration modes (with a slight tendency for minorities to score higher on the CAT than on the P&P test). Average scores for men and women were also reported to be largely unaffected by the mode of administration of the test.[10]

But more research is needed to study the effects of CAT administration on individuals with minimal computer skills. The fact that average performance on CAT and P&P tests is very similar doesn't eliminate the possibility that some test-takers are substantially affected by administration mode. There are also some typical features of CATs that could have implications for test fairness. For example, because a CAT uses the answers to previous questions to determine what item should be given next, test-takers are not permitted to skip items or to change their answers to earlier questions. Some test-takers may find this restriction to be especially stressful. Also, since there are no test booklets, it's not possible for test-takers to make notes right next to the text of a question. Notes can be made on scrap paper, but that may not be as helpful as, say, underlining portions of reading passages. Some nonnative speakers of English may rely on the ability to make notes directly on the test booklet, perhaps consisting of a partial translation of the item. Finally, features of the computer display may be problematic for certain individuals. On reading comprehension items, for example, it may not be possible to display the entire reading passage at one time. Also, some candidates may find computer displays to be harder to read than paper text. In one study, "older" candidates (those over 30) reported difficulty reading from the computer screen.[11] Finally, some candidates may not be used to writing essays with word processors; this could be a disadvantage in the GMAT writing test, which is administered via computer (though it is not adaptive).

Where Do the Test Questions Come From?

Whether a test is given on the computer, like the GRE or GMAT, or the old-fashioned way, like the SAT, ACT, LSAT, or MCAT, the test developers need a pool of test questions to work with. In the case of a CAT, the items administered to each candidate are drawn from this pool; in a paper-and-pencil exam, test forms are assembled from items selected from the pool. But who develops the pool itself?

When a standardized admissions test is constructed, the people in charge are the test's sponsors—for example, the College Board in the case of the SAT, or the Graduate Management Admission Council in the case of the GMAT. The sponsoring organization makes the broad policy decisions about the purpose, content, length, and method of administration of the test. The next step usually involves the development of a framework or blueprint that specifies the content areas—and sometimes the cognitive skills—that are to be included in the test, along with the importance to be accorded to each of these areas and skills. This framework is typically developed by a committee of testing professionals and subject-area experts and then submitted for review to numerous other individuals and panels.

The way items are composed varies to some degree across tests and testing organizations. Some companies rely mainly on in-house staff to write items; others primarily use hired consultants—usually classroom teachers or university professors. Sometimes one testing company even contracts with another for the development of test questions. After the items are created, they are reviewed by expert panels and by test editors who check the grammar, spelling, and format of the items.

Another type of evaluation that takes place somewhere along the line is a review of the test items to eliminate content that could be disturbing. According to the guidelines used at ETS, the test "must not contain language, symbols, words, phrases, or examples that are generally regarded as sexist, racist, or otherwise potentially offensive, inappropriate, or negative toward any group." For example, "[w]omen should not be portrayed as overly concerned with their appearance or as more intuitive than men." The ETS guidelines helpfully point out that phrases like "the little woman" are also unacceptable. In addition, "African Americans should not be characterized as people who live in depressed urban areas or who excel only in sports," and "[o]lder people should not be characterized as feeble, incompetent, or dependent."[12] Also prohibited is content that could be upsetting or inflammatory. For example, topics like abortion or euthanasia are usually taboo.

The items that pass muster are then tried out on real test-takers. This may be done by embedding a special section (which does not count toward the test-taker's score) in a test that is given at a regular administration, or by conducting a separate experimental administration. The results of this pilot test are analyzed to determine whether the new items meet the established statistical specifications, which dictate how difficult the items should be and how closely an item score must be associated with the overall test score. (If an item tends to have a low score for test-takers who do well on the test overall, something is wrong. Often, this means that the "key"—the alleged correct answer—has been incorrectly identified.) Analyses of item bias, or differential item functioning (see chapters 5 and 6) are typically conducted at this point too. The surviving items are deemed eligible for inclusion in a CAT pool or in a bank of items from which paper-and-pencil test forms can be constructed.

One fairly recent change in test development methods is that the initial versions of P&P test forms are sometimes assembled by computer, using a procedure called automatic item selection.[13] The computer program incorporates both content and statistical specifications, and can monitor the degree to which the test form conforms to the blueprint. If the test designer wants to make sure that "A" isn't always the right answer to the multiple-choice items, that a certain number of reading passages include content expected to be of interest to minority test-takers, or that a particular set of items stays together, the procedure can accommodate these constraints too. Test specialists can then select the best of the automatically produced test forms, and can modify them as needed.

Multiple-Choice Items on Standardized Admissions Tests

The limitations of standardized tests are sometimes attributed to their heavy reliance on multiple-choice questions. And indeed, although some admissions tests include short-answer items or even essays, most test questions are multiple-choice. It's often assumed that multiple-choice items test only "lower-order" skills like rote memorization. In contrast, performance-based assessments (or "authentic assessments"), which might require the test-taker to conduct a science experiment or write an essay on the pros and cons of a government policy, are assumed to test "higher-order thinking." But many creative test developers have demonstrated that it's possible to design multiple-choice questions that require complex reasoning, and other researchers have inadvertently shown that it's possible to develop "performance" questions that test trivial material. In short, the format of a test question does not determine the complexity of the thought process required to produce the correct answer.

Often, performance assessments are also assumed to provide a more equitable approach to testing that will lead to a reduction of the test score gap among ethnic groups. But reviews of the accumulated evidence have not supported this conjecture. In fact, adding performance sections to existing tests has sometimes been found to increase the performance disparities among groups. In particular, performance assessments that require advanced writing skills often reveal large score differences between native English speakers and students for whom English is a second language, and some types of performance assessment may be more susceptible to socioeconomic influences than conventional tests. For example, consider portfolio assessment, a type of evaluation procedure in which students assemble, over time, a collection of their best work—the portfolio. Performance assessment enthusiasts often claim that portfolios provide a more fair assessment of students' skills than multiple-choice questions, but portfolio assessment can provide an advantage to students who have access to high-quality materials, good opportunities for study at home, and motivated and educated parents who can help. Studies have found large score gaps between African Americans and Whites on portfolios of student writing, "extended-response" essay questions, and other forms of performance assessment.[14]

There's no doubt that performance assessment can have substantial instructional benefits when it is used in the classroom. By observing and personally evaluating the students' work, the teacher can learn about their creativity and strengths, as well as the flaws in their problem-solving strategies, but these advantages wouldn't apply in the case of admissions testing. Even the most elaborate and realistic form of assessment needs to be boiled down to no more than a few scores in large testing programs, which means that the complexity of the test-taker's response can't be fully captured.

In fact, a key feature of the more elaborate forms of performance assessment is that scoring the tests requires human judgment. This could present problems in the context of a large-scale admissions testing program. Because scoring these exams tends to be relatively difficult, performance tests tend to be less reliable, or precise, than multiple-choice or short-answer tests. And because the scoring process is so labor-intensive, these tests are also more expensive. Finally, in the admissions context, the subjectivity of the scoring procedures would most likely lead to concerns about fairness. Indeed, one reason for abandoning the early College Board essay tests in favor of multiple-choice exams in the 1920s was to increase the objectivity and equitability of the testing process.

As testing expert Robert L. Linn recently remarked, the "multiple-choice format has limitations, but they are nowhere near as severe as those assumed by critics. It is admittedly easier to write multiple-choice test items that require only factual recall, but the format can also require higher-order reasoning and problem-solving skills. . . . There is an unfortunate tendency in education to swing radically from one end of the pendulum to the other, discarding past practices in favor of those currently in vogue with little thought for trade-offs. The current attacks on multiple-choice testing by some advocates of performance-based assessment are in keeping with this tendency."[15] Nevertheless, it's true (as

Linn also notes) that tests can more easily assess a broad range of capabilities and can better capture the interest of test-takers if they aren't composed entirely of fill-in-the-bubble multiple-choice questions. In chapter 8, we will look at some new kinds of test items that are beginning to appear on the horizon.

Scoring the Test: Where Do the Numbers Come From?

In this section, we'll take a general look at the way admissions tests are scored. First we will consider the main portions of each of the four paper-and-pencil tests and the two CATs. Then we'll examine the essay components of the MCAT and GMAT. (The essay that accompanies the LSAT is sent to the law schools unscored.)

The Paper-and-Pencil Tests (SAT, ACT, MCAT, and LSAT)

For the P&P admissions tests, scoring consists of two basic steps:

Step 1 A raw score is computed, based on the number of correct answers.

Step 2 The process of test equating, explained later on, is used to translate the raw score to the reporting scale (for example, the 200–800 scale for the SAT). The equating process adjusts for differences in difficulty between test forms (say, last year's version of the SAT and this year's version).

For the ACT, MCAT, and LSAT, the raw score is simply the number of correct answers. But for the multiple-choice questions on the SAT, a special type of score, called a *formula score*, is used. The formula score includes what is sometimes called a *guessing penalty*, which is intended to "correct" the score for random guessing. The idea is that test-takers who guess randomly (in contrast to those who make informed guesses) should not be allowed to increase their scores by doing so. The formula score, which is obtained by subtracting a fraction of the number of wrong answers from the number of right answers, is an estimate of the number of items for which the test-taker actually knew the answer.[16] (No points are subtracted if the test-taker omits the item.) The formula score, which can include a fraction, is rounded to the nearest whole number before proceeding to Step 2.

Let's consider an example of how all this works on the verbal section of the SAT, which consists of seventy-eight questions. Suppose Athena answers seventy-one items correctly, gets four items wrong, and omits three items. Let's assume that the incorrect items all offered five alternative answers. Then Athena's raw (formula) score will be computed by subtracting $1/4$ point for each wrong answer from the number of right answers, yielding a score of 70. Now a complex test-equating process will determine the correspondence between raw and scaled scores for the particular SAT version that Athena took. The SAT *Admission Staff Handbook* shows that a raw score of 70 on the verbal section could correspond to a scaled score of 720 on a relatively easy SAT form, but could translate to a scaled score of 760 on a harder version of the test. Assuming Athena took an SAT form of middling difficulty, her verbal score will be 740.

Equating

If a test is to be administered more than once, multiple forms of the test are needed. One obvious reason is test security. These days, if it were known that a given test form were to be readministered, the test questions would be posted on a website in nanoseconds. Also, test disclosure legislation requires that the answers to some standardized test items be publicized (see chapter 2). Finally, tests are changed over time to update and improve them.

Even though the intention of test makers is to create new test forms that are equivalent in difficulty to the old ones, some differences will inevitably exist. The purpose of the equating process is to assure that scores on new test forms can be used interchangeably with scores on earlier forms. The mathematical procedures for determining how scores from a new test form can be tied to an established score scale are usually quite elaborate. To complicate things further, each testing program uses a somewhat different equating method. We will just skim the surface of this topic here.

Suppose we want to equate a new version of a test to an old version. To do this, we need one of two types of data. Ideally, we'd like to have scores from a test administration in which the groups of candidates who took the two forms had equivalent levels of skill. (Sometimes, it's possible to have a single group of test-takers do both forms.) If we are stuck with groups that are not equivalent, we need to have responses from both groups to a set of common items, called an *anchor test*. Why do we need these particular kinds of test score data? If we had two groups with different skill levels taking two distinct sets of test items, we would have no way to determine the relative difficulty of the test forms. If the average score for those who took the new form was higher, for example, we wouldn't know if it was because those test-takers were more skilled or because the new form was easier than the old form, or both.

If equivalent groups of students take the two forms and the scores on the new form are higher, then we assume the new form is easier, and we can use the test results from the two groups to figure out how to adjust scores on the new form to make them comparable to scores on the old form. Now suppose we don't have equivalent groups. We give one group the old form and another group the new form, and we require both groups to take an anchor test. By comparing the scores of the two groups on the anchor test, we can determine how different the groups' skill levels are. We can then determine what portion of any score disparity between the new and old forms is attributable to differences in the skill level of the groups, and what portion results from differences in the difficulty of the test forms. This gives us a basis for making the appropriate adjustments to the scores on the new form.

Scoring a CAT

The scoring procedure for a CAT takes into account the fact that test-takers receive different sets of test questions. Two candidates who answer the same number of questions correctly will not ordinarily get the same score on the test. In general, the more difficult the item, the more credit the candidate receives for answering it correctly.[17] On the GRE and GMAT CATs, the test-taker's estimated skill level is then converted to a raw test score through a statistical process that essentially asks the question, "How many items on a standard paper-and-pencil version of the test would be answered correctly by a candidate with this level of skill?" Finally, this raw score is converted to a score on a reporting scale—the 200–800 scale, in the case of GRE scores or GMAT total score. This last step, in effect, equates the CAT scores to scores from previous test administrations. The final score, then, should be comparable to scores on either P&P or CAT versions of the test.

The GMAT and MCAT Essays

"This is E-rater. It'll be scoring your essay today." That was the catchy headline of a 1999 *Business Week* article about the GMAT Analytical Writing Assessment.[18] Yes, it's true—a computer does the scoring, or half of it anyway. To illustrate just how radical a departure this is, we'll first consider a conventionally scored writing test, the MCAT Writing Sample, which consists of two essays. For each, the candidate is presented with a "statement that expresses an opinion, discusses a philosophy, or describes a policy," according to MCAT materials. The test-taker is asked to perform three tasks: interpret the statement, describe circumstances under which the statement could be contradicted, and present a resolution of the conflict between the statement and the contrary viewpoint offered in the response to the second task. The essays, which are handwritten, are scored by humans only. Two raters score the "overall effectiveness" of each of the two essays on a scale of 1 to 6. (Disagreements of more than one point are adjudicated by a third reader.) These four scores (two per essay) are summed and then converted to alphabetic scores that range from J to T.

In the GMAT writing assessment, test-takers also respond to each of two essay questions, but in this case, they use a simple word-processing system instead of writing out their responses in longhand. One requires the candidate to develop a reasoned argument; the other asks for a critique of a point of view. (Although they don't know which questions they'll receive, test-takers do have the opportunity to review in advance, on the Graduate Management Admission Council's website, the 175 essay questions from which their two will be drawn.) Each essay is then evaluated by E-rater and by one human rater, each of which scores the essay on a six-point scale. The candidate's writing score is the average of the four essay scores (two ratings for each of two essays), rounded to the nearest half-point interval.

How does this electronic wizard work? E-rater counts the occurrence of over sixty different linguistic features in each essay, including sentence complexity, rhetorical structure (identified by the presence of certain "cue" words or phrases), and topical similarity to essay responses to the same question which received high grades from humans in the past. The importance that E-rater assigns to each feature is determined through statistical analyses that attempt to maximize the correspondence of E-rater scores to human experts' scores. For example, if the degree to which the essay adheres to its intended topic figures heavily in the human experts' evaluation, that feature will receive a large weight in E-rater's scoring system too. Technophobes should feel reassured that, for the moment, E-rater is learning from its human counterparts, and not vice versa.

According to ETS, which created E-rater and conducted more than five years of research on its performance, E-rater agrees with its human counterpart about as often as two human raters agree: About 90 percent of the time, the two scores are within one point of each other.[19] (If the human and machine raters disagree by more than a point, another human rater resolves the disagreement. This is the same process used for pairs of human raters.) How is it possible that a machine-human pair can agree roughly as well as a pair of trained human beings? One reason is that grading essays is often less than straightforward for *human* raters. Even with training, the task of assigning a number to a piece of writing is still complex and, to some degree, subjective. The success of E-rater relative to humans is less remarkable in light of the biases, inconsistencies, and downright mistakes that live raters, alas, cannot avoid.

How Should Test Scores Be Interpreted?

Critics often describe standardized tests as "reductionistic." There's only one possible response to this claim: It's true! Standardized admissions test scores tell us about only a fraction of a person's capabilities. They don't tell us that one applicant can write stunning poetry, that another is designing a better computer mouse in his spare time, or that a third organized a soup kitchen in her neighborhood. But high school grades don't tell us about the complete array of an applicant's talents either, and we rarely hear an argument in favor of ignoring grades. It's indisputable that measurements we use in everyday life are severely limited—our blood pressure does not give a complete picture of our health, our car's gas mileage does not tell us everything about its performance—but no one would deny that these measurements are useful for certain purposes. So while it's hard to disagree with the assertion in a recent SAT commentary that "[n]o person's understanding or potential can be reduced to a number," the further claim that ". . . it is disrespectful to do so" simply doesn't follow. (It's ironic that the author of this expression of distaste about the reduction of humans to numerals is a professor of mathematics.)[20]

Just how much can we infer from a test score? We will consider two broad limitations of test scores. First, scores aren't meaningful without supplementary information: If you were told that an applicant earned a score of 17 on a newly developed admissions test, this would be utterly impossible to interpret in a vacuum. Second, scores are imprecise: In psychometric jargon, we say they contain *measurement error*. These shortcomings apply even to the very best tests. Of course tests may have much more serious flaws—they may be invalid or unfair for a particular purpose. We will consider those issues in chapters 4 through 6.

Although the idea sometimes strikes test-takers as odd, test score scales are entirely arbitrary. Scores on the ACT range from 1 to 36, while scores on the LSAT range from 120 to 180. Standardized test scores don't have any meaning whatever unless additional information is supplied. The information could be one of two types: *norm-referenced* data or *criterion-referenced* data. Norm-referenced information describes the test-taker's performance relative to a comparison group, such as "all people who took this test during the 2000 calendar year." By contrast, criterion-referenced data illustrate the capabilities of individuals who reach (or exceed) a particular score level. This information helps to show how successfully the test-taker has mastered the skills that the test is intended to measure.

Admissions test scores are most often interpreted in terms of normative data. Knowing that the average MCAT Verbal Reasoning score in 1999 was 7.7 or that 25 percent of high school seniors who took the ACT in 1998 received a Composite score of at least 24 provides a context for determining whether a particular score is high or low. The score report mailed to a test-taker includes a key piece of normative data—the percentile rank associated with the score. The percentile rank tells how well the candidate performed in relation to the other test-takers in a given administration or in relation to candidates who took the test within a given time period. (In the case of the SAT, for example, the percentile ranks are based on the most recent scores of high school seniors who subsequently graduated from high school.) Specifically, the percentile rank tells a test-taker what percentage of the group she exceeded. If her percentile rank is 60, she scored better than 60 percent of the group. (Contrary to what some media folks and even school officials think, a percentile rank does not say what percent of test questions were answered correctly.)

Some admissions testing programs, such as the ACT, provide criterion-referenced data as well. For example, the description of test-takers who earn top scores (33 to 36) on the ACT Science Reasoning Test says, in part, that these "[s]tudents can compare and combine data from two data sets. . . . They understand precision and accuracy issues. . . . [T]hese students can predict how modifying an experiment . . . will affect the results. . . . They are able to determine whether given data . . . supports or contradicts a hypothesis. . . ." So, even without normative information, we get an idea of what a score of 33 to 36 means on this test. As another example, consider the MCAT Writing Sample. Essays that receive scores in the top three categories (labeled R, S, and T) are described this way: "The writing demonstrates a strong control of language. The response is presented in a clear, organized, and coherent fashion. Ideas are well developed, and the topic is dealt with at a complex level." Of course, normative and criterion-based data are not mutually exclusive: Test score reports can and often do provide both types of information.

Measurement Error

Can a competently developed test give a distorted picture of a candidate's capabilities? Of course. All sorts of factors that are irrelevant to a test-taker's abilities can affect his score. Possibly the test-taker was inexperienced with standardized tests and had little opportunity to prepare, or he had a bad headache or was exhausted on the day of the test. Maybe the testing room was stuffy and uncomfortable or there was a battle of the bands taking place in the auditorium nearby. Testing professionals have a name for factors that influence scores but are irrelevant to the purpose of the test: measurement error. "Error" in this case means "imprecision," it doesn't imply a mistake in the everyday sense. Even on a high-quality test, the scores are not perfectly precise.

Measurement error can increase scores as well as decrease them. Let's say a candidate watched a TV special the night before that essentially gave the answers to a set of reading comprehension items. Ordinarily, these items require the test-taker to read a passage and then answer questions about it. Not only is our candidate lucky enough to have obtained the correct answers with no effort at all, he will also have more time to work on other parts of the test. A candidate could also get a lucky break if he attended a coaching school which supplied some sample questions that turned out to be nearly identical to those on the test. Or maybe the test administrator accidentally allowed the candidates a few minutes of extra time. Not surprisingly, test-takers don't ordinarily complain about these potential sources of error.

As an illustration of measurement error outside the academic world, let's take the assessment of weight as an example. If the weight displayed on our bathroom scale seems too high, we might make a case for measurement error of one kind or another: "It's not a 'real' gain, just a temporary surge because of that strawberry shortcake," or "It's just water weight," or "This scale always gives high readings when the battery is running down." (Like test scores, weights that are suspected of being "off" in the desirable direction are much less likely to be questioned.)

Some degree of measurement error is unavoidable, but we need to have a way to quantify it—to determine its likely impact on an individual's score. Two indexes used by testing professionals to assess the amount of measurement error on a particular test are the reliability coefficient and the standard error of measurement (SEM). We'll consider each of these briefly, without digging too deeply into the technical underpinnings.

Let's say that we're evaluating a test of eighth-grade algebra that yields scores ranging from 1 to 50. Imagine that every student has a "true" algebra ability, which will be imperfectly measured by the test. But how imperfectly? The reliability coefficient, which ranges from 0 to 1, is an index of precision—the higher the reliability, the smaller the impact of measurement error. In general, tests that consist of a cohesive set of items with unambiguous answers are more reliable than tests made up of loosely related items that are difficult to score. All other things being equal, reliability increases with the length of the test. The multiple-choice portions of standardized admissions tests typically have high reliabilities, exceeding .90.[21]

What about the SEM? According to typical psychometric assumptions, a test-taker's score will be within one SEM of his "true" score roughly two-thirds of the time, and within two SEMs of his true score about 95 percent of the time. The SEM is expressed in terms of test score points. Suppose Hank's true algebra ability corresponds to a score of 40 on our eighth-grade test, and suppose the SEM is equal to 2. Now suppose we could test him dozens of times, wiping out his memory of the test after each administration. We'd expect him to get a score between 38 and 42 on about two-thirds of those testings, and between 36 and 44 on 95 percent of them. The SEM depends on the test reliability and the standard deviation of test scores, a measure of how spread out the scores are.[22] For the verbal and math sections of the SAT, the SEM is about 30 SAT score points. For the ACT Composite, it is just under one ACT score point.

It's important to keep in mind that all forms of measurement are affected by measurement error. Reputable testing companies estimate and report the degree of precision of test scores, in the form of the test reliability or SEM. By contrast, the measurement error (and possibly bias) associated with classroom grades, ratings based on interviews, and judgments included in letters of recommendation is very difficult to quantify and is rarely discussed. Oddly enough, these forms of evaluation, which are often used in admissions decisions, are not typically subjected to the scrutiny applied to tests; instead, the distortions and imprecision involved in these measures tend to be ignored.

What Happens When the Scoring Changes?
The Case of the Recentered SAT

In a vacuum, test scores are meaningless, as we discussed earlier. Without either normative information or illustrations of the skills possessed by test-takers with a certain score, the numbers are uninterpretable. But people who have extensive experience with the scores, like admissions officials, develop a feel for what a particular score means.

And through relentless media exposure, even folks who aren't in the admissions business acquire ideas about the meaning of a score ("We can't move here—the average SAT score at the high school is only 950.") So entrenched are these beliefs that the College Board's decision to change the scale of the SAT I: Reasoning Test in 1995 led to a seismic upheaval. The move, which had the effect of boosting the math average by about 25 points and the verbal average by about 75 points was assailed from all political quarters.[23] Diane Ravitch, a former assistant secretary of education and a staunch proponent of educational standards, bemoaned the loss of the test's role as an unchanging yardstick: "With the stroke of a pen, extremely poor performance on the verbal portion of the test was turned into the new norm."[24] And the *Journal of Blacks in Higher Education*, noting that the Black-White score gap was reduced on the recentered scale, had this to say: "Whether intentional or not, the recentered scale . . . serves to take some of the heat off the College Board for the continuing poor performance of African-American students on the test. By statistical chicanery, the College Board was able to reduce the racial scoring gap during a period when Black students did not improve their actual test performance relative to White students."[25]

What was behind the widely unpopular decision to change the score scale? Before the recentering, SAT scores were reported on a scale established in 1941. At that time, it was decided that, on each section (verbal and math), scores would range from 200 to 800, with an average score of 500—the midpoint. Or, to put it another way, the average score of the 1941 test-takers was arbitrarily labeled "500."[26] Then, through the process of test equating, discussed earlier in the chapter, subsequent versions of the test were linked to the 1941 version. Under this scaling system, if a student had a verbal score of 600 and a math score of 625, then we could say that her math performance was better in the sense that it exceeded the average score by a larger amount. But over the years, the scores drifted and lost their intended meaning. A score of 500 was no longer the average on either section, and the math and verbal averages were no longer the same. By 1993, the math average was 478, while the verbal average was 424. Now, a student with a verbal score of 600 and a math score of 625 would actually have a more impressive verbal performance (176 points above average) than math performance (147 points above average). But this would not be apparent without consulting the percentile ranks corresponding to the scores.

What explains the downward drift of SAT scores? The reasons for the decline, most of which took place between 1963 and 1980, were the subject of a federally financed study. The federal advisory panel concluded that much of the decline up to the early 1970s resulted from changes in the academic backgrounds of the students taking the SAT: The percentage of high schoolers taking the test increased during this period, along with the percentage of test-takers from the lower ranks of their high school classes. (In 1941, the number of high school graduates in the United States was equal to about 50 percent of the 17-year-old population, compared with about 70 percent today, and only about 10,000 top students—fewer than 1 percent of graduates—took the SAT.)[27] By the early 1970s, this shift in the test-taking population stabilized, but test scores continued to drop. The advisory panel cited several other factors that may have contributed to the score decrease, including declining school and textbook quality, and a reduced emphasis on the teaching of writing (which could explain the greater decrease in verbal scores). William Turnbull was president of ETS during the second part of the decline, which was paralleled by a dip in scores on the ACT and other educational tests. Turnbull conjectured that this later phase of the decline was indirectly related to population changes as well: Because of reductions in the high school dropout rate, the average achievement level among high school seniors was decreasing, and high school education was becoming less rigorous. Turnbull also speculated that the decline in the verbal complexity and vocabulary level of textbooks may have contributed to decreasing scores on the verbal section of the SAT.[28]

The recentering was, in essence, an adjustment procedure that assigned a label of 500 on the "new" SAT scale to the average score obtained by a special sample of about one million 1990 high school seniors. This adjustment made it possible, once again, to interpret individual test scores relative to a mean of 500. The recentering did not change the percentile rank of an individual's score. If a student scored at the 65th percentile (better than 65 percent of students) on the old scale, he would be at the 65th percentile on the recentered scale, but the label attached to his score would have changed.

Equivalence tables were created showing how to make the translation between the old and new score scales, but this did little to cushion the blow. Five years later, the recentering was still making news: A June 2000 opinion piece in *Education Week* listed the "re-norming of the SATs" as one of the ten worst educational disasters of the twentieth century, leading to the destruction of "an accurate and valuable barometer of the nation's educational achievement."[29]

The SAT is not the only testing program that occasionally revises its scoring system. For example, the original ACT score scale was based on the 1942 scale established for the Iowa Tests of Educational Development. In 1989, a new score scale was introduced on which the average scores for each of the four ACT tests and for the Composite were set equal to 18 for a nationally representative sample of 1988 college-bound seniors. The nation seems to have taken the ACT adjustment in stride, without proclamations of disaster.

CHAPTER 4

Test Validity

How Well Do Admissions Tests Measure Academic Skills and Predict Achievement?

Research on the association between test scores and college grades has been going on for more than a hundred years. In the late 1800s, several studies at Columbia and Yale found that scores on psychological tests were nearly useless for predicting grades in various subjects,[1] but around 1920, researchers did have some success in predicting college grades using intelligence test scores.[2] While these early investigations focused on the psychological implications of the findings, present-day researchers often study the association between admissions test scores and subsequent grades as a way of evaluating the tests themselves: The validity of admissions tests as a selection tool for higher education institutions is judged largely by the degree to which test scores can predict later grades. Thousands of these prediction studies have been conducted—more than 3,000 for the SAT alone, according to one 1988 estimate.[3] Oddly enough, there isn't universal agreement about the results. While a chorus of critics insists that standardized admissions tests don't predict grades, testing professionals just as relentlessly defend the usefulness of tests for this very purpose.

What's the reason for this endless debate about a seemingly factual question? One source of disagreement is that the word "predict" has a specialized statistical connotation that is not identical to its everyday meaning. In the statistical world, prediction is not an all-or-nothing phenomenon. We can legitimately say, for example, that the number of years of schooling individuals have received predicts their income at age 30 if the amount of schooling contributes in a useful way to the prediction of income. It is understood that the income estimates won't be right on target in every case, but they'll be substantially more accurate than they would have been if the schooling data had been ignored. From a statistical perspective, a prediction procedure may be worthwhile even if it yields estimates that are far from perfect. We know that weather prediction methods are not infallible, for example, but we listen to the forecast anyway.

In contrast to the statistical meaning, the dictionary definition of "predict"—"to make known in advance, especially on the basis of special knowledge"[4]—seems to imply that prediction is by its nature highly accurate. Because of this discrepancy in meaning, we sometimes see a test defender declaring that a new study shows that test scores predict grades, while a test critic, looking at the very same research findings, disputes the claim that "prediction" has been demonstrated. Under the more stringent definition, a single error in prediction could be considered sufficient to discredit tests. But as testing expert William Mehrens, a professor emeritus at Michigan State University, points out, "one should *not* conclude that a test should not be used because it is possible to point to incorrect inferences made with the use of test data (for example, 'I scored 88 on an intelligence test and a counselor told me I could not succeed in college, but now I have a PhD in education; therefore all intelligence tests are invalid')."[5] It's important to take stock of the available evidence and evaluate it as a whole.

How Is a Test's Predictive Value Assessed?

Although they differ somewhat in what they are alleged to measure, all college, graduate school, and professional school admissions tests share one particular claim—that they are useful for predicting the first-year grades that students will receive in the programs to which they are applying. How can the predictive value of a standardized test be measured? To get a grasp of the nuts and bolts of this kind of research, it's helpful to consider a step-by-step account of a predictive validity study of the SAT. The specific question at hand is, "How much better can we predict first-year college grade-point average (CGPA) using test scores *and* high school grades than we could if we were to use high school grades alone?" (In the case of graduate or professional school admissions, we'd like to know whether our ability to predict first-year grades will be substantially improved by using admissions test scores in addition to undergraduate grades as predictors.)

These predictive validity studies are usually conducted within a single institution, although results may later be averaged across institutions. Conducting a study of this kind requires that the actual first-year college GPAs for the freshman class be available. This allows the predicted CGPAs (computed using test scores and high school grades) to be compared to the first-year CGPAs actually earned by the admitted students.

The effectiveness with which SAT scores and high school grades can predict CGPA is typically evaluated through linear regression analysis, a standard statistical procedure used in a variety of prediction applications—for example, stock market forecasting. Using the data from the freshman class, the regression analysis will produce an equation for predicting CGPA using high school GPA, SAT math score, and SAT verbal score. Each of these predictors will be multiplied by a weighting factor and then added to obtain the predicted CGPA. This regression equation can then be applied in future years to predict the CGPAs of college applicants.

To go beyond a superficial understanding of the use of tests in admissions, it's necessary to know something about regression analysis. This becomes particularly important in considering issues of test bias (addressed in chapters 5 and 6). To learn about the workings of regression analysis in a relatively pain-free way, it's useful to start with a simplified (and hypothetical) example: Let's say we want to see how well we can predict the CGPAs of the 100 members of the freshman class at Faux University, using their total SAT scores—verbal score plus math score. We can then evaluate our success by comparing these predicted CGPAs to the students' actual CGPAs. (Verbal and math scores are not usually added together in this situation, but using a combined score simplifies the example.)

The data for these students are displayed in figure 4-1. The horizontal axis corresponds to total SAT score; the vertical axis corresponds to college GPA. Each data point represents one of the 100 students. The circled point, for example, represents a student with an SAT score slightly below 800 and a college GPA of about 3.0. The shape of the "cloud" of data points shows that CGPA tends to be high when SAT is high. The line that goes through the point cloud, called the *regression line,* represents the predicted CGPAs. Clearly, the predictions are not perfect—the data points don't fall precisely on the line. The equation that corresponds to figure 4-1 is

Predicted College GPA = 1.2 + (.0014) × (Total SAT score).

The weighting factor of .0014 is the slope of the line, which means that each 1-point increase in total SAT score will raise the predicted CGPA by about one-thousandth of a point. Or we could say that a 100-point increase in SAT score raises the predicted CGPA by a little more than a tenth of a point. (The "1.2" in the equation represents the predicted college GPA for a person with an SAT score of zero. Since it's impossible to earn a zero on the SAT, this is not a particularly useful feature of the equation.)

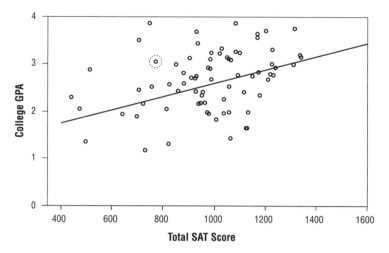

Figure 4-1 Illustration of a Correlation of .4 between Total SAT Score and College GPA

How would Faux University use this equation? Suppose a new applicant had a total SAT score of 1350. Then her predicted CGPA would be found by multiplying 1350 by .0014 and then adding 1.2, which yields a value of 3.1, equivalent to a B. The applicant's predicted CGPA, along with all other pertinent information in her application packet, would be used in deciding whether to admit her.

How can we tell how well this equation works? One product of a regression analysis is the correlation coefficient, an index of predictive effectiveness. When two factors are positively correlated (one factor tends to be high when the other is high), the value of the correlation coefficient will be between 0 and 1. In the SAT-CGPA example, the correlation indicates the degree to which the predicted CGPAs correspond to the actual CGPAs. A value of 0 would indicate that total SAT scores were of no use in predicting college GPA; a value of 1 would mean that CGPA could be perfectly predicted from total SAT score. In that case, all the data points would fall right on the regression line. In fields of research involving the prediction of human behavior (including test performance), correlations larger than .5 are usually considered fairly big; values of .3 to .5 are considered moderate, and values less than .3 are considered small. The six panels of figure 4-2 illustrate what happens as the correlation between SAT score and college GPA increases from .35 to .75. As the correlation rises, the regression line gets steeper, and the data points become more tightly clustered around the line.

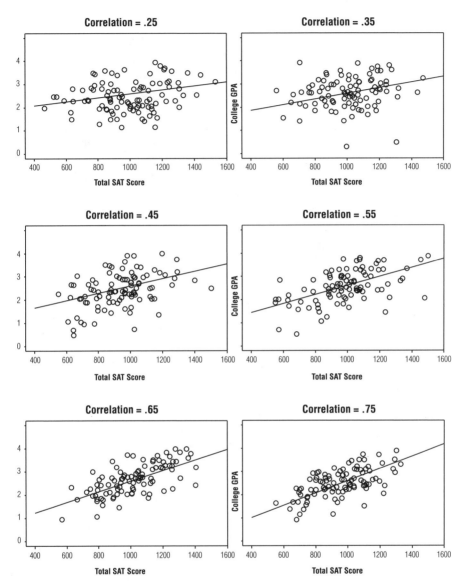

Figure 4-2 Illustrations of Correlations of Varying Size between Total SAT Score and College GPA

The correlation coefficient for the data in figure 4-1—often called a *validity coefficient* in this context—is .4, a fairly typical value for the association between SAT total and freshman GPA. To get a better feeling for the meaning of a correlation coefficient of this magnitude, consider table 4-1, which illustrates a situation in which total SAT scores and college grade-point averages have a correlation of .4. (The table note explains the assumptions that were made about the averages and the spread of the test scores and GPAs.) The table shows the probability of earning a CGPA above 2.25, 2.75, 3.25, and 3.75 for a variety of SAT score levels. For example, a student with a total SAT score of 1000 (the average, in this example) has a 16 percent chance of earning a CGPA of at least 3.25 (nearly a B+), while a student with an SAT score of 1400 has a 44 percent chance. What if we wanted to predict CGPA without taking advantage of what we knew about the association between SAT scores and CGPA? Using the average CGPA and the spread of the CGPA values, we could still make a statement about the likelihood of earning a CGPA of at least 3.25, but it would not be particularly informative: We could say only that 18 percent of students overall were expected to earn a CGPA this high.

Table 4-1 An Example of the Prediction of College GPA Based on SAT Score When The Correlation Coefficient is .4

	Estimated Probability of Earning a CGPA of at Least:			
Total SAT score	2.25 (C)	2.75 (B-)	3.25 (B)	3.75 (A-)
400	.22	.06	.01	.00
600	.37	.13	.03	.00
800	.54	.25	.07	.01
1000	.71	.41	.16	.04
1200	.84	.58	.28	.09
1400	.92	.74	.44	.18
1600	.97	.86	.62	.32
Prediction Ignoring SAT	.69	.42	.18	.05

Note: Total SAT score was assumed to have a mean of 1000 and a standard deviation of 200. College GPA was assumed to have a mean of 2.6 and a standard deviation of .7. Standard linear regression assumptions were made to produce the SAT-based predictions. Only normality of the CGPA distribution was assumed to produce the "prediction ignoring SAT."

Now consider a more realistic application of regression analysis, involving three predictors—high school GPA, SAT verbal score, and SAT math score. The equation might look like this one, which is similar to an equation obtained from an actual validity study:

Predicted College GPA =

.8 + .4 × (H.S. GPA) + .0009 × (SAT verbal score) + .0007 × (SAT math score)

Regression analysis is guaranteed to produce the best weighting of high school GPA, SAT verbal score, and SAT math score: The equation will produce predicted CGPAs that correspond as closely as possible to the actual CGPAs for the students in question.[6] To see how this regression equation can be used, consider a college applicant who has a high school GPA of 3.65 (a B+), an SAT verbal score of 690, and an SAT math score of 610. When we plug these values into the equation, we find that the predicted CGPA for this student is 3.31, lower than the high school GPA, but still a B+:

Predicted College GPA = .8 + .4 × (3.65) + .0009 × (690) + .0007 × (610).
= .8 + 1.46 + .621 + .427 = 3.31

Predictive effectiveness can again be measured by the degree to which the predicted CGPAs correspond to the actual CGPAs. When there is more than one predictor, the index of predictive effectiveness, which ranges between 0 and 1, is called the *multiple correlation*. (Here, we often refer to it simply as a correlation.) The regression analysis can then be repeated using high school GPA alone as a predictor. Comparing the predictive effectiveness of the two equations gives an estimate of the "value added" by using SAT scores.

To get a better idea of how to interpret the results of a test validity investigation, it's instructive to examine the most detailed and painstaking study ever conducted of the utility of the SAT as a predictor of college grades. The analyses, published in a 1994 College Board report, were conducted by Leonard Ramist, Charles Lewis, and Laura McCamley-Jenkins based on 1985 data from a total of about 45,000 students from 45 colleges. (All analyses were conducted separately within each school and then averaged.)

The regression analysis using only high school GPA as a predictor yielded a moderately high correlation of .39; using only the SAT produced a correlation of .36. When high school GPA, SAT math, and SAT verbal scores were used in combination, the correlation rose to .48, yielding an

"SAT increment" of .09 (.48 minus .39). These findings parallel the results of many other test validity analyses in two basic ways. First, prior grades alone were slightly more effective in predicting subsequent grades than were admissions test scores alone. Second, adding test scores to prior grades improved the prediction.

How important is this improvement? In their 1988 book, *The Case Against the SAT*, James Crouse and Dale Trusheim of the University of Delaware argued that the typical SAT increment is so small as to make the SAT useless. Essentially, their claim was that SAT scores are redundant with high school grades. It's certainly true that the SAT increment is not usually staggering in size. But for large schools that do not have the opportunity to interview candidates or review applications in elaborate detail, even a small improvement in prediction accuracy is often perceived as worthwhile. From the point of view of these institutions, in fact, admissions tests are often considered great bargains: The students themselves pay to take the tests, and the cost to the schools of collecting and processing the scores is minimal. Also, as we will see in chapter 5, using only high school grades (without test scores) to predict freshman grades tends to produce predictions that are systematically off target for some ethnic groups, a problem that can occur despite the sizeable correlation between high school and college grades. Including test scores in combination with high school grades to predict college performance often reduces these systematic distortions (see table 5-3, page 119).

In addition, it's quite possible that tests actually play a role in curbing grade inflation. If admissions tests were eliminated nationwide, the usefulness of high school grades as predictors of college achievement might well be diminished because of an increasing drift in grading standards.

Why Correlations and Regression Equations Can Be Misleading: Range Restriction, Criterion Unreliability, and Other Technical Pitfalls

The usual method of evaluating the usefulness of tests by examining the correlations between the scores and subsequent grades seems fairly straightforward, if somewhat narrow. But in fact, interpreting the test validity coefficients that result from these analyses is more complicated than it seems. One major reason is the effect of "selection," or "restriction of range." Because this phenomenon is complex and technical, it is often overlooked or misunderstood in media accounts of test validity. This is unfortunate, since it has important implications for the interpretation of testing research.

A very basic limitation of test validity research is that only a portion of the applicants is available for analysis. Why? Consider an SAT validity study within a particular institution—let's say the now-familiar Faux University. Students whose SATs were too low to allow admission will not, of course, have freshman GPAs. (Some high-scoring applicants who were, in fact, admitted may also be unavailable for analysis because they chose another school over the less reputable Faux.) This "restriction of range" (of the test scores, and, as a result, of the grades as well) curtails the size of the correlations. As a result, the apparent association between test scores and CGPA is smaller than it would be if the entire group of applicants could be considered.

To understand why range restriction has this effect, consider an example completely outside the realm of admissions testing. Suppose an insurance company researcher is interested in the association between age and driving ability for people who are 16 to 30 years old. He conducts a study and finds a very strong association: For 16- to 30-year-olds, driving skill increases substantially with age. Now suppose the researcher conducts new analyses based on only those policy holders who have recently purchased a new car. As shown in figure 4-3, he finds that the

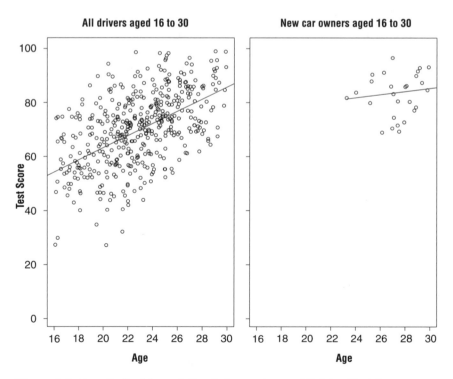

Figure 4-3 Hypothetical Association between Age and Driving Test Score

relationship between age and driving ability now appears to be slight. Why? Because most of the younger teenage drivers will have been excluded from the analysis, leaving the older, better drivers. Among these remaining drivers, individual variation in driving skills will easily obscure the association between age and driving ability that was evident in the larger group. So, if the researcher's goal was to estimate the association for 16- to 30-year-olds, the analysis based only on new car owners will give a distorted picture.

Similarly, a simple correlation or regression approach to the analysis of test validity will produce a more pessimistic picture than is warranted, given that the intended goal of a validity study is to estimate the usefulness of tests in selecting students from the overall applicant pool. The range restriction problems that affect validity analyses at the college level lead to even greater distortions in the case of graduate and professional school admissions, where the selection process is more stringent. To compensate for the effects of selection, statistical "corrections" are sometimes applied in an attempt to estimate how big the association would have been if the range had not been restricted. These adjustments are only approximate, though, since they require that unrealistically simple assumptions be made about the selection process. In college, graduate school, and professional school admissions, the determination of which applicants end up attending a particular institution is quite complex, involving a combination of self-selection and institutional selection.

An additional drawback of traditional validity studies is that they ignore the inaccuracies and inconsistencies of GPA as a criterion of academic performance. As in the case of range restriction, statistical corrections can be made for the imprecision—or unreliability—of grades. In evaluating the results of a validity analysis, it's important to determine whether validity coefficients have been adjusted for range restriction or criterion unreliability, since the effect of these corrections can be substantial. For example, the 1994 College Board study mentioned earlier found the uncorrected correlation of verbal and math SAT scores with college GPA to be .36. With adjustments for restriction of range and criterion unreliability, the correlation rose to .57, a sizable increase.

Several researchers, using approaches of varying sophistication, have attempted to improve the precision of grade-point averages by taking into account the fact that some college courses are harder than others and that some fields of study have more stringent grading practices than others.[7] Adjusting CGPAs for course difficulty—not a trivial task—usually leads to a slight increase (up to .1) in the correlation between test scores and CGPAs. Even a relatively simple refinement—achieved by using only specific academic courses as the basis for computing GPA—has been found to make GPAs more comparable across students and more highly correlated with test scores. A more troublesome question about the validity of GPAs is whether grades reflect biases against particular groups of students, such as people of color, individuals with disabilities, or foreign students. This issue is rarely investigated. In general, grades are subject to far less scrutiny than tests when it comes to investigating bias.

Another subtle and complex aspect of validity analysis is the problem of "underprediction" and "overprediction" mentioned earlier. Suppose a college uses data from all freshmen to obtain a regression equation for use in predicting college GPA for future applicants. Will this equation work equally well for all groups of students, or will it lead to distorted conclusions in predicting the CGPAs of certain groups, such as African Americans, Latinos, or women? Will we tend to get predicted college grades that are too high for some groups and too low for others? In fact, prediction errors of this kind *do* typically occur, whether high school grades or test scores are used as predictors. We will return to this issue in chapters 5 and 6.

How Well Do Admissions Tests Predict First-Year Grades?

What does current research say about the predictive validity of admissions tests in college, graduate school, and professional school? An examination of recent large-scale studies, most of which concern college admissions tests, reveals some consistent patterns.[8] The correlation of ACT score (all four section scores considered together) or SAT score (verbal and math scores considered together) with first-year college GPA is about .4, on average. This correlation—the validity coefficient—is usually slightly lower than the correlation between high school GPA and CGPA. (Correlations given here are not "corrected," except where noted. Corrected correlations are often larger by as much as .2.) Considering ACT or SAT scores as predictors along with high school grades yields correlations averaging about .5 with college GPA. (Adding the SAT achievement tests—now called the SAT II: Subject Tests—to the prediction equation has been found to further boost the correlation by a small amount.)

Occasionally, test scores are found to do a better job than high school grades in predicting CGPA, as in a 1990 study at Dartmouth,[9] and in the

1994 Ramist study, which found that SAT scores tended to work better than high school GPA in predicting grades in individual college courses. This study also showed that, among African-American students, SAT scores were slightly more effective than high school grades in predicting college GPA.

The correlations for the GRE are quite similar to those for the SAT and ACT. GRE scores (Verbal, Quantitative, and Analytical combined) typically have a validity coefficient of .3 to .4, and this is usually slightly smaller than the correlation between college GPA and first-year grad school GPA. When CGPA and GRE scores are considered in combination, their correlation with grad school GPA is typically .4 to .5. Including scores on the GRE Subject Tests (available in chemistry, physics, psychology, English literature, and other areas) as predictors usually boosts the correlation to between .5 and .6.

What about the professional school admissions tests? The GMAT (Verbal and Quantitative scores combined) has been found to have a correlation of .2 to .3 with business school GPA, similar to the correlation between college GPA and business school GPA. According to a 1999 summary, the LSAT typically does a better job of predicting law school GPA than do college grades, yielding correlations averaging about .4, compared to slightly under .3 for CGPA. A recent summary of MCAT validity studies reported that the typical correlation between MCAT and med school grades was over .4, higher than the correlation between college grades and med school GPA. Using college grades and MCAT scores together produced a correlation of .5.

In summary, test scores tend to be slightly less effective than previous grades as predictors of college and graduate school GPA. Including test scores in addition to past grades in the prediction equation tends to increase the validity coefficient by about .1. In predicting professional school grades, however, test scores are frequently found to be more effective than past grades.

Can Tests Predict Academic Performance beyond the First Year?

The evidence is fairly strong that tests can be useful in predicting grades beyond the first year of college, grad school, or professional school. A recent College Board report by Nancy W. Burton and Leonard Ramist summarized the results of nineteen studies (all appearing since 1985) of the association between students' SAT scores and their cumulative grade-point averages upon completing college. These studies were based on results from 227 institutions and over 64,000 students. SAT verbal score and SAT math score each had correlations averaging about .4 with the final college GPA, as did high school achievement (grades or class rank). These correlations are at least as large as those typically reported for first-year college GPA.[10]

In another new research project financed by the College Board, University of Minnesota researchers conducted a meta-analysis of more than 1,700 previous studies of the predictive value of the SAT. In a report of their initial findings, they concluded that the SAT was useful for predicting grades obtained both early and late in college, as well as other factors. The corrected correlations between SAT scores and grade-point averages earned in the second, third, and fourth years of college ranged from roughly .35 to .45.[11]

Recent MCAT research also found test scores useful for predicting grades beyond the first year. In a study of the 1992 and 1993 entering classes at fourteen medical schools, MCAT scores were found to have an average correlation of more than .4 with cumulative GPA for the first two years of medical school, and an average correlation of .3 with third-year GPA.[12] Another study showed that MCAT scores were useful for predicting performance in third-year clerkships, which are typically graded on the basis of both exams and ratings by supervisors.[13] A recent University of Michigan study found that a composite of LSAT scores and undergraduate GPA had a correlation of more than .6 with final law school GPA.[14] In my own 1993 study of doctoral programs in business, I found a smaller association between test scores and subsequent GPA. Although GMAT scores predicted final grades about as well as they predicted first-year grades, the correlations were quite low in both cases—about .2.[15]

Outside the realm of grades, several studies have found GRE scores to be moderately useful for predicting performance on departmental examinations and faculty ratings of students.[16] On the other hand, a well-publicized 1997 study at the psychology department at Yale yielded less favorable results about the predictive value of the GRE. Robert J. Sternberg, a Yale intelligence theorist, and Cornell professor Wendy M. Williams found that, although GRE psychology test scores were correlated about .4 with first-year GPA, GRE scores were not, in most cases, useful for predicting second-year grades or six different types of ratings of students by faculty.[17] "Tests like the GRE measure only a fairly narrow aspect of intelligence," Sternberg said. "They may predict grades, but they won't predict much beyond that."[18] In a flurry of responses to Sternberg and

Williams, GRE defenders pointed out that some studies *have* found GRE scores to be useful in predicting criteria other than grades. These critics suggested that the Yale study may have been marred by technical problems or that the faculty rating scales, rather than the GRE, may have been flawed.[19]

Can Test Scores Predict Who Will Graduate?

Isn't it more important to predict who will complete a degree than to foretell first-year grades? This very reasonable question often arises in discussions of the utility of admissions tests. In an article in *Science* almost thirty years ago, Warren Willingham, then a research director at ETS, neatly summarized the pros and cons of graduation as a measure of academic success. Although his article was about graduate education, his remarks are equally applicable at the college level:

> Regardless of what other judgments a faculty may make about a ... student, the acid test is whether he or she is granted the degree. Consequently, this is probably the single most defensible criterion of success. On the negative side, one must wait a long time for this criterion. Another difficulty is the fact that whether or not a student graduates may frequently depend upon extraneous influences. [Also,] this criterion places a premium on academic persistence and probably does not differentiate very well the most promising scholars and professionals.[20]

How well *can* admissions test scores predict who will graduate? As in so many aspects of admissions testing research, the evidence is frustratingly mixed, with some studies showing that tests are moderately useful for this purpose and others concluding that test scores are of little value in predicting who will attain a degree.

The College Board report by Burton and Ramist includes a review of the research conducted in the last twenty years about the association between SAT scores and college graduation. A 1996 study of more than 75,000 freshmen at 365 institutions showed a rather remarkable link between SAT scores and rates of college graduation within four years. Even among the 9,000 students with high school GPAs of A or A+, the SAT was a valuable predictor: The graduation rate was 28 percent for those with total SAT scores (math plus verbal) of less than 700. The rate rose steadily as SAT score increased, reaching 80 percent for the A and A+ students with combined scores over 1300.[21] And preliminary findings of a recent study sponsored by the College Board showed, based on eleven earlier analyses, that SAT scores were somewhat useful for predicting both persistence through the first year of college and completion of the bachelor's degree.[22]

A 1999 U.S. Department of Education report described a strong relationship between a "mini-SAT" (a one-hour test with items drawn from old SATs) and the likelihood of completing college. Results from a national sample of more than 7,000 college students showed that only 7 percent of those who scored in the bottom fifth on this test completed a bachelor's degree, compared with 67 percent of those who scored in the top fifth. High school grades were slightly less useful in predicting college completion; the rigor of the student's course background was a slightly better predictor.[23] In their extensive analysis of data from the National Longitudinal Study of the High School Class of 1972, which appeared in the widely acclaimed book, *College Choice in America*, Charles F. Manski and David A. Wise also found a strong relationship between SAT score and persistence in college, even among students with similar class ranks in high school.[24] On the other hand, several analyses of large national data bases have yielded correlations between SAT scores and graduation that were quite moderate (about .3, slightly greater than the typical correlation between high school grades and college graduation), and several analyses conducted within single institutions found correlations of only .1 or .2 between test scores and graduation.[25]

Results for graduate and professional school are quite scarce. In a 1974 review of more than 40 validity studies of the GRE, Willingham concluded that GRE scores tended to be moderately useful—and more useful than college GPA—in predicting Ph.D. attainment.[26] A recent study of 31 institutions by Gregory M. Attiyeh also found GRE Verbal and Quantitative scores to be useful in predicting completion of the doctorate.[27] On the other hand, my own 1991 research, based on an analysis of 11 graduate programs at each of three selective universities, showed that degree attainment was not well predicted by either GRE scores or CGPA,[28] and my 1990 analysis of data from 25 doctoral programs in business revealed very little association between degree completion and either GMAT scores or undergraduate grades.[29]

One pattern that becomes evident in the results of this body of research is that single-institution studies tend to find smaller correlations between test scores and degree completion than studies based on large national data bases. In a large study that includes many colleges, there will be a much larger range of test scores and graduation rates than in a single school. Multi-institution analyses of graduation are usually based on the combined data from all the schools (unlike multi-institution GPA prediction studies, which usually involve analyses that have been conducted *within* institutions and then averaged). To some extent, then, the apparent association between test scores and graduation will reflect the fact that some *schools* have both higher test scores and higher graduation rates than others.[30]

What's the final word on our ability to predict who graduates from college, graduate school, or professional school? Most students admitted to higher education are quite competent academically. In deciding whether to remain in school, they are influenced by an array of nonacademic factors, involving finances, mental and physical health, and family responsibilities. For these reasons, it's unlikely that any measure of academic performance can do a very accurate job of predicting who gets a degree. Admissions test scores may be of some use for this purpose, but their predictive value within a particular school is likely to be quite small.

Can Test Scores Predict Career Success?

Investigating the role of tests in predicting career accomplishments is a complex venture. Several studies have demonstrated that admissions test scores are correlated with scores on tests of professional knowledge. For example, LSAT scores have been found to be predictive of performance on the bar exam, MCAT scores have been shown useful for predicting scores on medical boards and medical licensing exams, and SAT scores have proved to be correlated with performance on nursing exams.[31] But, of course, the bar exam and medical and nursing tests do not directly assess professional competence. And, as test critics are quick to point out, the fact that one test score predicts another is not terribly impressive.

Before determining whether test scores predict career success, it's necessary to consider a basic question: How should success be defined and measured? Income is, of course, one criterion, but a mediocre businessman may earn far more than an excellent professor. Supervisor ratings may be useful in some occupations, but they are notoriously imprecise and subjective. Prizes and titles are another possibility, but customs for awarding these kinds of recognition differ widely across fields. Another knotty question is *when* people's career accomplishments should be assessed. If it's soon after they have finished school, individuals may not yet have had time to bloom. If it's late in their careers, countless life events that can affect career progress will have intervened. In addition to determining what and when to measure, researchers attempting to investigate career success are also faced with the practical problem of tracking down an appropriate group of individuals for study and attempting to locate their test scores, which may be decades old.

Further complicating this kind of research is the "credential effect"—the fact that employees with high test scores may have certain personal qualifications that are likely to lead to career advances, regardless of actual ability. As Harvard psychologist David McClelland described this phenomenon in a much-quoted 1973 article (based on a presentation at ETS), the same social class advantages that are associated with high test scores also confer certain credentials on the employee that facilitate his success: "the habits, values, accent, interests, etc.—that mean he is acceptable to management and to clients."[32] To explain the concept even more vividly, McClelland sketched out a hypothetical scenario in which a "ghetto resident" from Roxbury wants to be a policeman, but is condemned to being a janitor because he cannot "play analogy games" and define words like quell, pyromaniac, and lexicon. Data from the would-be policeman—his poor test scores and menial job—then contribute to the "celebrated correlation of low intelligence with low occupational status."[33] McClelland contended that any association between aptitude test scores and career accomplishments was probably due only to the credential effect, rather than to any actual predictive value of the tests. Although McClelland's claims are still being debated decades after his article,[34] it's wise to keep in mind the possibility that a credential effect may influence the apparent association between test scores and later success.

The credential effect may help to explain the results of a 1998 study of the LSAT. The analysis found LSAT scores to be highly predictive of post-law school earnings—each score point was "worth thousands of dollars to the test-taker"—but the effect diminished when the quality of the law school the graduate had attended was taken into account.[35] Those with higher test scores went to better law schools; the superior education, rather than the test scores themselves, may have been primarily responsible for the greater earnings. On the other hand, a recent University of Michigan study found that a composite of LSAT score and undergraduate GPA was *not* predictive of later income or career satisfaction. The composite, however, did have a slight negative association with the number of hours of postgraduation pro bono service—the higher the composite, the lower the service contribution. According to the authors, this might have occurred because "Michigan seeks ... students who subscribe to the legal profession's aspirational norms of service and so admits applicants who appear committed to serving others on somewhat weaker numerical records" than would otherwise be required.[36]

In a 1978 study of 215 Ph.D.-level psychologists, ETS researcher William B. Schrader found that the GRE Advanced Test (now "Subject Test") in Psychology and, to some degree, the GRE Quantitative test, were moderately useful in predicting the number of professional publications and the number of times the psychologists' work had been cited. On the other hand, SAT scores were of little value for predicting these criteria, and test scores were clearly of no use in predicting which psychologists were subsequently elected to fellow status in the American Psychological Association.[37] Schrader later conducted a similar study of Ph.D.-level historians, in which he examined the association between GRE scores and several indexes of career accomplishment, including citations, books, and awards. Although he concluded that the scores were "correlated with productivity as measured by citations," the reported relationships appear quite weak.[38] In yet another study conducted in 1982, Mary Jo Clark and John A. Centra found little relationship between either grades or GRE scores and the career accomplishments of Ph.D.s in the physical, biological, and social sciences.

A 1985 review of the literature on the prediction of career accomplishments concluded that, "[a]cross a rather large spectrum of the population, both test scores and grades tend to have modest predictive power for many kinds of 'later-life contributions.'"[39] Based on the information that has accumulated to date, this assessment seems a bit too rosy. For each study that shows a relationship, another does not. How well, then, do admissions test scores predict eventual career success? Overall, the answer appears to be "not very well." An equally accurate answer might be "better than expected." After all, a test is just a small sample of a candidate's skills. It is extremely limited both in duration and in breadth—a point often emphasized by test critics. Career success, on the other hand, depends on many factors that are unrelated to competence, including health, family situation, and national economic conditions, not to mention luck. From that perspective, it's amazing that tests *have* occasionally proven useful in predicting career accomplishments.

Beyond Statistical Prediction: A Broader Look at Test Validity

What would happen if you compared two methods of predicting first-quarter college grade-point averages—one method that used a regression equation that included the students' high school ranks and college aptitude test scores, the other based on the judgments of counselors, who would use the students' high school standings and test scores, plus additional background information and personal interviews to make the predictions? In 1939, T. R. Sarbin conducted this study based on 162 college freshmen, and the regression equation won—the counselors tended to overestimate the student's future grades.[40] Although the superiority of the statistical approach in the Sarbin analysis was small, two studies of the prediction of academic performance conducted thirty years later showed a substantial advantage for the statistical approach.[41] (And of course, the cost of obtaining statistical predictions is typically much lower than the cost associated with predictions based solely on human judgment.) The next three decades produced a fascinating body of literature that examined the accuracy of prediction methods, including a remarkable book, *Clinical versus Statistical Prediction*, published in 1954 by the psychologist Paul Meehl.

Despite recurrent findings that regression-based approaches can be superior to judgmental procedures in a variety of applications (including psychiatric diagnosis), some researchers find the very idea of statistical prediction to be anathema. A 1962 paper put it this way: "[B]y its opponents [the statistical approach] has been called atomistic, pedantic, artificial, static, and pseudoscientific" compared to prediction procedures based on human judgment (unaided by statistics), which are viewed as "dynamic, meaningful, deep, genuine, and sophisticated."[42]

Although the idea that it's more humane and meaningful to render predictions without relying on statistical analysis seems strikingly naive to most researchers, it is true that predictive accuracy alone is not sufficient evidence of test validity. For example, even if we demonstrated substantial success in predicting college grades using family income, we would not consider a question about income to be a valid admissions test. (SAT critics, of course, have long asserted that the SAT is, in effect, just such an "income test"; see chapter 5.) A judgment about the validity of an admissions test must involve an evaluation of the appropriateness of the test's content (see chapters 3, 5, and 6). But even if the test is useful for predicting grades and contains questions that are judged to be measures of academic competence, we cannot simply declare it valid. There is no across-the-board validity. According to Samuel Messick, one of the premier theorists in this area, "[v]alidity is an overall evaluative judgment . . . of the *adequacy* and *appropriateness* of *inferences* and *actions* based on test scores."[43] Although we often say, as a kind of shorthand, that a particular test is valid, what we really mean is that the test is *valid for a particular purpose* (say, selecting individuals for college admission) *for a particular population of test-takers* (say, high school students who want to attend college in the United States). Even the most ardent supporter of the SAT or ACT would not argue that these tests were valid for selecting students for a university system in which the language of instruction was Spanish or Arabic. And certainly a test score could be useful for picking a freshman class, but entirely inappropriate for, say, characterizing the quality of a neighborhood.

To illustrate some of the more complex aspects of validity, we now explore two special topics that are important in their own right. First we consider the validity of admissions testing for people with disabilities; then we examine the use of admissions test scores as general measures of educational quality. (Issues of test validity for people of color, language minorities, and women are addressed in chapters 5 and 6.)

The Validity of Admissions Tests for People with Disabilities

A standardized test is meant to be administered under uniform conditions and time constraints. But fairness dictates that test scores should not be affected by any limitations of the test-taker which aren't relevant to the skills being assessed. In this spirit, candidates with disabilities who are taking admissions tests are offered various types of special accommodations. Candidates with visual impairments, for example, are offered Braille, cassette, or large-type versions of the test, or are provided with assistants who read the test aloud. Other special arrangements that are typically available include adjustable desks for people in wheelchairs, scribes for individuals with physical impairments that make writing impossible, and sign language interpreters who can relay spoken instructions to deaf test-takers. Extended time is also permitted for candidates with disabilities. Although these accommodations are, by definition, departures from standard administration conditions, their purpose is to give candidates with disabilities an equal opportunity to demonstrate their skills. The rationale is that "the standard procedures ... impede [these] test takers from performing up to their ability."[44] Ideally, scores on the accommodated tests should be comparable to scores obtained from non-disabled test-takers under standard conditions—they should measure the same cognitive abilities and should be of equivalent difficulty.

The advent of computerized testing has expanded the range of accommodations that can eventually be provided to test-takers with disabilities. Already, keyboards and displays can be enlarged to make them more readable for candidates with visual impairments, and special input devices like trackballs or head-mounted mouse emulators can be made available as alternative ways for test-takers to enter their responses.[45] Computerized testing can also make it easier to monitor the provision of extended time or extra breaks. Computer displays can be used to present sign-language interpretations of instructions for deaf candidates. Proto-types already exist for speech synthesizers that could be used to administer tests to blind candidates, and speech recognition technology could allow candidates who cannot use a keyboard to give answers aloud.

The provision of special testing arrangements gives rise to a vast array of questions. What should "count" as a disability in an admissions testing situation? How can we be sure that testing procedures for people with disabilities are fair and reasonable? How can we determine whether the difficulty of an accommodated test for a candidate with a disability is equal to the difficulty of the standard test for a nondisabled test-taker? Should scores that are sent to schools be "flagged" if they have been obtained under nonstandard conditions? Do admissions test scores predict grades as well for people with disabilities as for other test-takers?

During the last two decades, researchers have investigated these issues extensively. At the recommendation of a National Academy of Sciences panel, a four-year research program was undertaken during the 1980s under the sponsorship of Educational Testing Service, the College Board, and the Graduate Record Examinations Board. These studies, conducted by Warren W. Willingham, Marjorie Ragosta, Randy E. Bennett, Henry Braun, Donald A. Rock, and Donald E. Powers, all of ETS, focused on issues involving candidates with disabilities who take the SAT or the (paper-and-pencil) GRE. The research showed that blind test-takers found some SAT math items with figures or special symbols (which must be described verbally or rendered in Braille) to be excessively difficult, and that deaf test-takers found the verbal content of the GRE to be particularly hard. In general, though, the scores of test-takers who received accommodations were roughly comparable to scores obtained by nondisabled test-takers under standard conditions. (The one major exception, which we will consider shortly, involved test-takers who were granted extended time.)

Prediction of subsequent grades was found to be somewhat less accu-rate for candidates with disabilities, whether test scores or previous grades were used as predictors. The researchers speculated that one reason may be the exceptionally wide range in the quality of educational programs and grading standards for these students. Individuals with disabilities may also be more likely than other students to experience difficulties in college or graduate school that affect their academic performance, such as inadequate support services or insufficient funds.

Evaluating score comparability is particularly complex for students who take tests under extended-time conditions. Students with disabilities are typically given up to twelve hours to complete the SAT and up to six hours for the GRE, compared to roughly three hours for the standard paper-and-pencil versions of these tests. In general, the students who receive extended time are more likely to finish the test than candidates at standard test administrations. Does this mean that time limits for students with disabilities are too liberal? Although the research of Willingham and his colleagues did not support this conclusion in general, results did show that this may be true for SAT-takers who claim to have learning disabilities. For these candidates, "the data most clearly suggested that providing longer amounts of time may raise scores beyond the level appropriate to compensate for the disability."[46] In particular, these students' subsequent college grades were lower than their test scores predicted, and the greater the extended time, the greater the discrepancy. By contrast, the college performance of these students was consistent with their high school grades, suggesting that their SAT scores were inflated by excessively liberal time limits. More recent analyses of ACT and LSAT results for candidates with learning disabilities have led to similar conclusions.[47]

Developing fair policies for candidates with learning disabilities has been particularly troublesome for testing companies because even the definition of "learning disability" is murky and subject to manipulation. In recent years, the number of students requesting special test accommodations for learning disabilities has skyrocketed. The College Board reported in 1998 that the "number and proportion of students with learning disabilities requesting accommodations on the SAT I has been increasing annually at a rate substantially faster than for students with any other type of disability, and represents approximately 90 percent of students receiving accommodations on the test."[48] Two-thirds of these accommodations involve only extra time.

Recent research suggests that some SAT-takers have sought to gain extra time by falsely claiming to have learning disabilities. Some schools in wealthy areas have in-house personnel who will conduct disability testing and aid students in their requests for extra SAT time. A *Los Angeles Times* analysis of national data from the College Board showed that students who received extra SAT time in 1999 because of supposed learning disabilities tended to be Whites from high-income families,[49] and a California audit released in 2000 produced a similar finding. The California auditors suspected that some students who were granted extra time didn't deserve it and that some students who needed it did not request it.[50] The SAT program has recently tightened up its criteria for granting extra testing time to candidates claiming learning disabilities. The College Board now turns down most such requests, and the number of requests has decreased dramatically.

Should Scores from Nonstandard Test Administrations Be Flagged?

A longstanding controversy about testing accommodations for people with disabilities is whether score reports should contain a "flag" indicating that the test was given under nonstandard conditions. Proponents of flagging (which include most college admissions officers and high school guidance counselors, according to a recent survey)[51] say that information about testing conditions is needed to interpret test scores correctly. Test users, such as universities, are misled when this information is withheld, the argument goes, possibly to the test-taker's disadvantage. Advocates of flagging say that it can also help to discourage dishonest "game-players" from requesting undeserved extra time, and can thus increase the fairness of the test to those who play by the rules. Those who argue against flagging, however, say that it stigmatizes test-takers with disabilities and constitutes both a privacy violation and a form of discrimination that is prohibited by law.

The flagging debate intensified when ETS announced in 2000 that it would discontinue flagging scores of test-takers who received extra time on some tests—the GRE, GMAT, Test of English as a Foreign Language, and certain teacher tests. The action came in response to a federal lawsuit filed against ETS by a GMAT test-taker with a disability. The decision did not affect the SAT, for which controversy is greatest, because it is owned by the College Board, which was not a defendant in the suit. The parties to the lawsuit and the College Board agreed, however, that an expert panel would be formed to address SAT flagging issues.

The *Standards for Educational and Psychological Testing* offer a reasonable guideline for determining when flagging is appropriate. "[I]mportant information about test score meaning should not be withheld from test users who interpret and act on the test scores," the *Standards* say, "and . . . irrelevant information should not be provided. When there is sufficient evidence of score comparability across regular and modified administrations, there is no need for any sort of flagging."[52] The one accommodation for which comparability evidence is clearly lacking is the provision of extended time to candidates claiming learning disabilities. Flagging the scores from these administrations, therefore, does seem appropriate. A possible long-term solution to the extended-time dilemma, which has been gaining attention over the last decade, is to do away with time constraints for all test-takers.[53] This would eliminate the need to rule on the legitimacy of thousands of extra-time requests and would minimize the likelihood of legal challenges. It would also reduce the anxiety of millions of students who take admissions tests each year.

If It Works for Admissions Counselors, Why Not Governors? Admissions Test Scores as a Measure of Educational Quality

In 1993, the *Wall Street Journal* published a table, produced by the conservative Heritage Foundation, which showed per-pupil expenditures for education in each state, along with two kinds of test score information—the state's rank in terms of average SAT scores and its rank on the eighth-grade math results from the National Assessment of Educational Progress (NAEP). The accompanying text noted that some states with very high expenditures had low test scores (New Jersey, New York, and Connecticut, for example), while some states with low expenditures had high scores (Iowa, North Dakota, Utah). Hence the caption on the table, "Money Doesn't Help." [54]

What's wrong with this conclusion? Quite a lot actually. Differences in the cost of living and in the student population were ignored, to name just two problems. But the article's discussion of the admissions test scores was especially misleading. For illustration, consider New Jersey, which had the highest average per-pupil expenditure ($9,159) and Utah, which had the lowest ($2,993). New Jersey had an SAT rank of 39; Utah's rank was 4. But nowhere did the report mention that New Jersey is in SAT country—at least three-quarters of high school grads typically take the SAT, while Utah is an "ACT state" in which no more than five percent of high school graduates ordinarily take the SAT. Students who live in ACT states, but take the SAT, tend to be the cream of the crop, academically speaking—the students who want to attend prestigious schools outside their home states.

In terms of average scores on the National Assessment of Educational Progress, New Jersey's rank of 14 wasn't that far behind Utah's rank of 8. Although NAEP results are not entirely adequate for the intended comparison either, they have a tremendous advantage over SAT scores—they are based on a random sample of students. The SAT ranks, which compare the academic elite of Utah to a broad sample of high school students from New Jersey, tell us little about the relative effectiveness of the two states' educational systems. And of course, admissions test results tell us nothing about the achievement of students who aren't considering college and therefore don't take the tests. So why would a reputable newspaper evaluate state educational systems on the basis of average SAT scores? In reporting these comparisons, the *Wall Street Journal* was just following the lead of the U.S. Department of Education, which, between 1984 and 1991, issued a "wall chart" that compared states in terms of educational resources and educational performance, including average SAT and ACT test scores.[55]

The College Board itself warns that using SAT scores "in aggregate form as a single measure to rank or rate teachers, educational institutions, districts, or states is invalid because it does not include all students. In being incomplete, this use is inherently unfair." But later portions of the same College Board document seem to waver from this firm position: "Average scores analyzed from a number of years can reveal trends . . . and can provide states and schools with a means of self-evaluation and self-comparison. . . . Aggregate data can also be useful to state, regional, and national education policymakers. . . ."[56]

The College Board's own statistics from 2000 help to illustrate the difficulties with state comparisons. Every year, the College Board publishes the percentage of high school graduates taking the SAT in each state (plus the District of Columbia), along with the average SAT scores. Tables 4-2 and 4-3 show the top five and bottom five states in terms of average verbal and math scores. As is typical, fewer than 10 percent of high school grads took the SAT in the top five states, while at least 50 percent of graduates took the SAT in the bottom five. (After the existence of this pattern sparked criticism of the original wall chart, the Department of Education began reporting either the ACT or the SAT for each state, depending on which test was taken by more students.)

If it were always the very top students in each state who took the test, it would be possible to use statistical adjustments to estimate the average score that would have resulted if all high school graduates in the state had

Table 4-2 States with the Highest and Lowest SAT Verbal Averages for 2000

Highest States	Average Verbal SAT Score	Percent of Graduates Taking SAT	Lowest States	Average Verbal SAT Score	Percent of Graduates Taking SAT
Iowa	589	5	Texas	493	52
North Dakota	588	4	North Carolina	492	64
South Dakota	587	4	Hawaii	488	53
Wisconsin	584	7	Georgia	488	64
Minnesota	581	9	South Carolina	484	59

Note: The District of Columbia is included along with the fifty states. Source: The College Board (2000), *College-Bound Seniors 2000.*

Table 4-3 States with the Highest and Lowest SAT Mathematical Averages for 2000

Highest States	Average Mathematical SAT Score	Percent of Graduates Taking SAT	Lowest States	Average Mathematical SAT Score	Percent of Graduates Taking SAT
North Dakota	609	4	North Carolina	496	64
Iowa	600	5	Delaware	496	66
Wisconsin	597	7	Georgia	486	64
Minnesota	594	9	District of Columbia	486	89
South Dakota	588	4	South Carolina	482	59

Note: The District of Columbia is included along with the fifty states. Source: The College Board (2000), *College-Bound Seniors 2000.*

taken the test. Although the students who take admissions tests do tend to be higher achievers, factors other than academic talent play a role in determining whether high school students will apply to college. Their financial resources, their friends' plans, and their immediate job opportunities all affect students' decisions. Because of the complexity of the college decision process, attempts to statistically adjust average ACT or SAT scores to "correct" for differing participation rates have had limited success. In fact, competing adjustment methods, based on seemingly sensible conclusions, have been found to produce very different rankings of the fifty states.[57] Not surprisingly, the percentage of students taking admissions tests varies not only over states, but over districts, schools, and ethnic groups. It also changes over time. Like assigning ranks to states, comparing average scores over time, schools, or student groups tends to be more complicated than it first appears.

There's another less frequently mentioned reason that admissions test scores are neither a good index of the overall achievements of American students nor an appropriate measure of the quality of a school or school system. That reason has to do with what's on these tests. College admissions tests are not designed as measures of instructional quality. The ACT has stronger links to curriculum than the SAT, whose creators actually try to choose questions that are not heavily dependent on course content. But both these tests cover only a limited number of subjects, and neither can claim to include a comprehensive assessment or even a representative sample of the material taught in American high schools. And since states, districts, and schools differ in curriculum, the tests may be a better match in some locales than others. This does not make for fair and reasonable comparisons of the quality of education.

Unfortunately, groundless comparisons of admissions test results abound. Politicians use SAT or ACT trends to draw conclusions about the changing quality of schooling in America, popular magazines publish college rankings based in part on average admissions test scores, and real estate brokers trot out the average SAT score at the local high school along with other features of the neighborhood. The national obsession with SAT averages has led to some absurd attempts to manipulate them. In 1984, Indiana's state superintendent recommended that only the most talented students be encouraged to take the SAT, and more recently, South Carolina legislators proposed banning students who had not completed certain math courses from taking the test.[58]

Although public awareness of the pitfalls of comparing average admissions test scores is much greater today than it was a decade ago, relying on SAT averages is a tough habit to break. Average SAT scores even entered the 2000 presidential campaign. When George W. Bush, then the Texas governor, criticized Vice President Al Gore's educational policies, the Gore campaign replied, "I think there is a bit of an irony here when Texas is ranked 45th out of 50 in SAT scores."[59]

Alternatives to Tests in Admissions

Just as a nonstatistical approach to prediction is often assumed to be more fair and humane than a statistical method, an admissions requirement that's not a standardized test is often regarded as a more equitable and benevolent alternative by definition. A case in point is the "noncognitive" approach of William E. Sedlacek, professor of education at the University of Maryland, which played a role in selecting the first crop of Gates Millennium Scholars. This group of 4,000 minority students received scholarships for college or graduate school, courtesy of the Bill and Melinda Gates Foundation. Sedlacek's Noncognitive Questionnaire (NCQ) is intended to assess such factors as positive self-concept or confidence, the ability to "negotiate the system," and the availability of a strong support person. The questionnaire asks applicants to indicate their degree of agreement with such statements as "If I run into problems concerning school, I have someone who would listen to me and help me" and "There is no use in doing things for people, you only find that you get it in the neck in the long run."[60]

According to Sedlacek, "[a]pplicants who do not have traditional, White, middle- or upper-middle class, mostly male-oriented experiences are less likely to show their abilities" on standardized tests. For these "nontraditional" students (defined to include "various racial and cultural groups," women, gay, lesbian, and bisexual students, athletes, and students with disabilities), Sedlacek claims that the noncognitive features included in his questionnaire are more predictive of success. If schools "would like to admit more of these individuals than the traditional admissions criteria and procedures allow," but do not want to "risk the perception of 'lowering standards,'" he recommends that they use his NCQ.

In a 1984 study that continues to be cited as a primary source of evidence for the NCQ's validity, Sedlacek and a colleague, Terence J. Tracey, found the NCQ useful for predicting college GPA and college persistence—sometimes more useful than the SAT. But the NCQ wasn't actually used in admissions in this study; it was administered to about 2,000 incoming freshmen.[61] In actual admissions settings, the NCQ questions would seem easy to fake: It's pretty easy to guess the right answer to questions like, "I want a chance to prove myself academically" or "My high school grades don't really reflect what I can do." And certainly an approach of this kind raises at least as many questions as standardized tests. For example, even if the availability of a strong mentoring figure in the student's life is predictive of success in school, do we want to give preference to someone who already has such a figure? What about the tremendously talented student who doesn't have one? Maybe the school should provide one instead of perpetuating this disadvantage, which is largely outside the student's control. And isn't it condescending to suggest that the selection criteria for people of color should be "noncognitive?" One person who took offense at the use of Sedlacek's approach in picking the Gates Millennium scholars was Shelby Steele of the Hoover Institution. "Don't excuse them from tests," he said. "For God's sake, have some faith in their minds."[62]

It's interesting that one of the items on the NCQ that looked most promising in the study by Tracey and Sedlacek may actually include a cognitive component. The item instructs the candidate to "List three things that you are proud of having done." Each response is rated on the perceived difficulty of the accomplishment. The finding that this type of information was useful in predicting college success seems quite consistent with a conclusion of Warren Willingham in his distinguished study of college success twenty years ago. Willingham identified a characteristic he called "productive follow-through," defined as "persistent and successful extracurricular accomplishment" in high school. Productive follow-through proved to be a poor substitute for high school grades and admissions test scores in predicting which students would be identified as most successful by their colleges. But taking this quality into account along with traditional academic qualifications improved the prediction of success substantially.[63]

Though Sedlacek's approach may be out of the mainstream, it's downright conventional compared to the Bial-Dale College Adaptability Index, which attracted media attention in 1999. In a pilot project financed by the Mellon Foundation to the tune of $2 million, nine colleges tried a new approach to student selection. These schools committed themselves to accepting a total of 100 students as part of this project. Most of the candidates, a prescreened group of New York City high school seniors, were Black or Latino. These students had less than stellar grades and test scores, but had been identified by their high schools as having potential. Most of the public attention focused on one component of the index in which applicants were asked to build a robot out of Legos, those plastic snap-together blocks sold as children's toys. Applicants were first shown a Lego robot; then they moved to another room where, in groups of ten, they tried to replicate the robot using loose Lego pieces. Each student was scored on a scale of 1 to 4 by six raters. While cynics might point out that the Lego exercise bears a passing resemblance to block design tasks found in widely used intelligence tests, the creator of the task, a Harvard doctoral student, explained that applicants were to be scored not on their Lego talents, but on their skills at interacting, taking initiative and thinking strategically. She hoped the scores would "predict whether a student will be able to persist in a selective college environment."[64] So far, the jury is still out.

A key principle to keep in mind is that demonstrating the validity of an alternative admissions criterion requires more than simply showing that it is radically different from conventional standardized tests. Supplements or alternatives to standardized tests need to be subjected to the same kinds of public scrutiny and rigorous research that is applied to the tests themselves. Is the proposed measure predictive of later achievements? Is it fair? Will its use affect the academic preparedness of the entering class? These are the kinds of questions that will determine whether an assessment procedure will survive or whether it will be added to the long list of bygone educational fads.

CHAPTER 5

Are Standardized Admissions Tests Fair to People of Color?

On a recent public radio show, the featured guest lamented that the affirmative action debate was often cast as a question of who should be allowed to occupy the seats around the table. Instead, she said, we should think about adding more chairs. It's a pretty metaphor, but one that is singularly inappropriate to the admission of students to selective colleges, graduate schools, and professional schools. When a resource is limited—in this case, places in a school—it's a zero-sum game: Including one person means excluding another. And of course, any discussion of educational resources in America leads inevitably to the issue of race. For Blacks, Hispanics, and Native Americans, the rate of participation in U.S. higher education is strikingly low. These groups constituted 27 percent of the enrollment in elementary and secondary schools in 1986, but they collectively earned fewer than 7 percent of the doctorates granted by U.S. institutions ten years later.[1]

How should spaces in institutions of higher education be allocated? As we discussed in chapter 2, one possible approach would involve a lottery—we could draw applicants' names from a hat until all slots were filled. But in sorting candidates for higher education, our society has typically assigned a fairly hefty weight to their presumed academic talent. The journalist Nicholas Lemann discussed societal sorting mechanisms in his 1999 book, *The Big Test: The Secret History of the American Meritocracy*. Oddly, Lemann portrays this preoccupation with sorting as an American phenomenon—perhaps even a creation of Educational Testing Service. He speaks of testing as "the all-powerful bringer of individual destiny," imposed from above (that is, from ETS) onto a "classless" nation[2]—a description of early twentieth-century America that few African Americans or descendants of turn-of-the-century immigrants are likely to endorse.

The idea that testing and ranking are American inventions can be refuted in one word: China. As we've seen in chapter 1, a society could hardly be more preoccupied with sorting than China, with its elaborate system of civil service examinations, which lasted for over two thousand years. I was reminded of this at a recent museum exhibit of Chinese calligraphy spanning several centuries. Although the biographical description provided for each artist was brief—only a few lines—it inevitably included information about which civil service examination he had passed. Some calligraphers who had never succeeded in passing any exams were evidently condemned to lifelong dishonor, despite their artistic talents.

Throughout the history of the United States, the process of allocating places in a university has provided an opportunity for intolerance to flourish. Educational institutions have used both informal and explicit policies to exclude people of color, women, Catholics, Jews, and other groups. Valuable resources—spaces in the most desirable classrooms—are thus reserved for those considered most deserving; at the same time, the learning environment is kept free of "contaminating" influences. African Americans have been the most obvious victims of this process. The "separate but equal" doctrine espoused in the 1896 Supreme Court ruling in *Plessy v. Ferguson*, a decision permitting the segregation of railway cars, was used to justify the segregation of public education, from elementary school to graduate school. Until a 1938 Supreme Court ruling, for example, Missouri excluded Blacks from the state university's law school, instead giving them money to attend an out-of-state school. And until a 1950 Supreme Court ruling, the University of Texas Law School refused admission to Blacks, claiming that they had access to another Texas law school. Legal application of the "separate but equal" principle to public education ended when the Supreme Court issued its landmark ruling in *Brown v. Board of Education* in 1954.[3] But in the 1960s, segregationist governors tried to prevent the enrollment of Blacks in publicly supported White universities. And nearly fifty years after *Brown*, the higher education systems of eleven states are still not certified by the federal government as being desegregated.[4]

Restrictions on the admission of other groups have been less formal, and, of course, far less entrenched. Limitations on the number of Jews at elite colleges in the early twentieth century, for example, were openly acknowledged but not legally sanctioned. In the 1930s, Dartmouth's president defended limits on Jewish enrollment, remarking that "[l]ife is so much pleasanter in Hanover, the physical appearance of the place is so greatly benefited … with the decreased quota of the Hebraic element. …"[5] In the 1980s, some colleges enacted admissions policies that restricted the number of Asian-American students. The University of California, Berkeley, which was among the elite institutions that had evidently thought there were "too many" Asian Americans on campus, later issued a public apology.[6]

Are standardized admissions tests merely a variation on these sorts of discrimination, clothed in a scientific disguise? Many critics say so, maintaining that admissions tests promote elitist policies by restricting access to quality education.[7] Some testing opponents go one step further, maintaining that test defenders have the explicit goal of denying opportunity to African Americans, Latinos, and Native Americans—groups whose access to higher education is already threatened by recent legislative and judicial attacks on affirmative action programs. The countervailing view of tests, of course, is that they serve as the thermometer and that the disease is to be found in our educational system. In this chapter, we will tackle the difficult issues of test fairness and examine the role of admissions tests from the perspective of the current affirmative action debates.

Standardized Tests: Common Yardstick or Rubber Ruler?

Yardsticks seem to crop up often in discussions of standardized admissions tests. Since high school grades don't have a common meaning across schools, say testing supporters, college admissions tests are needed to provide a "common yardstick" for measuring candidates.[8] On the other hand, a recent essay by Nancy Cole, then the ETS president, referred to "the myth of tests as a single yardstick," an article in *Change* magazine called standardized testing "meritocracy's crooked yardstick," and the executive director of FairTest told the *New York Times* that "the so-called common yardstick of the SAT is in fact a flexible rubber ruler."[9]

How well do admissions tests work as a measuring device for people of color? To some, the answer is obvious. According to a web page maintained by *Time* and The Princeton Review, a test preparation company, "[s]tudies show persistent … race bias in both the SAT and the ACT … the SAT favors white males, who tend to score better than all other groups except Asian-American males."[10] This familiar characterization of admissions tests is based on the fact that African American and Latino test-takers tend to score lower than Whites and Asian Americans. (The *Time*/Princeton Review web page doesn't explain why bias in favor of White males translates into higher scores for Asian-American males.)

But testing devotees are quick to deny any assertions of bias against minorities, and some researchers suggest that the bias runs in the opposite direction. In their acclaimed 1998 book, *The Shape of the River*, authors William G. Bowen and Derek Bok hint at this possibility, noting that, for Black students, standardized admissions tests tend to predict higher college grades than are actually attained.[11] Paradoxically, both sides of the bias argument can offer credible data to support their positions. So, are standardized admissions tests biased against people of color? Is their elimination an effective remedy for the dismantling of affirmative action that is taking place in our country? Before digging into the research literature, it is useful to consider the multiple meanings of test bias.

What Is Test Bias and How Is It Studied?

Differences in racial and ethnic group performance on standardized tests, including admissions tests, have been the focus of substantial research efforts since the civil rights movement of the 1960s, and have been analyzed extensively in academic journals and in the popular press. Researchers, social theorists, and politicians have offered an array of reasons for these score differences, including socioeconomic, cultural, linguistic, and genetic factors, and, of course, test bias. A recent incendiary contribution to this literature was *The Bell Curve*, by Richard Herrnstein and Charles Murray, published in 1994, which encouraged consideration of genetic explanations for group differences in test scores. But the test bias controversy is not limited to the reasons for performance differences: Even the determination of which groups are advantaged by standardized tests is less straightforward than it first appears. To illustrate this, we will consider two possible definitions of test bias: differences between groups in average test scores and differences between groups in prediction accuracy. These definitions, each of which has a claim to legitimacy, can lead to very different conclusions. Then we will take a broader look at fairness in testing and admissions.

Differences between Groups in Average Test Scores

In the popular press, the existence of bias in admissions tests is typically assumed to be demonstrated by the persistent pattern of ethnic group differences (and, to a lesser degree, differences between men and women) in average test scores. Ethnic group disparities in test performance show up long before students encounter the SAT. African-American preschoolers score much lower than Whites on tests of vocabulary,[12] and striking ethnic group differences are evident in fourth-grade performance on the National Assessment of Educational Progress (NAEP), a U.S. Department of Education survey: In the 2000 NAEP reading assessment, 73 percent of White and 78 percent of Asian-American fourth-graders performed at or above the "basic" level, compared with 37 percent of Blacks, 42 percent of Hispanics, and 43 percent of Native Americans. The 2000 fourth-grade mathematics results showed a similar pattern.[13]

The idea that score differences are sufficient evidence for bias is reflected in the language of a California standardized testing bill that was introduced in 1998 and 1999 (but did not pass). According to the initial version of the legislation, "a test discriminates ... if there is a statistically significant difference in the outcome on test performance when test subjects are compared on the basis of gender, ethnicity, race or economic status."[14] And in its first draft, a recent resource guide on test use by the U.S. Department of Education Office for Civil Rights (see chapter 2) took a similar view, stating that "the use of any educational test which has a significant disparate impact on members of any particular race, national origin, or sex is discriminatory, and a violation of [civil rights law], unless it is educationally necessary and there is no practicable alternative form of assessment which meets the educational institution's educational needs and would have less of a disparate impact...."[15]

Differences between Groups in Prediction Accuracy

It's clear, then, that one definition of test bias that has some public support—at least among test critics, journalists, and government officials—says that tests are discriminatory if a particular racial, ethnic, or gender group is disadvantaged by their use. But when academic researchers investigate the fairness of admissions tests, they don't ordinarily focus on the average scores achieved by each of these groups. Instead, they typically consider how well the test scores predict subsequent grades in each group.

The 1994 College Board study introduced in chapter 4, based on 1985 data from forty-five colleges, provides a useful context for illustrating these dueling definitions of test bias. As table 5–1 shows, the average SAT scores, high school grade-point averages (HGPAs), and college grade-point averages (CGPAs) show substantial differences

Table 5-1 Average SAT Scores, HGPA, and CGPA for the College Board Study

	Black	Asian-American	Hispanic	American Indian	White	Overall
SAT Verbal	436	484	462	462	513	505
SAT Math	466	595	516	511	564	559
High School GPA	3.18	3.58	3.43	3.26	3.40	3.41
College GPA	2.14	2.80	2.37	2.21	2.66	2.63
Number of Test-Takers	2,475	3,848	1,599	184	36,743	46,379

Adapted from Ramist et al., 1994, p. 7, 9. The GPA scales range from 0 to 4. The "overall" results include 1,530 students who did not fall into the five listed ethnic categories.

across groups. Average SAT scores are higher for Asian-American and White students than for Black, Hispanic, and Native American students. The difference is more dramatic for the math component than for the verbal; the average SAT math score for Asian Americans is about 130 points higher than the average for African Americans.[16] (National SAT results typically reveal similar patterns; see chapter 1.) If a difference in average performance were considered to be sufficient to demonstrate test bias, then these findings would appear to show bias against Black, Hispanic, and Native American test-takers. From this perspective, we would have to conclude that high school and college grades were biased as well.

But in the world of psychometrics—the statistical analysis of test scores—equality of average test performance for all ethnic groups is not considered to be a criterion for test fairness. Group performance differences, while certainly worthy of attention, can arise for many reasons that are not a function of the test itself—unequal educational opportunity being the most obvious. The typical psychometric investigation of bias in a college admissions test focuses on predictive validity: When used in combination with high school grades, is the test an equally effective and accurate predictor of CGPA for all groups? (For the moment, we focus on ethnic groups, but other demographic groups—men, women, native and nonnative English speakers—are often examined as well.)

Two distinct questions are typically asked about the validity of a test for particular ethnic groups. First, are the test scores as strongly correlated with later grades for all groups, or are they better predictors for

White students than for students of color? This is investigated by obtaining separate prediction equations for each group and then comparing them. Second, if we obtain a single prediction equation for students as a whole, what happens when we apply it to students in particular groups? Does the equation produce predicted CGPAs that are systematically "off" in one direction or another?

Comparisons of Validity across Ethnic Groups

First let's consider how the strength of the relationship between SAT scores and freshman grades—the predictive validity of the test—can be compared across groups. The central goal of a typical SAT validity study is to determine whether the SAT leads to better prediction of CGPA than would be attained using only high school grades as a predictor (see chapter 4). The effectiveness with which SAT scores and high school grades can jointly predict CGPA is evaluated through linear regression analysis, a standard statistical procedure. The analysis yields an equation for predicting CGPA using HGPA, SAT math score, and SAT verbal score, each multiplied by a weighting factor and then added up. (HGPA is included in the equation because tests are used in combination with high school grades in actual admissions decisions.) Predictive effectiveness is measured by the degree of correspondence between the predicted CGPAs and the actual CGPAs. The analysis can be repeated using HGPA alone as a predictor; comparing the results of the two prediction analyses gives an estimate of the "value added" by using SAT scores.

After these analyses are completed for the entire group of students, a separate prediction analysis can be performed within each ethnic group, and the resulting equations can be compared across groups. Table 5-2 shows the correlations between key predictors and first-year college GPA that were obtained in each ethnic group.[17] The first row of the table shows the effectiveness of high school GPA as a predictor. For Black students, for example, the correlation between HGPA and CGPA was .28. The second row refers to the combined predictive value of SAT math and verbal scores (.30 for Blacks), and the third row gives the correlation for all three predictors together (.39 for Blacks). The "SAT increment," obtained by subtracting the values in the top row from those in the third row, measures the degree to which prediction is improved by including SAT scores rather than using high school GPA alone. (For Black students, the increment was .11, obtained by subtracting .28 from .39.)

Table 5-2 Correlation with College GPA (Predictive Efficiency) for 1985 College Board Data

Predictors in Equation	Black	Asian-American	Hispanic	American Indian	White	Overall
High School GPA	.28	.37	.35	.42	.38	.39
SAT Verbal and Math	.30	.39	.27	.34	.32	.36
HGPA, SAT-V, SAT-M	.39	.48	.43	.55	.45	.48
SAT Increment	.11	.11	.08	.13	.07	.09

Adapted from Ramist et al., 1994, p. 11. The correlation coefficients in the first three lines of table entries are "uncorrected" (see chapter 4). Corrected correlations were typically larger by about .2, except in the American Indian group, where the corrected coefficients were larger by an average of .1. SAT increments for the corrected analysis were within .03 of those listed here.

Consistent with most earlier research, the Ramist results showed that HGPA and SAT scores were useful predictors in all ethnic groups, and that including the SAT did lead to better prediction than could be achieved using only high school grades.[18] Prediction tended to be somewhat more effective (that is, CGPA was more strongly related to the predictors) for White and Asian-American test-takers than for Black and Hispanic test-takers, regardless of whether HGPA, SAT math and verbal scores, or all three were used. (For American Indians, prediction was actually better than for Whites, regardless of which predictor was used. Because this group consists of only 184 people, however, results are less precise than for other groups.)

The finding of a weaker correlation for Blacks than for Whites is quite typical. For example, based on a study of 10,000 students who entered eleven selective colleges in 1989, Frederick E. Vars and William G. Bowen concluded that, "while SAT scores are related to the college grades of both Black and White students, the relationship is weaker for Blacks than for Whites."[19] The College Board study was unusual, however, in finding that, in the African-American group, SAT alone provided slightly more effective prediction than HGPA alone. What can we learn from the fact that the correlation between test scores and CGPA is typically lower for Blacks than for Whites? Does this mean that standardized tests lead to misleadingly low predictions of college grades for Black students? As we will see, it does not.

The Overprediction Mystery

Although separate prediction equations for each ethnic group are obtained in the course of research, admissions officers ordinarily use a common set of academic criteria in their initial screening of candidates. These standards are often based directly or indirectly on the results of a regression analysis. The reasoning goes something like this: We don't want to admit anyone who is likely to have a first-year GPA lower than X, so we'll restrict admission to those whose high school grades and admissions test scores produce a predicted CGPA at least that large. The regression results—based on all groups—can aid in the determination of who's likely to receive sufficiently high GPAs. Often the regression equation will be translated into an "academic index" that is a combination of test scores, prior grades, and possibly other factors.

Will the use of a single equation or index result in predicted college GPAs that are systematically too high or too low for certain groups? This question is at the root of the most prevalent definition of test bias in the psychometric world, articulated by Anne Cleary in 1968. Cleary's definition says that a test is biased against a particular subgroup of test-takers "if the criterion score [in this case, CGPA] predicted from the common regression line is consistently too high or too low for members of the subgroup."[20]

To get a better grasp of the meaning of over- and underprediction, consider figure 5-1, which shows hypothetical plots of the relationship between test score (plotted along the horizontal axis) and college GPA (plotted along the vertical axis). Assume that Population A is the majority group and Population B is a minority group. Case 1 illustrates the situation in which prediction is equally accurate for both groups: The same line "fits" the data points for both groups, and the data points are as likely to be above the line as below. (This is similar to the situation illustrated in figure 4-1, except that two groups are now included.) In the other three cases, the line that fits best for Population A does not fit well for Population B. (To keep the plots relatively simple, the line for the combined group is not shown, but because Population A is assumed to be considerably larger than Population B, the combined-group line will be similar to the Population A line.) In case 2, using the Population A line (or the combined-group line) to predict results for Population B will lead to underprediction: Population B's actual performance exceeds its predicted performance. Case 3 illustrates overprediction of Population B, discussed in this chapter. Case 4 shows a more complicated situation in which the strength of the association between test scores

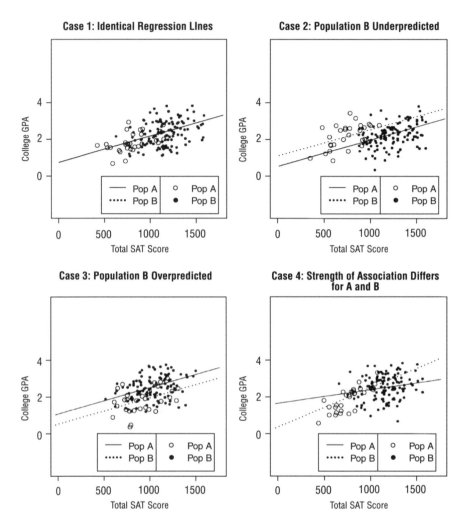

Figure 5–1 Illustration of Overprediction and Underprediction of College GPA in a Regression Analysis Involving Two Test-Taker Populations

and grades is greater for Population B than for Population A, leading to a steeper prediction line. Applying the Population A or combined-group line to Population B will lead to overprediction at lower test score levels and underprediction at higher test score levels.

To determine whether a test is biased according to this definition, we can compare the actual first-year CGPAs to the predicted CGPAs (obtained using the equation based on all students combined). Table 5-3 shows the average differences between actual CGPA and predicted CGPA for each group in the College Board study. CGPAs are on a scale of 0 to 4. A minus sign indicates overprediction (actual grades lower than predicted grades); a plus sign, underprediction (actual grades higher than predicted grades).

It's a property of regression analysis that the equation will, on average, predict perfectly for the overall group.[21] Because Whites constitute about 82 percent of the total group in this study, the differences between actual and predicted grades for White students will necessarily be quite small. (The values in the "White" column in table 5-3 range from .01 to .03.) But how do the results stack up for the remaining ethnic groups? The authors noted that, whether SAT, HGPA, or a combination of these factors was included in the equation, "there were, on average, underpredictions [of CGPA] for Asian-American students (and to a lesser extent, white students) and overpredictions for American Indian, Black and Hispanic students."[22] In other words, the SAT tended to predict higher college grades than were attained for African-American, Latino, and Native American students, while giving an erroneously low prediction of college grades for Asian-American and White students. So, using the Cleary definition, this study, like most admissions test research, found no evidence that the SAT was biased against African-American, Latino, and Native American students.

It is worth noting that overprediction was mitigated by the use of the SAT—it was even worse when only HGPA was used. For example, table 5-3 shows that CGPAs for Black students tended to be overpredicted by about a third of a point when only HGPA was used as a predictor. When SAT scores were included in the prediction equation, the average overprediction was reduced by more than half.

The perplexing combination of lower admissions test scores and overprediction of subsequent grades for Black students (and often for Latinos too) occurs for the ACT, GMAT, MCAT, and LSAT, but a 1985 study did not find similar evidence of overprediction on the GRE.[23] In his 1985 book, Robert E. Klitgaard described overprediction of minority grades on

Table 5-3 Average College GPA Minus Average Predicted College GPA

Predictors in Equation	Black	Asian-American	Hispanic	American Indian	White
High School GPA	−.35	+.02	−.24	−.32	+.03
SAT Verbal and Math	−.23	+.08	−.13	−.29	+.01
HGPA, SAT-V, SAT-M	−.16	+.04	−.13	−.24	+.01

Adapted from Ramist et al., 1994, p. 15. The CGPA scale ranges from 0 to 4.

the SAT, LSAT, and National Board of Medical Examiners tests, as well as job performance assessments. Concerning the LSAT, he added the following (perhaps facetious but still inflammatory) note of explanation: "To have unbiased predictions, how would we have to adjust the test scores and college grades of Black students? To compensate for overprediction . . . , we could subtract 50 points from Blacks' LSAT scores (on the old scale) and about .4 from Blacks' college GPA's—then we would have a roughly unbiased prediction of Blacks' law school grades compared to white students. Or, we could leave college GPAs alone and subtract about 110 points from the LSAT scores of Blacks."[24]

The "overprediction" of the academic performance of Black students and sometimes other minorities is one of the most pervasive and yet least understood findings in the admissions testing literature. In fact, those who comment on it in the popular press often get it backwards. In a 1997 article, journalist Peter Sacks claimed that "many minority students . . . on average, earn better grades in college than their test scores would predict."[25] And William Raspberry, in a 1999 column, referred to "the unexplained but apparently true fact that the SAT and other standardized predictive tests frequently *under* predict the performance of Black applicants."[26]

Testing professionals and educational researchers, however, have long been aware of the overprediction phenomenon—citations go back at least thirty years.[27] In 1983, Robert L. Linn, an eminent educational researcher, noted that this recurrent result is "contrary to a commonly held expectation that tests are unfair to certain minority groups in the sense that they give a misleadingly low indication of the likely performance . . . in school. The overprediction finding suggests that, if anything, just the opposite is true."[28] Recently, with the publication of two acclaimed books—*The Shape of the River,* by William G. Bowen and Derek Bok, and *The Black-White Test Score Gap,* edited by Christopher Jencks and Meredith Phillips—overprediction has become more widely recognized. (Bowen and Bok prefer the term "underperformance," implicitly attributing the phenomenon to the behavior of *students* rather than the functioning of *tests.*)

Let's take a look at some of the most prevalent theories about the overprediction of CGPAs for students of color. One conjecture, which might be called the *unmeasured difference theory,* is that minority and White students are likely to differ in ways that are not fully captured by either their test scores or their high school grades. For example, a Black student and a White student who both have high school GPAs of 3.5, SAT verbal scores of 600, and SAT math scores of 650 may nevertheless differ in terms of factors like the quality of early schooling, the environment in the home, and the aspirations of the family, all of which can influence academic preparation.

Vars and Bowen offered a related explanation for overprediction: Perhaps Whites earn higher college grades than Blacks with the same SAT scores because, among qualified applicants, a smaller percentage of Whites than Blacks are admitted to college. White college students, according to this reasoning, are therefore more likely to have been selected using stringent (though perhaps informal) criteria that involve academic factors not captured by SAT scores (or, presumably, high school grades). In fact, Robert Linn suggested twenty years ago that overprediction of CGPA for African Americans could result from the use of admissions criteria that differ across ethnic groups; he laid out an explicit statistical model that shows how affirmative action policies could explain the phenomenon.[29]

A somewhat related technical explanation that has been offered repeatedly in the psychometric literature is that overprediction occurs because both SAT scores and high school grades are imprecise measures of academic abilities. This "unreliability" can be shown to distort regression results in a way that produces overpredictions for lower-scoring groups and underpredictions for higher-scoring groups.[30] Seemingly, then, the imprecision of test scores and grades could explain overprediction for Blacks, Hispanics, and Americans Indians, and underprediction for Asian Americans and Whites—the pattern of results that occurred in the Ramist study. But one major research finding argues against this technical factor as an all-purpose explanation: As we will see later, female SAT-takers tend to score lower than male SAT-takers, yet their later grades tend to be underpredicted.

Another theory about overprediction—one that would undoubtedly draw the scorn of test critics—is that college (or grad school) grades are biased against Blacks and other people of color, and tests are not. (A variant is that both are biased, but the bias in grades is worse.) Under this scenario, raised by Klitgaard in his book, tests give a more accurate reading of students' capabilities than the subsequent evaluations of their academic performance. A testing official I contacted also offered this explanation. His belief was that testing companies, through a process of scrupulous research and refinement, had eliminated any existing biases in tests; college grading practices, on the other hand, have not been subjected to any such scrutiny. Even if this theory were true, however, we would still have to explain the fact that previous grades (when used alone as predictors) produce even more substantial overpredictions of the later grades of Black and Latino students. (See table 5-3, line 1; the same result has been found on the ACT and LSAT.)[31] In fact, there is a plausible explanation for this finding, at least in the case of college admission: High school GPAs reflect students' academic standing within their own schools. If Black and Latino students are more likely to have attended lower-quality high schools (and therefore to have "inflated" high school grades, compared to Whites and Asian Americans), this could explain the tendency for high school grades to overpredict the college performance of Blacks and Latinos.[32]

Another category of hypotheses about overprediction is based on the assumption that minority students in college (or graduate or professional school) are not fulfilling their academic potential, which is assumed to be accurately captured by the tests. This "underperformance" could occur because of outright racism or because of a campus environment that is inhospitable to people of color. Or it could be related to a greater occurrence among minority students of life difficulties, including financial problems, that interfere with academic performance. It has also been hypothesized that anxieties or low aspirations may interfere with the academic success of minority students. Anthropologists Signithia Fordham and John Ogbu, for example, have suggested that, in response to a racist society, African-American students have developed a culture in which achieving academic success is considered "acting White" and is therefore to be avoided.[33] In a recent controversial book, Berkeley professor John H. McWhorter contended that the implementation of affirmative action programs has led Black students to embrace anti-intellectual and defeatist attitudes that depress their academic achievement.[34]

Stereotype Threat and Overprediction

The "stereotype threat" theory of Claude Steele and Joshua Aronson, which has appeared widely in the popular press, has been offered as another possible explanation for overprediction. Stereotype threat—"the threat of being viewed through the lens of a negative stereotype, or the fear of doing something that would inadvertently confirm that stereotype"—produces stress, which causes students to "learn to care less about the situations . . . that bring it about" and, ultimately, to perform more poorly.[35] In some circumstances, merely asking test-takers to state their sex or ethnic group can be damaging to their performance, according to Steele and Aronson. In their chapter in *The Black-White Test Score Gap*, they focused on the impact of stereotype threat on African-American students in testing situations, and concluded by saying that their "analysis uncovers a social and psychological predicament that is rife in the standardized testing environment. . . ." The goal of their studies, they said, was to "seek to explain why Blacks underperform in college relative to equally well-prepared Whites."[36] Bowen and Bok, in *The Shape of the River*, and Frederick E. Vars and Bowen, in their chapter in *Gap*, suggest that stereotype threat might explain the recurrent "underperformance" finding.[37]

But, although the stereotype-threat research is certainly intriguing, it does not provide a straightforward explanation of the overprediction/ underperformance phenomenon. If stereotype threat depressed standardized test performance, but didn't affect subsequent academic work, it would be expected to lead to underprediction because the affected students would perform better in college than their (depressed) test scores would indicate. To explain the existing pattern of test results and college grades, we'd have to hypothesize that stereotype threat had more effect on college grades than on admissions test performance, which seems contrary to Steele's implication that standardized testing situations are particularly evocative of stereotype threat.[38]

Although some research has supported the Steele and Aronson findings—for example, a study by Margaret Shih, Todd L. Pittinsky, and Nalini Ambady on the mathematics performance of Asian-American women[39]—other investigations have found no evidence of stereotype threat. In studies of the Advanced Placement calculus exam, given to high schoolers, and the Computerized Placement Tests, administered to community college students, ETS researcher Lawrence Stricker was unable to demonstrate any effect of asking African-American and White candidates about their sex and ethnic group.[40] Similarly, Peggy Loveless found no evidence of stereotype threat for African Americans on the ACT.[41] The explanation for the contradictory results may lie in the experimental setting: The Steele and Shih findings are based on laboratory studies—controlled experiments in artificial surroundings. On the other hand, Stricker's studies involved actual test candidates who chose to take the exams for reasons of their own, and participants in the Loveless research took the ACT at their schools, in a special administration described to them as a practice test. The attitudes and motivation of test-takers in a laboratory study would certainly be expected to differ from those of candidates in real (or realistic) testing situations. Stereotype threat may be a subtle phenomenon that, outside the laboratory, is masked by more pervasive anxieties about test-taking.[42]

For now, the perplexing overprediction phenomenon must remain, at least in part, a mystery. Unmeasured differences between Whites and Blacks (or Latinos or American Indians) with the same test scores and previous grades certainly explain at least part of the overprediction. But it seems plausible that a greater incidence among minority students of life difficulties and financial problems in college, graduate school, or professional school contributes to the phenomenon as well. We'll revisit the issue of over- and underprediction in chapter 6, where we consider differences between men's and women's performance on standardized admission tests.

Validity of Admissions Tests for Students with Limited English Skills

Although countless researchers have studied the validity of college admissions tests for ethnic minorities, few have explicitly considered the language background of the assessed students. One exception is María Pennock-Román, who examined language proficiency in her investigation of SAT validity for Hispanic and non-Hispanic freshmen at six universities in the early 1980s. She concluded that English proficiency had very little impact on SAT validity: The degree to which SAT scores predicted freshman grades didn't depend on students' English language skills. "It seems likely that persons with somewhat limited English proficiency are handicapped both on test scores and in [freshman] college achievement . . . ," Pennock-Román said.[43]

The 1994 Ramist study compared the validity of the SAT for students who said English was their best language and those who said it was not. Both high school GPA and SAT verbal scores were more effective predictors of first-year CGPA in the "English best language" group than in the other group. When high school GPA, SAT math score, and SAT verbal score were all included, however, their combined effectiveness as predictors was the same in both groups.

For the "English not best language" group, systematic differences between actual and predicted first-year college GPAs emerged in some analyses. Any combination of predictors which included SAT verbal score led to predicted grades that were lower than actual grades. By contrast, predictions were quite accurate when SAT math score alone or high school GPA alone were used as predictors.[44] The findings from the Ramist study are difficult to interpret because these "English not best language" students did not share a common language or ethnic background: 57 percent were Asian American, 4 percent were Black, 9 percent were Hispanic, and 30 percent were White.

Although the Ramist findings seem to show that stressing verbal tests in admissions decisions unfairly disadvantages students with limited English skills, a different picture emerged from the analyses that Lizabeth Schlemer and I conducted of test scores and grades of 1997 and 1998 freshmen at the University of California, Santa Barbara.[45] Analyses focused on two groups of students who stated English was not their best language: those who were Latino and those who were Asian American. Correlations between test scores and CGPA were sometimes higher for these two groups than for White students who claimed English as their best language. Also, for the two limited-English groups, including the SAT verbal score as a predictor served to improve the accuracy of predicted CGPAs. Using high school GPA or SAT math score alone led to predicted grades that exceeded actual grades, sometimes by a substantial amount. As Pennock-Román noted, freshman GPA is likely to have a large verbal component. Including a verbal test as a predictor, therefore, can actually *increase* the accuracy of prediction for students with limited English skills.

How Does Test Content Contribute to Ethnic Group Differences in Test Scores?

Many testing professionals first heard the legal term "disparate impact" in connection with the Golden Rule insurance case. In 1976, the Golden Rule Insurance Company filed a lawsuit involving an employment test for insurance agents that had been developed by Educational Testing Service at the behest of the Illinois Department of Insurance. The company, along with five unsuccessful applicants for insurance licenses, charged that the test was biased against African-American test-takers because average scores of Black candidates tended to be lower than those of Whites. As part of an out-of-court settlement in 1984, ETS agreed to select test questions for future versions of this test in a particular order: Questions on which similar percents of Blacks and Whites had responded correctly in the past were to be selected first, provided that they were not very difficult for either group. Questions that were very hard or that resulted in large differences between Blacks and Whites in the rate of correct response (*disparate impact*) were to be used only as a last resort. The goal was to reduce the difference in average scores between Black and White test-takers.

After the settlement, this method of test development became known as the "Golden Rule procedure"—a name that seemed to convey a stamp of approval, although it was, of course, merely the name of a party to a lawsuit. The Golden Rule approach was proposed in legislation in at least five states as a general method for assembling tests.[46] The procedure drew harsh criticism from psychometricians, however, and was later formally disowned by ETS president Greg Anrig, who had agreed to the initial settlement.[47] Legal scholar Michael A. Rebell cited the Golden Rule decision as an example of court actions that have been detrimental to testing policy. As Rebell explained, "[t]he major difference between the Golden Rule approach and previous use of statistics to indicate differential performance by racial groups on particular items is that under Golden Rule decisions would be made solely on the basis of statistical indicators, without any necessity to identify questionable content in the targeted items."[48]

What would happen if the Golden Rule procedure were applied to admissions tests? An ETS study conducted by Gary L. Marco used existing test data to predict the effect of various test assembly procedures on SAT results. One of the main findings of the SAT study was that "selecting items with the smallest differences [between Blacks and Whites] in proportions correct tend[s] to eliminate middle difficulty items. Yet these are the items that . . . contribute most to the measurement power of the test for both Blacks and Whites."[49] (Measurement power here refers to the ability of an item to distinguish between more skilled and less skilled test-takers.) Marco found that the tests produced using the Golden Rule approach were substantially less reliable (yielded scores that were less precise) than existing SAT forms. Also, because the test forms assembled under the Golden Rule procedure had fewer difficult items than real SATs, Marco concluded that they could not do a good job of screening applicants for selective colleges. Another ETS study, which involved an unnamed "graduate-level admissions test," also found that picking test items that minimized Black-White differences produced tests that were significantly less reliable for both Blacks and Whites.[50] Summarizing the psychometric view of the Golden Rule procedure, eminent psychometrician William Angoff said that "the inevitable outcome" of its application would be a test with lower reliability and less measurement power—an "ultimately less valid instrument."[51]

As ETS president Anrig noted in declaring the settlement a mistake, the Golden Rule procedure appears to endorse the premise that items on which Blacks and Whites score differently are biased by definition. Yet, as testing experts Robert L. Linn and Fritz Drasgow remarked in yet another Golden Rule commentary, tests like the insurance exam "*do not measure innate abilities or aptitudes. Instead, they assess a test taker's current repertoire of knowledge and skills* . . [which] . . . is certainly affected by his or her 'environment.' . . . ."[52] If the test questions are based on material that insurance agents do indeed need to know, eliminating them solely on the basis of group differences or unusual difficulty is not a sound test construction procedure.

The remarks made by Linn and Drasgow bear serious consideration because they could be applied to standardized admissions tests as well. Admissions tests, too, assess a "repertoire of knowledge." To argue that group differences in test performance are sufficient to demonstrate test bias, it is necessary to claim that opportunities to acquire this repertoire of academic skills are equal for all groups in our society—a claim that, unfortunately, would be impossible to support.

What's Better Than the Golden Rule?

If the Golden Rule approach isn't sensible, how can biased test questions be identified? Doing a good job of screening items for bias takes both expert judgment and statistical analysis. Before an item is approved for inclusion in an admissions test, it undergoes a "sensitivity review" to make sure its content is not disturbing to certain ethnic or national groups or offensive in some other way (see chapter 3). Later, when the item is administered, a statistical screening is performed. From a statistical perspective, a test question is *potentially* biased if equally skilled members of two groups have different rates of correct response. All major testing companies routinely perform analyses to look for this kind of difference in item results among ethnic groups and between men and women.

Let's say we wanted to see if any questions on a math test were biased against women or against men. Essentially, what we would do is to group all the candidates according to their total scores on the test. Then, within each score level, we would compare the performance of men and women on each test item. The goal would be to make comparisons between men and women of equivalent overall math ability.[53] Suppose that men were found to be more likely to answer a certain question correctly than their female counterparts. This test question would be flagged as a potentially biased item because, evidently, some factor other than overall math skill affected the candidates' ability to answer correctly. At this point, math experts would be called in to determine whether the content of the question was consistent with the purpose of the test.

Suppose it turned out that the suspect question was this one: *The width of a football field is 160 feet. What is the area of the portion of the field that lies between a team's goal line and the 50-yard line?* Even if you know the formula for the area of a rectangle, you can't solve the problem without knowing the distance between the goal line and the 50-yard line—a piece of trivia that is obvious to football fans but obscure to football ignoramuses like me. Because the test is intended to assess math skills, not sports knowledge, and because we know that more men than women have mastered football facts, most experts would consider this item to be biased against women. The offending test question would not count toward test-takers' scores, and it would not be given again without modification. (Chapter 6 gives a real example that involves hunting jargon.)

Research on the detection of item bias (now often called *differential item functioning*) dates back to the 1960s—the era of the Civil Rights movement.[54] In reality, the causes of item bias are often far more obscure than in the football example, but some consistent patterns have been found.

What kinds of items have shown statistical evidence of possible bias in ethnic group analyses? Findings about verbal items tend to be somewhat more consistent and interpretable than results for math questions. It has been a recurrent finding that African-American, Hispanic, and Asian-American test-takers don't do as well as a matched group of Whites on verbal analogy items[55] (examples of which appear below and in chapter 6). The same is true for test questions containing homographs—words that have two (or more) completely different meanings, such as "light," which can mean "not heavy" or "not dark."[56] Here's an example of an SAT verbal analogy question on which Mexican-American and Puerto-Rican test-takers did not perform as well as a matched group of Whites. The item has two homographs—*bark* and *wake*.[57]

BARK : TREE ::
(A) skin : fruit   *[correct answer]*
(B) dew : grass
(C) seed : flower
(D) peak : hill
(E) wake : boat

SAT test questions reprinted by permission of the College Entrance Examination Board, the copyright owner. Permission to reprint SAT materials does not constitute review or endorsement by Educational Testing Service or the College Board of this publication as a whole or of any other questions or testing information it may contain.

ETS researcher Alicia Schmitt and her colleagues also found that analogies containing similar words with common roots in English and Spanish—*true cognates*—favor Hispanic test-takers if the Spanish version is used more frequently than its English cognate. Consider the following SAT antonym item, which contains five true cognates.

TURBULENT
(A) aerial
(B) compact
(C) pacific   [correct answer]
(D) chilled
(E) sanitary

Reprinted by permission of Lawrence Erlbaum Associates, Inc.

Hispanic test-takers performed better on this item than a matched group of Whites.[58] One reason may be that the correct answer—"pacific"—is a more unusual word than its cognate, the Spanish "pacífico" (peaceful). There is some evidence that Hispanic test-takers are disadvantaged by false cognates—similar words that have different meanings in the two languages.

Findings of potential bias on math items are quite murky. Some studies have found that minorities perform better than a matched group of Whites on "pure math" items—those involving algebraic manipulations in the absence of any context—and do worse on word problems. One speculation about the reason for this is that pure math items tend to resemble textbook problems, which may be the focus of instruction at schools with fewer resources.[59] Some research has also found that Black test-takers don't do as well as a matched group of Whites on test questions that include graphs, charts and diagrams, although the reasons for this remain unclear.

Some findings from a study that Kadriye Ercikan and I conducted show why it's not a good idea to have a blanket policy of discarding all items that show statistical evidence of bias. We compared the performance of Black and White eighth-graders on a U.S. history exam that was part of the National Assessment of Educational Progress. On three test questions, Black test-takers performed substantially better than their White counterparts; there were no items with equivalent performance differences in the other direction. The "culprit" items turned out to be about Martin Luther King, Harriet Tubman, and the Underground Railroad. Hispanic test-takers performed much better than a matched group of Whites on one question about Latin-American and Asian immigration to the United States; again, no items showed equivalent differences in favor of Whites.[60]

These real-life examples are distinct from the hypothetical football item in a fundamental way: The Black history items and the immigration question involved content that was clearly a legitimate part of the subject that the test was intended to measure—U.S. history. But they are questions that were particularly captivating for minority test-takers. These results illustrate the fact that apparent bias can be caused by differences in test-takers' interest in the content of the test items. Other studies have shown that questions on topics of minority interest show statistical evidence of bias in favor of people of color. For example, one study of the SAT found results of this kind on a reading comprehension passage about a Black mathematician and on passages about civil rights and poverty.[61] In other cases, differences across groups in training and course background may also result in statistical evidence of bias. Obviously, then, we should not be too quick to remove items solely on the basis of statistical results. Only a few of those that are flagged prove to have identifiable flaws.

To what degree do problem test items contribute to overall *test score* differences among ethnic groups? In a 1993 study, Elizabeth Burton and Nancy W. Burton examined ethnic group performance differences on the SAT before and after statistical screening of items for bias began at ETS in 1989.[62] Essentially, there was no change over time in the score disparities among ethnic groups. For one thing, the number of test questions found to have problems was fairly small. Also, on some items that were eliminated, ethnic minorities had an advantage. Even in the absence of evidence that it affects overall SAT results, however, item screening is important as a precaution against the inclusion of unreasonable test content and as a source of information that can contribute to the construction of better tests in the future.

Standardized Tests and Ethnic Diversity in Higher Education

As we saw in chapter 2, the controversy about the legitimacy of admissions testing has been fueled by the growing legislative and judicial challenges to affirmative action. In 1996, Californians approved Proposition 209, which banned consideration of race or ethnicity in admissions to the state's public colleges and universities. Texas has been grappling with the effects of the 1996 Hopwood decision, which also outlawed the use of race in admissions programs, and the state of Washington has been faced with the consequences of Initiative 200, a Proposition 209 clone that passed in 1998. Ward Connerly, father of Proposition 209, has promoted similar ballot measures throughout the country.

Fearing that minorities would be left out in the cold without the protective cloak of affirmative action, some educators and government officials advocated a de-emphasis of standardized admissions tests, which, they argued, serve to limit opportunities for people of color. Bills that would reduce the role of standardized testing in admissions decisions were intro-duced in several states and in the U.S. Congress in 2000, and a U.S. Educa-tion Department document issued in 2000 advised that colleges could be in legal jeopardy if they relied too heavily on standardized tests in making admissions or financial aid decisions.[63] In a dramatic development in 2001, Richard Atkinson, the president of the University of California, made a surprise speech advocating the elimination of the SAT: I as a crite-rion for admission to UC. The idea of abandoning the SAT at the Univer-sity of California had been hotly debated years earlier but had faded from public awareness. In his speech, Atkinson advocated an immediate switch to college admissions tests that are tied closely to the high school curricu-lum, and said that he hoped to eventually move away from quantitative admissions formulas in order to "help all students, especially low-income and minority students, determine their own educational destinies."[64]

Would Eliminating the SAT Boost Diversity?

What would be the likely effect on the diversity of University of Cali-fornia campuses if the SAT were dropped as an admissions criterion? This very topic was addressed in a December 1997 report issued by the Office of the President of UC, based on supplementary analyses of data from a study conducted by the California Postsecondary Education Commission. Transcripts, test scores, and background information from a random sample of more than 15,000 students who graduated from California public high schools in 1996 were analyzed to determine the effect of applying various admissions criteria. In particular, the study considered the impact of eliminating standardized admissions test requirements on the rates of "UC eligibility." At that time, eligibility for the university was based on the completion of certain college preparatory courses, GPA for those courses, and, if the GPA was below a certain level, scores on the SAT or ACT. (Students who are judged UC-eligible are then subject to the admissions criteria of the individual UC campuses.)

The study's conclusion was surprising to some: Eliminating considera-tion of test scores, while maintaining other mandated features of UC admissions policy, would produce very small changes in the eligibility rates for Latinos (from 3.8 percent to 4.0 percent), African Americans (from 2.8 percent to 2.3 percent), and Asian Americans (from 30 percent to 29 percent). The largest change would be an increase in the eligibility rate for Whites (from 12.7 percent to 14.8 percent).

The minimal change in the predicted eligibility rates for Black and Latino students in the California study are less remarkable in light of the finding that "[l]ow test scores rarely are the only reason for a student's ineligibility." In fact, only 2.5 percent of California public high school graduates were ineligible solely on the basis of inadequate admissions test scores. (It is perhaps ironic that this key piece of information comes from the office of the same university president who has become an instant hero of the anti-SAT movement.) Most students—63 percent of graduates overall—were ineligible because they had major course omissions or grade deficiencies, or because they attended "schools that did not have a college preparatory curriculum approved by the University." The percentage of students in this ineligibility category was much higher for African Americans (77 percent) and Latinos (74 percent) than for Whites (59 percent) and Asian Americans (39 percent).[65]

How much do course completion rates and grades vary among ethnic and socioeconomic groups in the nation as a whole? The National Center for Education Statistics conducted a study of the transcripts of about 25,000 students who graduated from high school in 1994. Examination of course-taking patterns in science and mathematics shows that, for basic courses such as biology, geology, algebra I, and geometry, differences across ethnic groups are relatively small. For higher-level courses, however, a clear pattern emerges: Asian Americans and Pacific Islanders are the most likely to take these courses, followed by White, Hispanic, Black, and Native American students in that order. For example, 44 percent of Asians, 26 percent of Whites, 16 percent of Hispanics, 15 percent of Blacks, and 10 percent of Native Americans took physics. Twenty-four percent of Asians, 10 percent of Whites, and 4 to 6 percent of the other groups took calculus.[66]

Further evidence comes from a nationwide study called "Making the Cut," conducted by the National Center for Education Statistics. Researchers examined 1992 data from a national sample of about 7,000 college-bound high school seniors and determined what percentage of these students met criteria similar to those used in admissions to selective colleges. The study determined which students had earned high school grade-point averages (HGPAs) of at least 3.5, achieved SAT scores (math and verbal combined) of at least 1100, completed a certain number of course credits (four in English, three in math, three in science, three in social studies, and two in a foreign language), received favorable evaluations from teachers, and participated in at least two school-related extracurricular activities. Overall, only about 6 percent of the grads met all the criteria.[67]

The researchers looked at each factor separately and compiled results for various groups of students. As table 5-4 shows, differences among ethnic groups were small to moderate for the criteria involving extracurricular activities, teacher perceptions, and course credits. (At first blush, the relatively small differences among ethnic groups in course completion rates seems to be at odds with the results of the transcript study mentioned earlier. In Making the Cut, however, researchers merely counted credits; they didn't determine how advanced the courses were.) High school grades and SAT scores differed substantially across groups, however, and the ethnic group pattern for the HGPA criterion closely paralleled the results for the SAT: The percentage of students with grade-point averages of at least 3.5 was highest for Asians, followed by Whites, Hispanics, and Blacks in that order. The group differences in high school grades were quite large. For example, 29 percent of Asians received a high school GPA of at least 3.5, compared with only 4 percent of Black students. (The percentages for the very small American Indian/Alaskan Native group are less precise than those for other groups, but it is evident that few students in this group met the GPA or SAT criteria.)

It is clear that, contrary to what is often believed, grades, like test scores, show large disparities across ethnic groups. What about the association of family income and education with students' test scores and grades? The correlation between standardized test scores and income has often been invoked as a reason to avoid the use of tests. It is frequently suggested that the relationship between test scores and family income occurs because test coaching is available to only the wealthiest test-takers. "The only thing the SAT. predicts well now is socioeconomic status," a University of California dean claimed recently.[68] "Call it the 'Volvo Effect,'" said journalist Peter Sacks, noting that "one can make a good guess about a child's standardized test scores simply by looking at how many degrees her parents have and at what kind of car they drive."[69] Sacks refers to several studies to demonstrate that SAT scores and socioeconomic status are related, including the same national study that served as the source of table 5-4. What he neglects to mention is that this study showed that socioeconomic status was related to high school grades too. Table 5-5 shows the percentages of students in each of three socioeconomic categories (high, medium, and low, as measured by parental education, occupation, and income) who met each of the five criteria considered in the study. It's obvious that socioeconomic status—SES for short—is related to the likelihood of meeting the SAT criterion (32 percent of the high-SES students versus 9 percent of the low). But it's also a fact that, across the board, the percentage of students satisfying the academic criteria increased with socioeconomic level. In particular, 24 percent of the high-SES group, compared to only 10 percent of the low-SES group, had high school GPAs of at least 3.5.

Table 5-4 Percentage of 1992 High School Graduates Meeting Typical Admissions Criteria for Selective Colleges, by Ethnic Group

Admissions Criterion	White	Black	Hispanic	Asian	American Indian/ Alaskan Native
HGPA at least 3.5	21	4	10	29	5
SAT total at least 1100	25	3	8	28	2
Specified course credits completed	56	56	47	60	24
Teacher perceptions positive	42	40	41	49	26
At least two extracurricular activities	68	68	63	68	58
All five criteria met	7	< 1	3	9	0

Adapted from Owings, McMillen, & Burkett, (1995). *Making the Cut: Who Meets Highly Selective College Entrance Criteria?* National Center for Education Statistics. (NCES publication 95–732). Retrieved August 18, 1999, from http://www.nces.ed.gov. The study was based on analyses of a sample of 6,760 students from the National Education Longitudinal Study of 1988: Second Follow-up, 1992. "Specified course credits completed" indicates that the student had four credits in English, three in math, three in science, three in social studies, and two in foreign language. Teacher perceptions were obtained from a questionnaire.

Table 5–5 Percentage of 1992 High School Graduates Meeting Typical Admissions Criteria for Selective Colleges, by Socioeconomic Status

Admissions Criterion	Socioeconomic Status		
	High	Middle	Low
HGPA at least 3.5	24	16	10
SAT total at least 1100	32	15	9
Specified course credits completed	65	50	40
Teacher perceptions positive	48	38	36
At least two extracurricular activities	72	66	57
All five criteria met	9	4	2

Adapted from Owings, McMillen, & Burkett, (1995). *Making the Cut: Who Meets Highly Selective College Entrance Criteria?* National Center for Education Statistics (NCES publication 95–732). Retrieved August 18, 1999, from http://www.nces.ed.gov. The study was based on analyses of a sample of 6,760 students from the National Education Longitudinal Study of 1988: Second Follow-up, 1992. "Specified course credits completed" indicates that the student had four credits in English, three in math, three in science, three in social studies, and two in foreign language. Teacher perceptions were obtained from a questionnaire.

Another illustration of the association between family income and educational achievement comes from College Board data on about 870,000 high school seniors who took the SAT in 1997. SAT averages are certainly higher for students from families with larger incomes. But so are average grades: As income goes from less than $20,000 to more than $100,000, the percentage of students with an A average increases from 30 percent to 46 percent; the percentage with a C or below decreases from 19 percent to 10 percent.[70]

So, if we were to condemn any admissions criterion related to parents' income and education, we'd have to cross high school grades and course background off our list along with test scores. It's a sad reality that educational disparities in our country make it unlikely that we could find any reasonable measure of educational achievement that was unrelated to socioeconomic status.

Class Rank Admissions Plans: Will They Increase Diversity?

During his presidential campaign, George W. Bush declared his support for college admissions policies that replace the use of race with programs that admit the top students in every high school. This announcement came soon after Governor Jeb Bush of Florida proclaimed that he would eliminate affirmative action in college admissions, and would guarantee places in the state's public university system to the top 20 percent of students in each of Florida's high schools. Florida's retreat from affirmative action and its introduction of the "Talented 20" program, which began in 2000, constituted a sort of preemptive strike: Jeb Bush calculated (correctly, it turned out) that by taking these actions, he could keep a measure banning affirmative action off the November 2000 ballot—the same ballot on which brother George's name would appear as the Republican presidential candidate.

The "X percent plan" bandwagon had started up a few years earlier. Texas initiated its 10 percent admissions plan after the 1996 Hopwood decision, and the University of California began implementing its 4 percent plan in 2001 in response to Proposition 209 (see chapter 2).[71] Backers of these class rank plans argue that admitting students on the basis of high school record alone is more equitable than relying on a combination of test scores and grades.

But in 1999, the heavily Democratic U.S. Commission on Civil Rights issued a statement harshly denouncing the class rank admission plans as public relations ploys that are ineffective substitutes for race-based affirmative action. And from the other side of the political spectrum, the Hoover Institution's Shelby Steele said in the *National Review* that "...

X percent plans spread lowered standards" and diminish ". . . precisely the first-rate state universities that have historically offered superb educations to hard-working students from modest backgrounds."[72]

Politics aside, how well do these X percent plans work, given that high school grades, like test scores, vary across ethnic and income groups? In exploring the effectiveness of these programs, it is important to note that the existing class rank plans differ from each other in fundamental ways. Consider the Texas and California programs. One major difference between the two involves the definition of a high school grade-point average. A Texas GPA, it turns out, is not the same as a California GPA. In Texas, a GPA is whatever the high school says it is. Not so in California, where students must complete at least eleven of fifteen required courses by the end of their junior year, and the GPA considered for UC admission is based on these courses. Another key way in which the two plans differ is the level of enforcement. The Texas legislation requires that *each* public college accept all applicants who qualify under the 10 percent plan. In contrast, students admitted to the University of California through the 4 percent plan are guaranteed only "UC eligibility;" individual campuses still impose their own admissions criteria.

What are the implications of the differences between the Texas and California programs? The Texas plan has been touted as a success in a host of news stories because the ethnic makeup at the University of Texas at Austin closely mirrors pre-1996 levels. But the Texas plan may be more of a reallocation of minority students than an increase: Students who are guaranteed admission to the particular school of their choice will gravitate toward the most prestigious campus in the system—UT Austin. Data on the statewide effect of the Texas 10 percent plan are hard to come by.

What about the effects of the class rank plan at the University of California, where strict course requirements are in effect, and students are not guaranteed admission to a particular campus? My own institution, UC Santa Barbara, provides an interesting example of 4 percent plan results (although it is only one of eight UC campuses affected by the plan, and can't be considered representative of the university as a whole). Out of 34,000 applicants to UCSB for the fall of 2001, over 3,300 were eligible for UC admission under the 4 percent plan, including more than 700 from ethnic groups considered to be underrepresented (Native Americans, Alaskan Natives, African Americans, Chicanos, and Latinos). At first glance, this suggests that the plan had a substantial impact. But of these 3,300, all but 77 would have been eligible even without the 4 percent plan, and only 37 of these 77 were from underrepresented groups. Most dismaying of all was the finding that *none* of these 77 were admitted to UCSB. So although a headline claiming "3,000 apply to UCSB under 4 percent plan" would be literally true, a more blunt assessment would be as follows: Under the 4 percent plan, UCSB considered 37 minority students who would not otherwise have been eligible, but ultimately admitted none of them.[73]

Florida's Talented 20 program is similar to California's 4 percent plan in that the program guarantees each eligible student admission to one of Florida's ten public universities, not to the student's first choice. And, as in California, certain college prep courses are required. In contrast to the California situation, however, Florida districts apparently had a lot of leeway in determining how high school GPAs were to be computed. How well did the Florida plan work in its initial year? Although the state reported an increase in the number of minorities among the state's fall 2000 freshmen, most of those slots had been filled under earlier admissions policies, which permitted affirmative action. The Talented 20 program, in fact, had been frozen by the courts until mid-July 2000.[74] Furthermore, according to an analysis reported in the *St. Petersburg Times*, more than 99 percent of the students who were part of the Talented 20 already met previously existing admissions standards.[75] A more definitive analysis of the success of the program will be possible when data for the 2001 entering classes become available.

The problems faced by class rank plans are emblematic of the central dilemma of college admissions policy. On one hand, the more rigorous the academic requirements, the less effective an admissions plan is likely to be in increasing ethnic diversity. On the other hand, the absence of strict criteria may doom the students admitted under these programs to academic failure because of inadequate preparation. From the university perspective, a potential danger of the percent plans is that accepting students who rank highly within poor-quality high schools could lead to academic mediocrity and higher dropout rates on campus.

Relying heavily on grades and eliminating test requirements may have other unintended effects as well. According to some educators, the existence of tests serves to "keep grades honest." In the absence of test scores, grades may be subject to rampant inflation. Under the X percent plans, after all, teachers and principals have the power to alter a borderline student's eligibility for college by changing a single grade. And what about the incentives created by these plans? Students stand to gain by moving to schools where achievement is low, taking the easiest courses possible, and ensuring the failure of their peers. A cynical view, perhaps, but it's important to keep in mind that abolishing tests won't necessarily create a more benign, less competitive environment.

On the positive side, the class rank plans do seem to be having at least one beneficial effect: Colleges and universities are paying more attention to the academic preparation that students are receiving in high schools, and are stepping up their efforts to recruit talented students of color. Ultimately, this may be the greatest contribution of the X percent admission plans.

Should Test Scores Be "Corrected" for Student Background? The "Strivers" Controversy

If eliminating tests doesn't provide a straightforward path to a more equitable admissions policy, is it possible to calculate adjusted SAT scores that give "credit" to test-takers with disadvantaged backgrounds? This is the question behind a research project that led to a public relations disaster for Educational Testing Service in 1999. The so-called "Strivers" project was the brainchild of ETS Vice President Anthony Carnevale. The uproar began with a *Wall Street Journal* article, which quoted Carnevale as saying that ETS would soon meet with colleges who were interested in implementing a new program that "works a lot like a golf handicap."[76] A media frenzy followed, as the story was picked up by the nation's major newspapers, magazines, and TV news shows.

Some of the reactions were predictable: The Princeton Review applauded the research, adding that the existence of the Strivers project was an acknowledgment by ETS of "the biases inherent in the SAT."[77] Conservative commentator Abigail Thernstrom, who called the Strivers score a "victimology index," criticized ETS for "reinforcing the already-too-widespread belief that demography is destiny."[78] But there was one surprising response: Among the most explicit critics was Gaston Caperton, the newly appointed President of the College Board, who said he would block any attempt by ETS to implement the Strivers idea. "There is a real art and a real skill to blending these factors together for an institution to decide what its student body should look like," Caperton told the *New York Times*. To think that you could do that with some scientific formula just wouldn't work." Although squabbling between the College Board and its contractor, ETS, is hardly unprecedented, it's rarely quite so public.

The media reaction turned into an event in itself, with columnists commenting on each other's viewpoints for weeks. Amidst the ricocheting op ed pieces, ETS backed off from the Strivers idea with lightning speed. According to an internal ETS communication dated September 1,

1999, just a day after the *Wall Street Journal* article, Strivers was strictly a research venture, not a product, program, or service. A report that would explain all would be issued in about two months. (In fact, as of December 2001, it has not yet appeared.) Adding to ETS's woes, Nicholas Lemann claimed in his book, *The Big Test*, that a Strivers-like study by ETS researcher Winton Manning had been curtailed by ETS in the 1990s.

Oddly enough, despite all the charges of suppression and back-pedaling leveled at ETS, the Strivers research had already been unveiled publicly years before. Early results appeared in a chapter by Anthony Carnevale and Elhum Haghighat in a 1998 volume called *Hopwood, Bakke, and Beyond*. The book is an account of a 1997 "policy summit" on diversity in higher education organized by the American Association of Collegiate Registrars and Admissions Officers. Intriguingly, the acknowl-edgments section offers "special thanks . . . to our sponsors ETS and The College Board, who have been supportive of both the . . . Summit and this publication."[79]

The chapter by Carnevale and Haghighat presents the Strivers project as "a new method for evaluating test scores of students" that uses statis-tical analysis to identify "students who score better than expected on SATs, given their economic and social backgrounds." The report goes on to say that, "[w]ith race-based affirmative action now under political and judicial assault," the method can be used to award "extra credit to these newly identified 'strivers,' who can be identified without relying solely on their racial or ethnic background."[80]

As described in the 1998 report, Strivers works like this: Using regres-sion analysis (see chapter 4), a candidate's SAT score is predicted on the basis of social and economic factors, such as family income, parents' education, school location, and school quality. If the candidate's actual SAT score exceeds this predicted score by at least 100 points (later changed to 200 points), he's an "educational striver."[81]

Many criticisms can and have been made of this idea on philosophical, statistical, ethical, and practical grounds. But the most striking aspect of the Strivers method (as described in 1998) is that, when applied to actual data, it didn't work! The 1998 analysis used data from a large national study on students who had graduated from high school by 1992. While 84 percent of the individuals who constituted the college "applicants" in the analysis were White, more than 90 percent of the students identified as strivers were White. Among the strivers, the percentages of Hispanic and Black students were almost the same as in the applicant pool, and the percentage of Asians was smaller. In other words, applying this version of the Strivers approach admitted a freshman class that was less diverse than the pool of applicants.

A second version of the method was then applied, in which the candidate's race was used in the initial prediction equation. In effect, the kind of inquiry that underlies this procedure is, "How well did this student score on the SAT, considering that he is African American"—a deeply offensive question to many. (Opponents of affirmative action often argue that it engenders similar patterns of thinking.) The race-based Strivers method increased the percentage of African Americans (from 3.3 percent of the pool to 5.6 percent of those admitted) and, to a small degree, the percentage of Hispanics (from 2.5 percent to 2.8 percent), but it also increased the percentage of Whites (from 83.7 percent to 88.2 percent). Only the percentage of Asians decreased. If Carnevale's numbers are to be believed, the race-based Strivers approach reallocated some college slots from Asians to Hispanics and Blacks, and increased the number of Whites.[82] This outcome would certainly not be universally applauded; it also has the distinct disadvantage of being illegal in the parts of the country where the use of race in admissions has been banned.

Perhaps the most troubling aspect of this controversial approach to admissions is that the identification of "strivers" involves no evidence whatever of actual striving. To be labeled a striver requires only that the student have higher scores than other students with similar background characteristics, regardless of the reason. For example, an alleged striver may have obtained his score by attending coaching school, which is not the kind of striving that most proponents of the plan would choose to reward. And of course, there may be students who did in fact strive, but did not meet the statistical criteria for strivers. In contrast, affirmative action policies allow admissions officers the flexibility to determine who the real strivers are, using student records and interviews.

The Strivers project can certainly contribute to our national conversation about higher education by providing useful information about the effects of various alternative college admissions policies, and by provoking discussion of the thorny issues of fairness in testing and admissions. But, as an actual modification to admissions procedures, the Strivers method is a long way from being ready for prime time.

What Can Be Done to Increase Campus Diversity?

A point on which individuals of every political stripe can agree is that ultimately, we must fix "the pipeline"—that is, improve K–12 education so that college applicants of all ethnic and income groups will be better prepared. Inequalities in academic preparation are unsurprising in light of the enormous variation in the quality of K–12 education across districts and states, as reflected in teacher-pupil ratios, teachers' educational level and years of experience, and school resources. According to an *Education Week* survey, for example, state per-pupil expenditures for 1999 ranged from about $4,000 to about $8,700, after adjustment for regional cost differences. Even more glaring is the range in spending among districts within a state, which exceeded $3,000 in several states, according to 1997 calculations.[83]

But the proposal that we focus on shoring up K–12 schooling has drawn an impatient response from some educators. Said Harvard law professor Christopher Edley at a 1997 affirmative action colloquium, ". . . [O]bviously we all would prefer the great day in which the pipeline is repaired and students of all kinds show up at our doorsteps prepared, ready, eager to take the best of what we have to offer. But that day is not with us. What do we do in the meantime?"[84]

First off, we need to acknowledge that, in the short term, an admissions policy cannot simultaneously maximize the college grades and the ethnic diversity of our freshman classes. If the intent of our admissions policies were simply to use resources as efficiently as possible by maximizing the expected GPAs of the entering class, we would need to rely heavily on students' previous academic records. And any admissions policy that assigns a great deal of weight to evidence of past achievement will tend to reward those who have had the greatest educational opportunities—often White students from higher economic brackets. The indisputable fact is that both grades and admissions tests are reflections of the same educational system with all its flaws and inequities. As Christopher Edley noted, "the SAT simply recapitulates . . . all of the class advantages, all of the access advantages . . . in the K–12 experiences of the student."[85] In fact, the same can be said of grades. By using grades rather than SATs as an admissions criterion, said sociologist Christopher Jencks in a 1989 essay, "you are simply substituting tests designed by high school teachers for tests designed by the Educational Testing Service. . . ."[86]

Attaining campus diversity in the immediate future requires flexible admissions polices that allow for the consideration of a wide range of student characteristics. Among the student attributes that warrant further investigation are motivation, perseverance, and "spike talents" in particular areas. Such factors are already considered at many schools, but we need more research to determine how best to measure these characteristics and to assess their predictive value.

Of course, the most effective means of achieving ethnic diversity is through affirmative action programs. If we as a society want to increase the enrollment of under-represented racial and ethnic groups, the best way is to incorporate this goal explicitly by considering an applicant's membership in these groups to be a "plus" in the admissions process, rather than letting tests take the flak for admissions decisions that do not produce the desired ethnic balance.

CHAPTER 6

Are Standardized Admissions Tests Fair to Women?

"Next time your daughter comes home with a college board score that's about 40 points below what you thought she'd get, don't blame yourself for not making her the right breakfast the day of the exam. Instead, you can blame the Scholastic Assessment Test itself. The exam . . . continues to have a bias that favors boys. . . ." That's according to a 1997 *Washington Post* article.[1] Not so, says Christina Hoff Sommers in the May 2000 issue of the *Atlantic Monthly*: "A careful look at the pool of students who take the SAT . . . shows that the girls' lower scores have little or nothing to do with bias or unfairness. Indeed, the scores do not even signify lower achievement by girls."[2]

Here we are again in the Alice-in-Wonderland world of standardized testing. What are the facts about the fairness of standardized admissions tests to women? Like the findings about the test performance of people of color, the evidence turns out to be surprisingly complicated. The particular patterns of test scores and grades for women, however, are substantially different from the results for under-represented minorities, described in chapter 5. Although Black and Latino candidates tend to have test scores below those of Whites and Asian Americans, their subsequent grades are actually lower than their test scores would predict. Women, on the other hand, tend to score lower than men, and to receive higher grades than predicted. Why does this happen and what does it mean? This is the topic of chapter 6.

Differences between Men and Women in Average Test Scores

As a starting point, let's use the now-familiar Ramist College Board study.[3] In table 6-1, we can see that women had higher GPAs than men, both in high school and college, a typical finding. But here, in contrast

Table 6-1 Average SAT Scores, HGPA, and CGPA for the College Board Study

	Men	Women	Overall
SAT Verbal	512	499	505
SAT Math	586	535	559
High School GPA	3.37	3.44	3.41
College GPA	2.58	2.67	2.63
Number of Test-Takers	22,412	23,967	46,379

Adapted from Ramist et al., 1994, p, 7, 9. The GPA scales range between 0 and 4.

with the ethnic group results, the test score differences go in the opposite direction from the differences in GPAs: Men score better than women, with a larger difference on the SAT Math test than on the Verbal test. The 2001 SAT results in chapter 1 also show this pattern, although the score differences are considerably smaller. At one time, women scored better than men on the verbal SAT but this changed beginning in 1972. Ironically, some researchers have speculated that the reversal may have resulted from ETS attempts to make the content of the verbal exam more "gender neutral" in order to improve the scores of men.[4]

On average, men also score better than women on the ACT Math test, the ACT Science Reasoning test, and the ACT Composite; the MCAT Verbal Reasoning, Physical Sciences, and Biological Sciences tests; the GRE Verbal, Quantitative, and Analytic tests; the GMAT Verbal and Quantitative tests, and the LSAT. Women tend to score better then men on the ACT English and Reading tests and the GMAT Writing Assessment, and the same as men on the MCAT Writing Sample.[5]

At the high school level and beyond, women typically earn considerably lower scores than men on standardized tests in math and science. Often, they outperform men on reading and writing assessments; in other cases, men have a small advantage. The relatively strong performance of secondary-school girls on writing tests played a key role in the controversial resolution of a gender bias complaint involving the Preliminary Scholastic Assessment Test (now called the PSAT/NMSQT), which serves as a practice test for the SAT and is used in screening applicants for National Merit Scholarships. In 1994, the American Civil Liberties Union, acting on behalf of FairTest, filed a complaint with the Office for Civil Rights of the U.S. Department of Education charging that the PSAT was biased against girls: Fewer girls than boys won scholarships even though girls outnumbered boys among test-takers and went on to earn higher college grades. To settle the complaint, the College Board and ETS added a multiple-choice writing skills test to the PSAT in 1996. While critics accused the testing organizations of caving in to political manipulation, the College Board contended that the addition of the writing test was done for educational reasons and would lay the groundwork for a similar, long-planned addition to the SAT.[6]

Although the inclusion of a writing section did boost girls' PSAT scores, as expected, it was not a public relations success. The change did not appease the critics, who claimed that it amounted to a tacit admission that the earlier version of the PSAT, as well as the current version of the SAT, were biased. And even though their PSAT scores improved, girls continued to win fewer National Merit Scholarships than boys, leading testing watchdogs to complain that the PSAT was still biased against females. "This was a Band-Aid for a fundamental problem, and one that would not close the wound," a FairTest representative said in 1998. "Girls are still cheated of their fair share of National Merit Scholarships. . . ."[7]

What accounts for the fact that men perform better than women on most standardized admissions tests, especially on the math sections? It has been suggested that this test score gap results in part from differences in economic and academic background. More young women than men take the SAT, for example, and, according to a 1998 College Board report, "a much higher proportion of females than males taking the SAT come from families with lower levels of income and parental education."[8] (With the exception of the GMAT, more women than men take all the admissions tests discussed in this book; see chapter 1.)

The College Board also said that "important differences still persist in the proportion of males and females completing advanced courses in math, science, and computer programming" in high school.[9] But a recent College Board profile of high school seniors shows that disparities in course background have decreased substantially over the last ten years. The Board reported that in 2000, male and female SAT-takers were equally likely to have taken at least four years of math, and that 22 percent of girls and 26 percent of boys had taken calculus. Girls and boys had each taken an average of 3.4 years of natural science courses; 45 percent of girls and 53 percent of boys had taken physics. On ACT's 2000 survey of course background, about 6 percent of girls and boys reported that they had taken a math sequence consisting of algebra 1 and 2, geometry, trigonometry, and calculus. Thirty-three percent of boys and 28 percent of girls reported having taken general science, biology, chemistry and physics.[10]

Along with differences in course preparation, countless other reasons have been offered to explain the gender gap in test scores, including test bias, biological differences, diverging interests and aspirations, societal influences, and, more recently, the "stereotype threat" phenomenon described in chapter 5. This threat— the fear of inadvertently confirming a cultural stereotype—"dramatically depresses the standardized test performance of women and African Americans" in areas in which society regards them as inferior, according to Professor Claude Steele of Stanford, the primary developer of this theory.[11] According to Steele and others, this phenomenon could explain the typically lower math scores earned by women. "[T]he stereotype threat that women experience in math-performance settings derives from a negative stereotype about their math ability that is disseminated throughout society," says Steele.[12] Research findings have been inconsistent, with laboratory experiments tending to support the occurrence of stereotype threat, and studies in real testing situations failing to find any evidence of it (see chapter 5).

Differences between Men and Women in Prediction Accuracy

As in chapter 5, we can get another perspective on group differences in test performance by examining the strength with which SAT scores and high school grades predict first-year college GPA. Table 6-2 shows that in the Ramist study, test scores and high school GPA were a little more strongly related to CGPA for women than for men. When all three predictors were used in combination, the (uncorrected) correlation for women was .50, compared to .46 for men. It's typical to find that validity coefficients are higher for women, although the reasons aren't clear. One frequent speculation is that men are more likely to skip classes and homework assignments, making their college grades less predictable.[13]

Table 6-2 Correlation with College GPA (Predictive Efficiency) for 1985 College Board Data

Predictors in Equation	Men	Women	Overall
High School GPA	.38	.40	.39
SAT Verbal and Math	.35	.41	.36
HGPA, SAT-V, SAT-M	.46	.50	.48
SAT Increment	.08	.10	.09

Adapted from Ramist et al., 1994, p. 11. The correlation coefficients in the first three lines of table entries are "uncorrected" (see chapter 4). Corrected correlations were larger by about .2. SAT increments (obtained by subtracting the correlation in line 1 from the correlation in line 3) for the corrected analysis were .07 for men and .10 for women.

What about the phenomena of over- and underprediction that we saw in chapter 5? Table 6-3 shows that when a common regression equation, based on men and women, was used to predict college grades, women's predicted grades tended to be lower than the CGPAs they actually earned, and the reverse was true for men. When both SAT and high school grades were used as predictors, women's CGPAs were underpredicted by an average of .06 of a grade point. (Figure 5-1, case 2, page 118, illustrates a situation in which the college GPAs of Population B—in this instance, women—are underpredicted.)

Research on underprediction of women's grades dates at least as far back as 1973. The SAT, the ACT, and most of the SAT II subject-area tests have been found to underpredict women's college grades.[14] In a widely publicized study based on data from the University of California at Berkeley, David K. Leonard and Jiming Jiang argued that even a small degree of underprediction can disadvantage women in the admissions process. They analyzed the records of 10,000 Berkeley freshmen admitted between 1986 and 1988. At every level of Berkeley's academic index score—a composite of high school grades and SAT scores—women received higher cumulative college GPAs than men.[15] For the most part, this finding held up even when results were examined within each major.[16] This makes it unlikely that differences between men and women in their selection of college major had a large influence on the results. Leonard and Jiang claimed that, because of this pattern of underprediction, 200 to 300 White and Asian-American women per year were unfairly denied admission to UC Berkeley during the course of the study— women whose academic index scores would have reached the cutoff, were it not for SAT bias. Leonard and Jiang said they restricted their conclusion to White and Asian-American women because they determined that, under affirmative action guidelines, women of other races with index scores slightly below the cutoff would have been admitted anyway.

Table 6-3 Average College GPA Minus Average Predicted College GPA (1985 Data)

Predictors in Equation	Men	Women
High School GPA	−.02	+.02
SAT Verbal and Math	−.10	+.09
HGPA, SAT-V, SAT-M	−.06	+.06

Adapted from Ramist et al., 1994, 15. The CGPA scale ranges from 0 to 4.

Do SATs Help or Hurt the Prediction of Women's Grades?

According to a 1998 College Board research summary, both the SAT and high school grade-point average "slightly underpredict [CGPA] for females. When these measures are used together, however, this underprediction is reduced to a lower level."[17] But this is a somewhat misleading portrayal of the findings, as is evident from table 6-3 and from the "Gender Total" results in table 6-4. (The remainder of table 6-4 is discussed later.) The tabled results, based on the College Board's own research, show that underprediction is smallest when high school GPA alone is used as a predictor of CGPA. When the combination of high school GPA and SAT scores is used, the underprediction actually increases. Leonard and Jiang found similar results.

It may seem odd that this underprediction occurs despite the fact that the SAT is actually a better predictor of college grades for women than for men (see table 6-2). How can the SAT add substantially to the size of the validity coefficient and yet produce a greater distortion of the predicted grades? A dartboard analogy may help. When we predict CGPA with high school GPA, there's very little bias (for either women or men), but the predictions are not very precise. So, at the end of the game, the bullseye is well-centered in the cluster of darts, but the darts are, on the average, several inches away from the bullseye. When we add SAT scores to the equation—a new game of darts—we shorten the average distance between the darts and the bullseye, say, to an inch, but the darts are more likely to fall below the bullseye than above. Now the bullseye is no longer in the center of the dart cluster. Ideally, we'd like to have a prediction method that's both unbiased and precise—a bullseye centered in a tight

Table 6-4 Average College GPA Minus Average Predicted College GPA (1995 Data)

Predictors in Equation	Gender Total		African-American		Asian-American		Hispanic/Latino		White	
	M	W	M	W	M	W	M	W	M	W
High School GPA	−.04	+.04	−.22	−.12	−.04	+.01	−.20	−.15	−.01	+.09
SAT Verbal and Math	−.11	+.10	−.22	+.03	−.09	+.06	−.19	−.01	−.11	+.14
HGPA, SAT–V, SAT–M	−.08	+.07	−.14	+.01	−.07	+.03	−.15	−.02	−.07	+.09
Number of Test-Takers	46,916		2,891		7,669		3,383		30,600	

The "M" and "W" columns indicate results for men and women. Adapted from Bridgeman et al., 2000, p. 7. The CGPA scale ranges from 0 to 4.3. The overall sample is 52 percent women.

cluster of darts. Several researchers have investigated ways to achieve this, and their results may provide clues to the underprediction puzzle.

Ramist and his coauthors, for example, found that a portion of the underprediction of women's CGPAs could be explained by the fact that women are less likely than men to take college courses that are stringently graded. When a measure of the grading severity of students' courses was included in the prediction equation, the validity coefficients for both men and women increased, and the average underprediction of women's CGPAs shrank from .06 to .03, a small fraction of a grade point. (Compare this to the size of the prediction errors in the ethnic group analysis of table 5–3.) The researchers found that similar reductions in underprediction could be achieved by predicting the grades in individual college courses and then averaging those results, rather than predicting the CGPA. And some researchers have found that including college major in the prediction equation served to decrease the underprediction of women's grades (although this did not occur in the UC Berkeley study).[18] In the same vein, a study conducted a decade ago at a large university showed that underprediction could be reduced by including in the regression model various measures of academic preparation, attitudes toward mathematics, and studiousness.[19]

Another frequent finding is that underprediction of women's grades is reduced when writing test scores play a substantial role in the prediction equation. For example, Ramist found that if the Test of Standard Written English (a separately scored exam administered with the SAT between 1974 and 1994) was included in the regression equation along with SAT and high school GPA, underprediction of women's CGPAs was slightly reduced. And Leonard and Jiang reported that at Berkeley, giving a heavy weight to the College Board English Achievement Test was found to eliminate underprediction.[20]

A possible clue to the puzzling pattern of grade predictions for men and women is the recurrent finding that underprediction is slight or even absent at very high academic levels (although again, the UC Berkeley research appears to be an exception). The Ramist study found that "[a]t more selective colleges, the typical underprediction for females and overprediction for males was substantially reduced; there was no under- or overprediction using HSGPA, SAT scores, and [Test of Standard Written English] to predict course grade." And in recent studies, underprediction has not occurred at the graduate or professional school level.[21] Some researchers speculate that underprediction is minimized at graduate and professional schools and at elite colleges because nearly all students at these institutions take difficult courses. In this situation, differences between men and women in the grading stringency of their coursework is likely to be reduced. At typical colleges, by contrast, men may be more likely than women to gravitate toward fields of study with stricter grading standards.

A New Perspective: What Can We Learn by Studying Men and Women of Different Ethnic Backgrounds?

Some intriguing results on prediction accuracy have emerged from a new College Board study of SAT validity. In their research, Brent Bridgeman, Laura McCamley-Jenkins, and Nancy Ervin grouped students on the basis of both sex and ethnic background and then studied the patterns of over- and underprediction. What happens when CGPA is predicted using a single regression equation for the entire group of students? As in tables 5-3 and 6-3, the effect was examined by comparing predicted CGPAs to actual CGPAs within each group. Results of the analysis, based on about 47,000 students from twenty-three (mostly selective) colleges are given in table 6-4. Although it's never wise to make sweeping conclusions based on a single analysis, the findings suggest that it is primarily White women who are affected by the underprediction problem, while the college grades of men from all ethnic groups tend to be overpredicted.[22] Within each of the four ethnic groups, men's CGPAs were found to be overpredicted by amounts ranging from .07 to .15 when high school GPA and SAT verbal and math scores were included in the equation. College grades were underpredicted by small amounts for African-American (.01) and Asian-American (.03) women and overpredicted by .02 for Hispanic women. For White women, however, CGPAs were underpredicted by nearly a tenth of a grade point (.09).[23]

What Does It All Mean?

How can we make sense of the puzzling combination of lower test scores, higher validity coefficients, and underpredicted grades for women? Whereas a disparity in the quality of past education is a plausible explanation for ethnic group differences in test scores, that hypothesis is much less compelling in the case of the gender gap. Although at one time, differences between men and women in high school course background may have been a substantial factor, these disparities are much smaller now. From a strictly statistical perspective, then, the claim that college admissions tests are biased against women could be considered more convincing than the case for ethnic bias: Women tend to receive lower test scores than men and (at least in the case of White women) to earn higher college GPAs than predicted by their test scores.

But the bias conclusion is mitigated by the finding in several analyses (including those of Bridgeman and colleagues) that underprediction of women's grades is reduced when the grading stringency of college courses is taken into account. Also, some researchers paint a picture of female "overperformance" in college, suggesting that underprediction occurs because women are more serious than men about their studies, more diligent about attending class and doing assignments, and more likely to be neat and careful in their work. According to this conjecture, then, women actually do perform better in college than men with equivalent academic preparation, and this is appropriately reflected in their college grades. We haven't yet explored the further possibility that the tests themselves are flawed in ways that are particularly detrimental to women's performance. It is to this topic we now turn.

From Decoy Ducks to Gravel Trucks: Is Test Content Biased against Women?

"As a rule women object to the information test more than men because the test samples rather heavily the fields of sport, mechanical interests, etc. The chances are that this test would penalize women rather heavily. . . ."[24] This comment from Carl Brigham, a rather unlikely forefather of today's test critics, was written in 1923 about the Army Alpha exams. How little times change! Although today's standardized tests would be unlikely to ask who makes revolvers (Swift & Co., Smith & Wesson, W. L. Douglas, or B. T. Babbitt), and would certainly not ask where the Pierce Arrow car is made, latter-day equivalents of these Army Alpha questions did exist a decade or two ago. Consider the "decoy duck" analogy item, which appeared on a 1977 SAT verbal test. The test-taker was asked to determine which of the five possible answers contained a pair of words that are related in the same way that "decoy" is related to "duck."

    DECOY: DUCK ::
    (A) net : butterfly
    (B) web : spider
    (C) lure : fish   *[correct answer]*
    (D) lasso : rope
    (E) detour: shortcut

Reprinted by permission of Lawrence Erlbaum Associates, Inc.

Women were less likely to answer this question correctly than men with equivalent SAT verbal scores, presumably because it required knowledge of hunting and fishing jargon that is more familiar to men in our society.[25] This is the kind of bias that tends to get a lot of press, and many people believe that these sorts of items are common in educational tests. In fact, major testing companies today take great pains to avoid test questions about topics that might be relatively unfamiliar to women or people of color.

As described in chapter 3, test items go through "sensitivity review" to eliminate content thought to be racist, sexist, or potentially offensive in some other way. An ETS document decrees that among the types of test questions that should generally be avoided are those that involve violence or harm, sports knowledge, or military topics, particularly "specialized military language such as rapier or muzzle."[26] Test items that unnecessarily include these subjects are thought to put men at an unfair advantage. Some testing professionals find these kinds of regulations themselves to be insulting: Are men predestined for success and women doomed to failure if the test question is about war or sports? And some test developers complain of the "blandness problem"—so many topics are taboo, officially or unofficially—that it's hard to make test questions interesting. But today, these complaints are outweighed by concerns about fairness (or, as cynics would have it, lawsuits).

Although the initial review of item content occurs before candidates ever see the test, statistical analysis, of course, must wait until the test items have been administered. Usually, test questions are first given on a tryout basis as part of a regular test administration. (Tryout items don't count toward the candidate's score.) When item responses become available, testing companies conduct statistical analyses of item bias (also called differential item functioning). As described in chapter 5, these analyses are intended to determine whether comparable test-takers from different groups perform equally well on each test question. On the decoy duck question, for example, the goal would be to compare men and women with the same SAT verbal score. Essentially, all the SAT-takers would be grouped on the basis of their verbal scores, responses to the duck question from men and women would be compared at each level of SAT verbal score, and then the results from all score levels would be averaged. (To analyze math questions, test-takers would be matched on their math scores.)

If one group is found to outperform its matched counterparts on a test question, the item is discarded or "flagged" for further study. Typically, a flagged item is reviewed by panelists from a variety of backgrounds who are expert in the subject matter of the test. If the question is considered legitimate despite the gender difference, it remains on the test. But if the item is judged to contain a source of "irrelevant difficulty," such as sports content in a mathematics test, it is modified or eliminated.

Are there any consistent findings on sex differences in item performance? Reviews of item bias findings by two teams of ETS researchers— Kathleen A. O'Neill and W. Miles McPeek, and Brent Bridgeman and Alicia Schmitt—describe some of the common threads. Women tend not to do as well as a matched group of men on verbal SAT and GRE items about scientific topics or about stereotypically male interests, like sports or military activities. An example is this item from the SAT:[27]

CONVOY : SHIPS ::
(A) flock : birds   *[correct answer]*
(B) ferry : passengers
(C) barn : horses
(D) dealership : cars
(E) highway : trucks

Reprinted by permission of Lawrence Erlbaum Associates, Inc.

On the other hand, women tend to perform better than their male counterparts on questions about human relationships or questions about the arts, like the following GRE analogies item:[28]

TILE : MOSAIC ::
(A) wood : totem
(B) stitch : sampler   *[correct answer]*
(C) ink : scroll
(D) pedestal : column
(E) tapestry : rug

Reprinted by permission of Lawrence Erlbaum Associates, Inc.

Similar conclusions have been drawn from analyses that simply compared the proportions of men and women answering correctly (without first matching the test-takers on their overall scores). For example, in a 1989 study of the SAT that garnered a great deal of press attention, Phyllis Rosser of the Center for Women Policy Studies concluded that women performed better on verbal items about human relationships and about such topics as jewelry and fabric, while men did better on test questions about "physical science, sports, and the stock market."[29]

It seems likely that these particular performance disparities stem from differences in interests and pastimes, and perhaps high school course work (although these course preparation differences are vanishing). But for the vast majority of items that show statistical evidence of bias, the reasons are murky at best. In general, it's harder to understand the findings about math questions than the results for verbal tests. In their review of item bias findings, O'Neill and McPeek noted that on several ETS tests and on the ACT, women perform better on algebra questions than men with equivalent quantitative scores; men do better on geometry and mathematical problem-solving. Also, analyses of the GRE, GMAT, SAT, and ACT have shown that women do better on "pure mathematics" problems ($23/_2 + 23/_3 + 23/_6 = ?$), and men tend to perform better on word problems framed in terms of an actual situation. The authors gave this example of a word problem:[30]

> The rectangular bed of a truck is 6 feet wide and 7 feet long and has sides $1\frac{1}{2}$ feet high. A type of gravel weighs about 95 pounds per cubic foot. If the truck bed were filled level to the top of its sides with this gravel, approximately how many tons would the gravel weigh? (1 ton = 2,000 pounds)
>
> (A) $\frac{1}{2}$
> (B) $\frac{2}{3}$
> (C) 3   *[correct answer]*
> (D) 8
> (E) 36
>
> *Reprinted by permission of Lawrence Erlbaum Associates, Inc.*

Why women should have more difficulty with this question is not clear. (Could the presence of a truck be off-putting?) And the finding is hard to reconcile with the conclusion of a later study that women have an advantage on GRE items that require "modeling of a word problem as an algebraic expression."[31]

For another example of a mystifying result, consider this finding from a study that Kadriye Ercikan and I conducted.[32] The test we considered, a U.S. history exam for eighth graders, wasn't an admissions test; it was part of an ongoing federal survey of student achievement. But it provides a good illustration of the puzzling results that are often found in item bias analyses. We found that more than half the items that were easier for boys than for a matched group of girls involved historical dates. The items were similar to the following:

During which of these periods was Abraham Lincoln the president of the United States?

   (A) 1760–1800
   (B) 1800–1840
   (C) 1840–1880   *[correct answer]*
   (D) 1880–1920
   (E) 1920–1960

What could this result mean? Could there be something about "date" items that is conducive to lower performance in females? A closer look at the U.S. history results revealed twenty-one date items that did *not* show any differential performance. A cloudy picture indeed! Much of the research exploring the reasons for test performance differences between men and women has led to similarly obscure results.

Over the years, various conjectures about sex differences in test performance have become psychometric legends: "If they'd write math items about recipes instead of chemistry experiments, then girls would do better," or "Girls don't do as well because they're more nervous and are afraid to guess," or "Multiple-choice items are biased against women." Each of these speculations has gleaned support in some studies, but none have held up consistently. Consider, for example, the role of the multiple-choice format. On essay questions, which require writing skill, women often perform better than men. But this doesn't hold true for all items that depart from the multiple-choice format. On free-response math items—questions that don't offer a list of answer choices—men typically do better. The same is true of "figural response" items in science, which involve such tasks as completing graphs or drawing trajectories of objects. The Advanced Placement examinations, taken by high school students in advanced classes, are a good source of information on the effect of item format because twenty-seven of the twenty-nine exams include both free-response items and multiple-choice items. (Two art exams contain no multiple-choice items.) On sixteen of the tests, boys do better on both the free-response and multiple-choice sections, typically with larger advantages on the multiple-choice items. On six exams (four language and literature tests, plus art history), girls do better on both sections, with larger advantages on the free-response items. But on only five of these twenty-seven exams do girls perform worse than boys on the multiple-choice section and better than boys on the free-response section.[33]

Item Bias and Underprediction of Women's Grades

If we could weed out any flawed or biased test questions, would this fix the underprediction problem? Unfortunately, it's not that simple. As we saw in chapter 5, it's possible for a group (for example, Asian Americans) to have high average test scores and still be underpredicted. A further complication is that the items that turn out to be the culprits in item bias analysis need not be items that are responsible for underprediction of women's grades. The fact that women don't perform as well as men on a particular test question tells us nothing about the relationship between the item score and subsequent grades. So there's no guarantee that removing all items on which men perform better would change the underprediction result. In fact, screening out items that show statistical evidence of bias need not change the pattern of average test scores for men and women at all. A study by Elizabeth Burton and Nancy W. Burton (mentioned in chapter 5) found that there was essentially no change in the SAT score differential between men and women after statistical screening of items for bias began at ETS in 1989.[34] A fairly small number of items were found to have problems, and some of those eliminated were items on which women had an advantage.

What Can Be Done about the Gender Gap and the Underprediction Problem?

How should the testing industry tackle the persistent score differences between men and women and the underprediction of women's college grades? First of all, it's certainly worthwhile to continue research on the effects of test content and format on the performance of men and women. Ideally, this research should consist of designed experiments in which test questions are specially tailored to allow exploration of particular hypotheses. How much does the context matter in a math word problem? Are women really more reluctant to guess? How important is item format? Different versions of test questions can be administered to randomized groups of students and the results compared. Some work of this kind has been conducted, but because these experiments are very expensive, many studies have been based on analyses of existing tests. This restricts the conclusions that can be drawn. Designed experiments also have the advantage of allowing adequate numbers of students in various groups to be recruited. This makes it easier to look at the test performance of men and women within each ethnic group, rather than conducting separate studies of gender and ethnic group performance.

Second, item bias studies and validity research need to be unified. Collecting CGPA data for students who participate in item bias studies would make it possible to determine the role of certain item types in predicting CGPA. Following the lead of Ramist, Lewis, and McCamley-Jenkins, research on the role of college grading patterns in underprediction should also continue.

Third, the idea of including a writing measure in the SAT I—and the ACT—should not be abandoned. Of course, the impact of this change on language minorities needs to be explored, but if writing is a strong predictor of college performance, then its inclusion in college admissions tests is legitimate. (See chapters 5 and 8 for more discussion of these issues.) As we saw earlier, the incorporation of writing test scores in the prediction equation has been shown to reduce the underprediction of women's grades.[35]

Finally, test information booklets should be very clear about the meaning and magnitude of underprediction. In their article, Leonard and Jiang, who claim to be "in despair" about the underprediction phenomenon, conclude that the College Board should provide institutions using the tests with "an unambiguous, highly visible 'users warning label' that their appropriate use requires some kind of gender-sensitive corrective."[36] Although the authors' prose may be heavy on melodrama at times, their advice is nonetheless sensible: It is important for test users to be aware that women tend to earn higher grades than predicted by their scores.

CHAPTER 7

Gaming the Tests

How Do Coaching and Cheating Affect Test Performance?

Among the countless inflammatory issues in admissions testing, coaching probably ranks second, taking a back seat only to test bias. The public focus on test preparation is fueled by articles like the splashy cover story on coaching that appeared in the *New York Times Magazine* in 1999, to be followed just a few months later by another *Times* article—this time on upscale coaching in the Hamptons—called "Multiple Choice and Margaritas."

Coaching isn't a new phenomenon or a uniquely American one. The test-preparation industry at the time of the Sung Dynasty (960–1279 A.D.) is described this way in the book, *China's Examination Hell*:

> Despite repeated ... injunctions to study the Four Books and Five Classics honestly, rapid-study methods were devised with the sole purpose of preparing candidates for the examinations. Because not very many places in the classics were suitable as subjects for examination questions, similar passages and problems were often repeated. Aware of this, publishers compiled collections of examination answers.... Reports from perturbed officials caused the government to issue frequent prohibitions of the publication of such collections of model answers, but since it was a profitable business with a steady demand, ways of issuing them surreptitiously were arranged....[1]

Much later, in the 1800s, companies called crammers prepared students for exams in the British Isles.[2] And today, Japan reportedly has over 36,000 cram schools, or juku. The most prestigious juku have their own admissions tests, giving rise to jokes about attending juku for juku.[3]

What kind of test coaching is available in the United States in the twenty-first century? It can range from a competently taught yearlong course in math and verbal skills that is offered free of charge to a one-hour presentation of stolen test questions and test-taking tricks from a poorly informed novice who charges several hundred dollars. While most testing professionals would concede that the first type of coaching is legitimate, few would embrace the second variety. Often, though, the line between coaching and cheating is a bit fuzzy. Cheating (in one of its infinite variants) might be considered an extreme case of coaching in which actual test questions are obtained by test-takers in advance. In a *New Republic* commentary titled "Cram Scam," Joshua Hammer argued in 1989 that even some "shortcuts" taught by the well-entrenched Princeton Review coaching school "are equal in effect to common cheating." The Review, according to Hammer, a *Newsweek* editor, helps "dumb, rich, white kids" to get into college at the expense of "smart, poor, minority kids—and smart kids of all kinds."[4] And Nicholas Lemann's 1999 book, *The Big Test*, contains this fascinating index entry: "cheating, organized, *see* test-preparation industry."[5]

How do coaching and cheating affect test results? What is their impact on test fairness? What should testing companies do about coaching and cheating? In this chapter, we explore these controversial questions.

Coaching for College Admissions Tests

The most common types of coaching fall somewhere between an enriching year of high-quality education and an offer to help the student cheat. The kind of coaching that's examined in the *New York Times* articles consists of paid instruction that informs students about the types of questions contained in the test, recommends test-taking strategies, and provides for practice on items similar to those on the actual exam. Prospective test-takers can choose between private coaches, who may charge as much as $500 per hour, and commercial test preparation programs, such as the ubiquitous Kaplan organization or the relative upstart, The Princeton Review.

The Princeton Review, which says that it's "the country's leading test preparation organization," was begun by a Princeton University student in 1981 and now offers courses in seventy cities. In its website, the company asserts that its "presence fosters accountability (and intelligence) in the unjust world of standardized testing," and its president, John Katzman, considers the SAT "a disease that has to be eradicated."[6] (The Princeton Review's attempts at hip irreverence attracted a bit of unsolicited publicity in 1999, when one of its study guides was found to include this illustration of the meaning of *cardinal*: "The *cardinal* rule at our school is simple: no shooting at the teachers. If you have to shoot a gun, shoot it at a student or an administrator." Distribution of the guide was halted.) Kaplan Educational Centers, which one-ups the Review by claiming to be the *world's* leader in test preparation, was launched by Stanley Kaplan in 1938 in his parents' basement. The former one-man shop was sold to the Washington Post Company in 1984 for $50 million;[7] it now has 1,200 locations worldwide. Princeton Review and Kaplan offer preparation programs for all the tests included in this book, and more. Commercial SAT preparation courses typically last several weeks and cost about $800. Both companies also sell test preparation books and software; more recently, they have begun advertising other services such as online test prep courses, admissions counseling, and assistance with college applications.

Battles over coaching practices have led ETS to sue both Kaplan and Princeton Review for copyright infringement, prompted Kaplan to sue Princeton Review for false advertising, and even sparked an investigation by the Federal Trade Commission in the 1970s. The hefty 1978 report from the Boston regional office of the FTC was less than complimentary about coaching schools, which were said to "have a universal propensity for engaging in making unsubstantiated advertising claims . . . and engaging in other unfair and deceptive marketing practices. . . ." But the report also took aim at standardized admissions tests, which were labeled racially discriminatory, and, because of their alleged coachability, invalid and unreliable. The 1978 report would no doubt have made a greater splash had it not been issued along with a government memo stating that the study had "several major flaws in data analysis, making the results unreliable."[8] The analysis problems were mainly related to differences between the coached and uncoached groups in terms of high school grades, parents' income, ethnic background, and other factors. (As in most studies of test preparation methods, random assignment of students to coaching and no-coaching conditions was not possible.) A later reanalysis of the data by the national office of the FTC arrived at substantially reduced estimates of the effects of coaching.[9]

One reason that coaching continues to be a hot topic is that testing companies persistently say that coaching has very little effect on scores, while coaching schools make extravagant claims about the score gains they can produce. In 1997, Kaplan claimed that on the average, its students increase their SAT scores by 120; The Princeton Review boasted an average score gain of 140 points.[10] Of course, neither the testing companies nor the coaching schools can be considered disinterested parties. Testing companies prefer to promote their products as assessments of important intellectual skills that are developed through long-term educational processes; claims of coachability cast doubt on the tests' legitimacy. Also, if successful test coaching is accessible only to affluent test-takers, this throws the fairness of the tests into question. The president of The Princeton Review remarked that "The College Board's assertion that the SAT is not coachable is not unlike the tobacco industry's claims that cigarettes don't cause cancer."[11] On the other hand, test preparation companies can hardly be counted on for a balanced perspective—they obviously have a lot to gain by claiming that coaching works wonders.

But why have the controversy and overheated rhetoric gone on for so long? Isn't it a simple matter to show whether coaching works? Actually, it's not. First of all, it's not ordinarily possible to randomly assign students to "coaching" or "no-coaching" conditions the way you'd assign rats to the experimental and control groups in a laboratory study.[12] If you could, you'd be able to assume that on the average, the two groups of students were equivalent before the test preparation began. In the laboratory of real life, however, students who receive coaching are different from uncoached students to begin with. This came to light once again in a recent large-scale coaching study, published in 1999 by ETS researchers Donald Powers and Donald Rock.[13] The investigation was based on a national sample of over 4,000 candidates who took the SAT I: Reasoning Test, of whom about 500 were coached. The authors found a multitude of differences between the coached and uncoached students: Compared to the uncoached test-takers, the coached students tended to come from more educated and affluent families, to have better grades, stronger course backgrounds, and higher educational aspirations, and to have had more exposure to test preparation materials, apart from formal coaching. The groups also differed in terms of ethnic makeup: 21 percent of the coached group was Asian American, compared to 8 percent of the uncoached group.

A further complication in coaching research is that the duration, focus, and quality of coaching vary so widely. And even students who don't go to coaching schools typically prepare in some way for standardized tests, further clouding the research results. Another difficulty in assessing the effects of coaching is that a score increase that occurs after coaching can't automatically be assumed to be the result of coaching. Like previous studies, the ETS analysis found that students who took the SAT twice, without undertaking any formal coaching in between, tended to increase their scores. Why does this happen? The most obvious explanation is that the first testing is useful as a practice round.[14] Another reason may be that students who choose to retake the SAT, rather than relying on their first set of scores, have reason to believe they can do better the second time—for example, they were sick on the first go-round. Finally, even without coaching, students may learn some useful math or verbal skills between testings.

Powers and Rock found that the coached group gained an average of about 30 points on the verbal section of the SAT and 40 points on the math section, compared to 20 points on each section for the uncoached group. (Each section is scored on a 200–800 point scale.) The initial differences between the coached and uncoached students complicate the interpretation of this result. Were these larger gains due to coaching, or would the coached students, with their stronger academic backgrounds and higher aspirations, have made greater gains even if they'd played hooky from coaching school? The authors conducted a number of elaborate statistical analyses to adjust for the initial differences between the groups, but all the analyses, from the simplest to the most complex, tell the same story: At best (ignoring the initial academic superiority of the coached group), formal coaching had a positive effect of about 8 points on the verbal section and 18 points on the math section.

Needless to say, the Powers and Rock study is not without its detractors. The authors themselves pointed out some flaws. First of all, the study was not a randomized experiment. Second, only 63 percent of the original sample responded to questionnaires; those who did so may not have been typical test-takers. (One critic seized on this point, suggesting that the uncoached students who responded scored much higher than typical uncoached students.)[15] Finally, the information about students' coaching experiences was based on their own reports, which prompted an indignant response from FairTest: The authors "based their conclusions on a questionnaire mailed to students after they had taken the SAT but before their scores were returned. . . . The notion that anxious teenagers would give testmakers truthful answers in such a setting is preposterous."[16] FairTest also suggested the ETS researchers should have used a different research design. Students should have been given a "baseline" SAT, then assigned either to a coaching group or a control group. After the coaching group received its instruction, all the students should then have been given another SAT. (In yet another phase, the control group would be coached, and everyone would take a third SAT.)

But such a design, while just fine on paper, could well become a researcher's nightmare in the implementation phase. How would you get students to participate? If you paid them, what effect would that have? Would students really put in their best effort on SATs given as part of a research study? Would they experience the same pressure and anxiety, or respond in the same way to coaching, as students who were preparing for a real SAT? How would you get participants to stay in the coaching program? How would you stop the control group from getting coached? And so on. In research with human beings, there's always a trade-off between laboratory-style experimental research and naturalistic research. The formal experimental studies allow better control and should in theory yield more reliable conclusions. Unfortunately, human beings have a pesky tendency to behave differently in the lab than they do in everyday life.

In the view of some critics, the worst problem with the Powers and Rock study is that it was conducted by ETS authors who received sponsorship from the College Board. So let's compare the Powers and Rock findings to the results of two large studies that did not emerge from testing organizations. In 1990, Betsy Becker, a Michigan State University researcher, performed a meta-analysis that synthesized the results of forty-eight previous studies of coaching conducted between 1953 and 1988.[17] Becker's conclusion regarding the twenty-one published studies that included uncoached comparison groups (presumably the best studies) was remarkably consistent with those of Powers and Rock: The expected gain from coaching was nine points on the verbal section of the SAT and sixteen points on the math section. She also found that the most effective coaching programs were those that included practice on sample test items. (In addition, Becker discovered what at first seemed to be a very intriguing phenomenon. Studies that were conducted or sponsored by ETS tended to show smaller coaching effects than non-ETS studies. It turned out, however, that the non-ETS studies were less likely to include comparison groups. Because they did not take into account the improvements made by uncoached test-takers, these studies were more likely to overestimate coaching effects.)

A coaching study based on a large government data base was conducted by Derek C. Briggs of UC Berkeley. Briggs analyzed data collected in 1990 and 1992 as part of the National Education Longitudinal Study. The NELS data base includes information about students' background, test-preparation activities, and test scores. The analyses of SAT coaching were based on roughly 4,000 students. As in the Powers and Rock study, the students who received coaching tended to be wealthier and more motivated than uncoached students; they were also more likely to be Asian American. Briggs's estimates of coaching effects, after adjusting for background differences, were similar to those of Powers and Rock, and Becker: fourteen to fifteen points on the SAT math section and six to eight points on the verbal section. The Briggs article, published in 2001, was accompanied by an unusual editor's note pointing out that "the author is not affiliated with either a coaching service or a testing service." The note went on to say that commentaries on the study from ETS and from a coaching service had been solicited. The ETS commentary, by Donald Powers, appeared with the Briggs article, but a commitment from "a researcher at a coaching service" was not met. According to the editor, "[P]hone calls and emails have gone unanswered for more than a month."[18]

The fact is that the findings by Powers and Rock, Becker, and Briggs aren't necessarily at odds with the claims of large differences which have appeared in the press. Test tutors who are interviewed by the media focus on star pupils who showed dramatic improvements, not on the average student. And these three coaching studies do not contradict the claim that large score gains sometimes occur. Sixteen percent of the coached students in the Powers and Rock study showed score increases of at least 100 points on the math section; 12 percent had increases this large on the verbal section. (Eight percent of the uncoached students had math gains this large; the same percent had verbal increases of this magnitude.) So the research by academics and testing professionals doesn't say that it's impossible for coached students to achieve dramatic score gains—only that it's somewhat unusual.

The definition of a "large" score increase is also a matter of some dispute. For example, although the College Board spin on the latest research was that "coaching has a very small effect," an average gain of twenty-six points (verbal and math combined) is large from the perspective of Walter Haney, George Madaus, and Robert Lyons, authors of a 1993 book on testing. They concluded that score increases of the magnitude found by Becker (and now reaffirmed in other research) "can hardly be viewed as modest." According to their analyses, these coaching effects "rival in magnitude the amount of gain evident normally over a full year of maturation and school instruction."[19]

The ongoing warfare between testing and coaching companies about the value of test preparation raises an intriguing question: Why haven't coaching companies published their own research in professional journals? Instead, they make statements like "our average score increase of 140 points has been verified by Roper Starch Worldwide."[20] What exactly are these studies? I've looked at one, obtained by a testing professional who requested a report of The Princeton Review's research on the effectiveness of its test preparation courses. The "report" is a copy of a November 1994 letter from Christian J. Donahue of Roper Starch Worldwide to John Katzman, president of The Princeton Review.

The letter evidently constitutes the entire account of the "1994 Princeton Review SAT Performance Study." Roper Starch, the research contractor, phoned 700 Princeton Review "graduates" randomly sampled from a list of more than 5,000. The plan was to consider the 700 students' test scores from before and after The Princeton Review course and see how much change had occurred. The initial test, completed before the course, would be either the PSAT or a The Princeton Review "diagnostic test" consisting of old SAT questions.[21] The second test would be the SAT, taken after completing the course. It is remarkable that (except for Princeton Review's own diagnostic test) no actual test scores were retrieved from data files for use in the study. Instead, students were asked to recall their scores on the PSAT and SAT. The average change in reported scores between the first and second tests was assumed to result from The Princeton Review course.

Of the 700 students in the sample, only 203 (29 percent) provided data considered suitable for the score change calculations. The average score increase for these 203 students was reported to be 126.7 points (from an average of 1046.2 to an average of 1172.9). But what does this mean? How much improvement might these students have made on the second test without coaching? Can students be counted on to remember and provide accurate accounts of their PSAT and SAT scores? (It's noted in the report that some students were excluded from the analysis because they did not recall their scores.) Is The Princeton Review diagnostic test a legitimate pretest—are its scores comparable to SAT scores? Interestingly, the Roper Starch letter notes that for the 53 students who took The Princeton Review diagnostic test as the pretest, the average score gain was especially large—about 171 points. How do the 203 students whose scores were analyzed compare to the original sample of 700? How do Princeton Review students compare to typical SAT-takers in general in terms of motivation, financial resources, educational experiences, and ethnic background? None of these questions are addressed in this report, which is less than three pages in length.

Studies on ACT preparation are much more scarce than SAT coaching research. One recent study examined the effect of test prep for students who took the ACT in 1997. Unfortunately, only about a third of the original sample of 20,000 responded to questionnaires about test preparation activities. Researchers Roberta J. Scholes and Tina R. McCoy nevertheless concluded that preparation could raise scores one or two points on the ACT Composite score (which ranges from 1 to 36), even after allowing for the fact that the coached students tended to have better high school grades than the uncoached test-takers. Commercially available software and workbooks were found to be particularly effective.[22] The recent coaching study by Briggs also included an analysis of the effects of coaching on the math, English and reading sections of the ACT based on a national sample of over 2,000 students. He concluded that the effect of coaching on each of these section scores was less than one point. Surprisingly, the estimated effect of coaching on the ACT reading score was negative, suggesting the possibility that coaching had been detrimental. In his commentary, Donald Powers offers one possible interpretation of this finding: "For reading comprehension questions ... some coaching firms have advised students that they can save time by proceeding directly to the questions ... without first consulting the passages on which the questions are based. This strategy has been shown to be, at best, inefficient."[23]

Coaching for the GRE, MCAT, LSAT, and GMAT

Could a coaching company endanger the security of a major standardized admissions test simply by sending in a bunch of stooges to memorize test questions? Probably not, if enough different versions of the test were in use. But in 1994, Kaplan Educational Centers capitalized on a weakness of the computerized-adaptive test (CAT) version of the GRE and managed to throw the entire operation into disarray.

As explained in chapter 3, a CAT is a computer-administered test that tailors the content of the exam to the skills of the candidate. Test-takers who provide correct answers to a question are given more difficult questions next; those who answer wrong are given easier items. In CATs, some kinds of cheating, such as copying, are virtually impossible. On the other hand, the fact that these tests are offered on a year-round basis, rather than just two or three times a year, increases the opportunities for memorizing test questions. The problem with the GRE CAT in its early days was that not enough test questions were in circulation. In particular, there was a shortage of difficult questions, meaning that many high-scoring test-takers might receive certain questions in common within a short period of time. Kaplan sent in twenty "researchers" who were able to collectively memorize a substantial number of these questions. The company portrayed its actions as something of a public service effort, saying that the goal was to see whether the GRE CAT was vulnerable to cheating. Kaplan denied that it planned to use the questions in its coaching courses or as part of a promotional campaign. Kaplan's GRE "research" led to the redesign of the GRE CAT, a postponement of the termination of the paper-and-pencil GRE, and a lawsuit by ETS that Kaplan eventually settled for $150,000.

The latest uproar about GRE coaching took place on foreign soil: In 2001, ETS sued China's most popular test coaching school, the New Oriental School in Beijing. According to ETS, the school had been improperly using copyrighted materials from the GRE and the Test of English as a Foreign Language in its test preparation courses. "We urge you . . . to treat all GRE and TOEFL test scores from China with caution," said ETS officials in a letter to admissions personnel. A tip-off to the alleged theft of test questions that were in active use was the sharp increase in average GRE scores of mainland Chinese candidates between 1999 and 2000. [24]

So far, there haven't been any formal studies of the effectiveness of coaching on the GRE CAT (which was overhauled to include more test questions in its item pools after the Kaplan incident). In the 1980s, however, ETS researchers investigated the effects of test preparation on the paper-and pencil GRE. Donald Powers found in 1980 that coaching produced small benefits on the Quantitative section and essentially no effect on the Verbal section. On two of the four types of test questions on the Analytical section, however, Powers reported that coaching yielded substantial benefits (a public acknowledgment by a testing company researcher that certain test questions are coachable). The two particularly susceptible kinds of test items, called "analysis of explanations" and "logical diagrams," were subsequently eliminated. As is usual in these studies, interpretation was complicated by the fact that the coached and uncoached students differed in certain ways. For example, responses to a questionnaire on educational aspirations showed that coached candidates tended to be more motivated than uncoached test-takers.[25] In a 1983 study, Powers and Spencer Swinton found that test-takers who received about seven hours of preparation earned GRE Analytical scores that averaged about 66 points higher than those of a comparison group. (The Analytical section is scored on a 200–800 point scale.) In a later study, Powers and Swinton found that an "independent study" version of the test preparation program was also effective.[26]

What about test prep for professional school? MCAT test-takers have been flocking to coaching schools in recent years. The proportion of repeat test-takers who reported having taken a commercial coaching course rose from 15 percent in 1977 to 38 percent in 1994. A study of more than 12,000 candidates who took the MCAT in 1993 and 1994 showed that second-time testers tended to increase their scores by about half a point on the Verbal Reasoning, Biological Sciences, and Physical Sciences subtests, all of which are scored on a 1–15 scale. On the Writing Sample, scored on a 1–11 scale, the average gain was 0.3. The size of the increase, though, was not substantially greater for those who used some kind of test preparation method than for those who didn't. A 1986 study of an earlier version of the MCAT had found that candidates who took commercial coaching courses showed slightly larger gains than other repeaters on the science subtests.[27]

Research about the effects of coaching on the LSAT and GMAT is sparse. According to one recent estimate, the LSAT prep course industry takes in $30 million a year.[28] Both Kaplan and Princeton Review claim that they can increase LSAT scores by about seven points on a score scale that ranges from 120 to 180. A 1983 analysis of GMAT candidates who took the paper-and-pencil version twice showed that those who attended a prep course between testings gained an average of 48 points in GMAT total score (which ranges from 200 to 800), compared to 32 points for those who did not. This study was conducted before coaching took off: Only 8 percent of first-time test-takers and 17 percent of second-time test-takers reported having attended a prep course.[29] The Princeton Review (whose claims about its GMAT coaching products has led to suits by both ETS and Kaplan) says its students gain an average of 80 points on the paper-and-pencil GMAT.[30]

If You Can't Beat 'Em, Join 'Em: Test Prep Products from Testing Companies

As coaching schools have always been quick to point out, claims by ETS and other testing companies that coaching doesn't work are undercut by the enthusiastic participation of these companies in the test preparation marketplace. The SAT is definitely the main target of test preparation products. After several years of selling SAT prep books, ETS and the College Board in 1988 introduced a computer program called "One-on-One with the SAT" to help students prepare for the test. Then in 1999, the nonprofit College Board announced that it would create a for-profit Internet subsidiary, collegeboard.com, which would offer free and low-cost tutoring for the SAT and other College Board tests, as well as advice on the college application process. The collegeboard.com website, which has had a somewhat slow and rocky start, is intended to go head-to-head with similar sites established by Kaplan and The Princeton Review. The College Board's web venture got a boost in 2001 when ETS invested $15 million (a move that FairTest called "inside dealing with no apparent benefit to the public").[31] What about other admissions tests? ACT, Inc. sells ACTivePrep for the ACT, the MCAT's sponsors sell test prep books and videos, and the Law School Admission Council sells LSAT prep

Students take the LSAT Administration at Princeton University, 1955.
Reprinted by permission of Educational Testing Service.

A student completes the LSAT, Princeton University, 1955.
Reprinted by permission of Educational Testing Service.

books. In a refreshing departure from business as usual (and also a good public-relations move), ETS, which used to sell Powerprep software for the GRE and GMAT for $45, now gives it away.

Testing organizations also offer other forms of free help, including booklets of sample questions, and in some cases, online practice opportunities. When I tried the SAT Learning Center on the College Board website in April 2000, questions from the January 2000 administration of the SAT were on offer, along with hints, explanations of the answers, and tutorials about particular types of test questions. One item I tackled was the following verbal analogy:

PRUDENT : INDISCRETION ::
(A) frugal : wastefulness
(B) proud : accomplishment
(C) generous : wealth
(D) disqualified : competition
(E) disgruntled : cynicism

SAT test questions reprinted by permission of the College Entrance Examination Board, the copyright owner. Permission to reprint SAT materials does not constitute review or endorsement by Educational Testing Service or the College Board of this publication as a whole or of any other questions or testing information it may contain.

The "hint" explained the meanings of *prudent* and *indiscretion*, and suggested that I "make up a short sentence that shows how the two words in capital letters relate to each other. . . ." The explanation of the answer (A) defined *frugal* and *wastefulness* and pointed out that "someone frugal is not characterized by wastefulness just as someone prudent is not characterized by indiscretion." Although the College Board website sells an array of test preparation products—videos, software, sample questions, and books—the lively and useful SAT Learning Center is, for the moment, free.

Coaching and Test Fairness

Do test preparation courses magnify the inequities they claim to combat? Is test coaching just another impediment to test fairness for poor and minority test-takers—"another privilege of privilege," as the *New York Times Magazine* put it?[32] Although this point of view is often expressed in the popular media, testing companies have challenged the belief that Whites are much more likely than people of color to receive coaching. According to a test-taker survey conducted by the Law School Admission Council during the 1996–1997 academic year, about 38 percent of

Hispanic candidates, 31 percent of Whites, and 28 percent of African Americans had attended a commercial LSAT-preparation course;[33] a 1989 LSAC study revealed a similar pattern.[34] And a 1983 study of the GMAT showed that minority test-takers were slightly more likely to have participated in a prep course than White candidates.[35]

Regardless of the racial breakdown, it's certainly legitimate to question the fairness of a system in which some test-takers can afford coaching and others can't. Coaching programs are here to stay, and despite the perpetual controversy about their effectiveness, there's no doubt that they can help some of the people some of the time. If coaching is inaccessible to some test-takers, fairness is threatened. What, then, can be done?

Fortunately, the availability of test coaching is not limited to those who can pay $500 per hour for a private tutor or even $800 for a commercial coaching-school course. According to a 1996 survey, slightly over half of secondary schools offer SAT coaching, and many of these programs are free.[36] In 1998, the California legislature made a bold move to improve access to college education by passing a bill that established the College Preparation Partnership Program. The legislation set aside $10 million for a five-year program of SAT and ACT coaching aimed at students from low-income households. Students can be charged no more than $5 for a course that must provide at least 20 hours of instruction. The money provided under this program is used to supplement other federal, state, local, or private money, and is allocated to public high schools to offer the test prep courses. The schools can choose to contract with test-prep providers such as school district employees, public agencies, or private companies. (The Princeton Review claimed in early 2000 to have won contracts covering one-third of the California students in this program.)[37]

Other states and school districts have also adopted test preparation plans. Georgia's legislature, for example, approved a quarter of a million dollars to provide commercial SAT prep software to every public high school, Florida funded a program to train teachers in test preparation, and districts in Maryland, North Carolina, and Texas developed subsidized test preparation programs as well. And in a sure sign of the high profile of standardized admissions testing, Bill Clinton championed test preparation subsidies in his final State of the Union address, asking Congress to allocate $10 million for this purpose in fiscal 2001.

The National Association for the Advancement of Colored People, which says that standardized tests should be de-emphasized in the admissions process, has nevertheless urged the adoption of programs like California's state-sponsored test preparation plan.[38] The best way to get around the "rich get richer" aspect of commercial coaching—the fact that it's most accessible to those who have already benefited from a lifetime of educational advantages—is to make good-quality, low-cost test preparation available to everyone.

Cheating on Standardized Tests

"Some kinds of test preparation and coaching can wholly undermine test validity," Walter Haney and his coauthors said in their 1993 book. "The most obvious is usually called cheating."[39] Of course, obtaining the test questions in advance is only one kind of cheating. The varieties are limited only by the imagination of the cheater. In 1996, a California man known as George Kobayashi devised a unique method of assisting candidates for the GMAT, the GRE, and the Test of English as a Foreign Language: First, he instructed his clients to fly to Los Angeles to take the tests. Next, he hired expert test-takers to sit for the exams in New York, surreptitiously record the answers, and relay them to him in California by phone. Taking advantage of the three-hour time difference, Kobayashi then set to work encoding the answers on pencils, which he sold for as much as $6,000 to the test-takers in L.A. In a diabolical twist, Kobayashi had all his clients write letters saying that they had cheated and requesting that their scores be canceled; if they failed to pay up, the letters would be mailed to ETS. Kobayashi—whose real name turned out to be Po Chieng Ma—was eventually arrested by federal investigators and pleaded guilty to federal mail fraud charges.[40]

In another "made for TV" cheating case, two would-be lawyers, Danny Khatchaturian and Dikran Iskendarian, devised an ambitious cheating scheme that also exploited time zone differences. In 1997, after arranging to take the LSAT in Hawaii, they hired one accomplice to steal the test while it was being given in L.A. and another to relay the answers to them via pager. The plan was intriguing in its combination of high-tech gimmicks and old fashioned thuggery—the appointed test thief reportedly scuffled with the proctor of the LSAT session and pulled "what appeared to be a switchblade." Khatchaturian and Iskendarian, caught reading their pagers during the test, were convicted of felonies, received jail sentences, and were ordered to pay restitution to the Law School Admission Council.[41]

Is Test Cheating on the Rise?

"Cheaters Paradise" and "Evil House of Cheat" are just two of the cheating resources available on the web. Recent surveys suggest that at least half the students in America's high schools and colleges have cheated on tests or homework; some estimates are as high as 80 percent. Cheating on standardized tests has led to lawsuits, FBI investigations, and jail sentences. What's going on? Some recent news stories may provide a clue. In 1999, a massive test cheating scandal in the New York City schools was revealed. The cheating effort, which involved city and state exams, was especially notable because of who was behind it—more than forty teachers and two school principals. In some cases, teachers used palm-size crib sheets to check the initial answers that students scribbled on scrap paper. If the answers weren't correct, the students were told to redo them before marking the official answer sheet. In other cases, teachers or principals simply changed the students' answers themselves.[42] In recent years, at least twelve states have reported outright cheating on standardized tests by principals and teachers. Seven teachers in the Sacramento area made unauthorized copies of the Stanford Achievement Test, which is used to rate the state's schools, and then taught its content. An Arizona school employee copied a draft version of the state's graduation test and gave it to consultants who had been hired to prepare teachers for the exam. And in Massachusetts, a teacher sent e-mail to colleagues at other schools containing questions from a statewide test.[43] So maybe the reported increase in test cheating by students is not so mysterious.

Despite its prominence in America today, cheating on tests is, of course, universal and timeless. Recently, 75 Thai students were found trying to cheat on a college entrance exam by using radio receivers tucked into their underwear, 81,000 Nigerian students were caught cheating on a university admissions test, and more than 3,000 students in Bangladesh were expelled for cheating on a compulsory English test, amid rioting and violent attacks on teachers who tried to intervene. Descriptions of Chinese civil service examinations hundreds of years ago include accounts of impersonation (detected through tip-offs or handwriting discrepancies), copying, and even the use of "cribbing garments," inscribed with essays based on Confucian writing. Candidates were subjected to body searches to make sure they weren't smuggling in notes, miniature books, or money to bribe the officials. The inspectors, who were rewarded if they found contraband materials, were said to be so zealous that they would cut open the dumplings that candidates brought for lunch.[44]

How Is Cheating Detected?

At ETS, an investigation into a particular test score may be triggered for a number of reasons: a report from a test-center supervisor about suspicious behavior, an improbably large score gain over a previous attempt at the same test, a striking difference in handwriting among the materials submitted by the candidate, a concern expressed by a college about seemingly implausible scores, or an anonymous tip from another test-taker. These kinds of evidence are brought to the attention of a test security office, which then conducts an investigation. Cases for which substantial evidence of "irregularity" exists are ultimately considered by three members of the Board of Review, an esteemed committee of senior staff members. Unless all three agree that the case should be pursued further, the investigation is dropped.

The history of the Board of Review was chronicled in 1984 by Gary Saretzky, then the ETS archivist.[45] Before its establishment in 1969, procedures for investigating incidents of possible cheating were somewhat informal. Amazingly, in the first decade of SAT administrations, no cheating investigations were conducted, according to Saretzky. It was not until 1958, when ETS hired a trained investigator as its security officer, that cheating investigations took off. During the next year, fifty-nine cases of impersonation were confirmed, and five other scores were canceled for other types of cheating. Today, ETS reportedly investigates 2,000 to 4,000 SAT candidates per year, a fraction of a percent of all test-takers.[46]

Are testing companies vigilant enough in their efforts to curb test-taker deception? In 1997, the *New York Times* ran a cover story, based on a four-month investigation, charging that ETS "keeps quiet on cheating" and "is all too eager to sweep its dirt under the rug to protect its lion's share of the testing business. . . ." As examples, the article mentioned the security problems with the GRE CAT and the magic pencil scheme, as well as stolen tests and possible instances of fraud and bribery.[47] Soon after the *Times* investigation, ETS hired an outside company to conduct a full review of its test security procedures and also contracted with the National Opinion Research Center to survey candidates about their test-taking experiences and attitudes toward cheating.

On many an occasion, though, ETS has been taken to task for being *too* aggressive in ferreting out possible cheaters. FairTest, for example, has accused ETS of "the persecution of apparently innocent students." A more measured critique came from testing expert Walter Haney of Boston College, who in 1991 (six years before the *New York Times* investigation) told ETS that some of its security procedures appeared to violate professional standards. Haney charged that ETS failed to fully explain the procedures it used to determine if a test-taker's score should be canceled and that, in evaluating cases of possible cheating, it ignored some types of evidence favoring test-takers. As Haney later recounted it in the *Chronicle of Higher Education*, ETS officials "politely told [him] to buzz off."[48]

But then came the case of Brian Dalton, a New York high school student whose increase in combined SAT score (math plus verbal)—from 620 in May to 1030 in November—brought him to the attention of ETS officials in 1991. ETS also found an apparent handwriting discrepancy between the two sets of test materials and determined that Dalton's fingerprints did not show up on the November test booklet. Suspecting that someone else had taken the November test for him, ETS refused to release his score to colleges. Dalton, in turn, declined the standard offer of a free retest. He claimed the large score increase occurred because he had been sick during the May test; he'd also taken a Princeton Review prep course before retaking the test. Dalton submitted some evidence supporting his claim that he had personally taken the second test, including a statement from the exam proctor saying that he had indeed been present, but ETS was not convinced. So, with financial backing from The Princeton Review, Dalton took ETS to court. In a 1992 hearing, the judge accused ETS of "failing to make even rudimentary efforts to evaluate or investigate information furnished by Brian, information that was clearly relevant to a rational decision-making process...."[49]

The Dalton case dragged on for four years. In December 1995, an appeals court issued a ruling that prompted dueling headlines: An ETS press release bore the title, "Appeals Court Upholds ETS's System of Investigating Suspicious SAT Scores," while an *Education Week* piece was headed, "Court Backs Test-Taker in Suit Against ETS." In fact, the ruling *was* mixed: The court said that ETS had breached its contract with Dalton by refusing to adequately consider his explanation for the score increase, but it did not rule that ETS's procedures were unfair, nor did it order ETS to release Dalton's scores.

The Dalton case and its relentless newspaper and television publicity served as something of a watershed in ETS's treatment of potential instances of cheating. The case prompted Professor Haney to renew his criticism of ETS, this time much more publicly. Haney accused the company of violating the testing standards established jointly by the American Educational Research Association, the National Council of Measurement in Education, and the American Psychological Association in "hundreds, if not thousands, of cases."[50] He again faulted ETS for failing to fully explain its investigation procedures and for failing to consider all evidence presented in defense of students whose scores were being questioned.

Since then, ETS's procedures have become more public. Soon after the initial decision in the Dalton case, ETS invited an external panel of experts to study and document its test security process. In another manifestation of its new openness, ETS published a detailed report by statistician Paul Holland on the numerical index that has long been used by ETS to detect cases of copying.[51] When a potential copying case comes to the attention of the test security office, one piece of evidence that is routinely examined is the so-called K-index, a statistical measure of unusual agreement between the responses of pairs of test-takers on a multiple-choice exam. The K-index, developed by Frederick Kling in 1979, was mysterious even to ETS staff until the company decided that its workings should be published. Roughly speaking, the K-index considers the degree of agreement between the incorrect responses of two test-takers, and tells us how unusual it would be to find agreement this extreme if the test-takers were working independently. If the answer is "very unusual," this is consistent with the theory that one test-taker copied from the other.[52] The K-index information is used in combination with other data, typically including a seating chart for the test administration.

The K-index is one of many statistics that have been developed to assess the degree of unusual agreement between test papers. ACT, Inc. and other testing companies use similar measures. The literature on the use of statistical evidence in cheating investigations dates at least as far back as 1927, when Charles Bird wrote a paper called, "The detection of cheating on objective examinations." It's not a coincidence that this occurred just one year after the administration of the first SAT: The introduction of tests consisting of multiple-choice questions quite naturally increased the opportunities for cheating by copying, and created an interest in detection methods.

Today, both the SAT and ACT registration bulletins include information about test security issues. The SAT bulletin, for example, says that "ETS reserves the right to cancel any test scores when, in its judgment, a testing irregularity occurs, there is an apparent discrepancy in a test taker's identification, a test taker engages in misconduct, or the score is invalid for another reason." Before canceling scores, ETS says it "gives the test taker an opportunity to submit information that addresses the concerns, considers any such information . . . and offers the test taker a choice of options . . . [including] voluntary score cancellation, a free retest, or arbitration. . . ." ETS also offers a booklet titled, "Why and How Educational Testing Service Questions Test Scores." In its booklet, ACT, Inc. too "reserves the right" to cancel scores and notes that the "final and exclusive remedy available to examinees who want to appeal . . . [a cancellation decision] shall be binding arbitration. . . . The issue . . . shall be whether ACT acted reasonably and in good faith in deciding to cancel the scores."

In 1993, Walter Haney suggested that, "[r]ather than rely on procedures to try to detect cheating after the fact, testing companies should devote more attention to ways to prevent cheating in the first place."[53] It's possible that at least one testing company was listening. In 1999, ETS and the Advertising Council embarked on a three-year anticheating campaign. In addition to launching print, radio, and TV ads featuring "the ref in your head," they started a telephone hotline and a website, www.nocheating.org, featuring the slogan, "Cheating is a personal foul." The campaign is targeted at 10- to 14-year-olds, presumably to set them straight well before they take their first ETS test.

CHAPTER 8

New Directions for Admissions Testing

What Does the Future Hold?

A recurrent criticism of standardized multiple-choice admissions tests is that they are outdated and slow to change—the antique remains of a bygone era. Everyone agrees they need to evolve. But what would the ideal admissions test look like? It's intriguing that expert opinions on this issue are sharply divided. One camp advocates that advances in cognitive psychology be used to produce a more sophisticated test of reasoning abilities and creative thinking. The opposing view is that admissions tests should become less arcane and more curriculum based—they should test the specific knowledge that students will need in the program to which they're applying.

On the "cognitive" side of the argument, eminent Yale psychologist Robert Sternberg commented a decade ago that "[c]ognitive theory is evolving very rapidly, and tests will have to change with it."[1] Tests, he said, need to do a better job of "characterizing the nature of intelligent behavior in the world."[2] In a 1997 article about the GRE, Sternberg and co-author Wendy Williams recommended that graduate admissions tests be modified to include "creative and practical as well as diverse analytical abilities"[3] Sternberg is involved in an effort at the University of Michigan Business School to develop an alternative to the GMAT. This fledgling test, called the Successful Intelligence Assessment, is intended to measure "a combination of analytical, creative, and practical intelligence."[4] He is also working with the College Board to develop college admissions tests that are in keeping with his theories; these are being tried out on an experimental basis. Striking a note similar to Sternberg's, Stanford psychologist Richard Snow argued in a 1999 volume on higher education assessment that "psychological theory has now caught up with, and outdistanced . . . testing technology."[5] These theoretical advances, he said, should be used to expand admissions testing to include such skills as visualization, mechanical reasoning, creative and critical thinking, and flexible reasoning in the face of novel situations.

While some cognitive psychologists may wish to make admissions tests more like IQ tests, a chorus of commentators has adopted an entirely opposite view: Admissions tests—at least at the college level—should be more closely tied to the curriculum. Professor Howard Gardner of Harvard told the *Christian Science Monitor* in 1999 that if the SAT "magically disappeared and a law was passed that it could not be reinvented," it would be possible to develop much better tests based on mastery of historical, scientific, mathematical, and artistic modes of thinking. Somewhat unexpectedly, given his prominence as an intelligence theorist, Gardner then cited the Advanced Placement exams, which are firmly tied to high school course work, as examples of useful tests.[6]

The surprise recommendation in 2001 by University of California president Richard Atkinson to discontinue the use of the SAT I in UC admissions is also consistent with the growing push toward curriculum-based testing. Atkinson (a cognitive psychologist by training, ironically enough) said he opposed the SAT I partly because it is viewed as being "akin to an IQ test." He recommended that standardized tests be developed that are directly tied to the college prep courses required of applicants to the University of California.[7] In the short term, he recommended an increased role for the SAT II: Subject Tests in admissions decisions.

Stanford education professor Michael W. Kirst, too, has proposed that colleges substitute "subject-based state external exams" or the SAT II: Subject Tests for the SAT I or ACT in order to better align college admissions criteria with what's actually studied in high school.[8] And in his widely publicized 1999 book, *The Big Test*, journalist Nicholas Lemann went one step further, recommending that high schools "prepare their students for college by teaching them a nationally agreed-upon curriculum. Tests for admission to college should be on mastery of this curriculum—not the SAT or some dreamed-of better, fairer alternative test of innate abilities."[9]

So should admissions tests aim to be more aptitude-oriented or should they focus on testing past achievement? At the college level, the resulting admissions decisions would probably be much the same either way. In a 1987 report, Isaac I. Bejar, Susan Embretson, and Richard E. Mayer concluded that cognitive psychology could help test developers to design SAT items with certain characteristics, but that "the predictive power of the test is not likely to increase significantly because of this research. . . ."[10] And even as he argued for the inclusion of spatial visualization, imagery, and mechanical reasoning tasks in admissions tests, Snow acknowledged that these skills don't add much "to the prediction of gross criteria such as college grade-point average."[11] (In fact, the SAT did try including a test of spatial ability in 1930, but later dropped it, apparently because it was not useful in predicting college grades.)[12]

We can do more than conjecture about the impact of substituting curriculum-based tests for the SAT I. Consider the fact that the ACT, which is linked to instructional goals, and the SAT I: Reasoning Test, typically regarded as more IQ-like, are very highly correlated (over .9), and that they have similar correlations with freshman GPA (about .4, on average). How do scores on the SAT I and the SAT II compare? Applicants to the University of California constitute a particularly rich source of data because they are required to take the SAT I, the SAT II writing test, the SAT II math test, and a third SAT II test of their own choosing. Among the roughly 40,000 applicants to UC Santa Barbara in 1997 and 1998, the correlation between SAT I verbal scores and SAT II writing scores was about .75, and the correlation between SAT I and SAT II math scores exceeded .85. (Correlations for recent UC Berkeley applicants were nearly identical.) For those who went on to enroll at UCSB, the two verbal tests had similar correlations with freshman GPA (about .3); as did the two math tests (.22).[13] Preliminary results of a recent analysis that combined data for all the campuses of the University of California found a correlation of .84 between the SAT I and the SAT II.[14]

A further comparison of the SAT I and the SAT II comes from a recent College Board study, which used data from students at ten colleges to investigate the effects of applying various admissions criteria. High school grades were used in combination with either SAT I or SAT II scores to select (hypothetical) entering classes. Freshman grade-point averages "were virtually identical for students selected by the different models," according to the authors, which is not surprising given that admissions decisions were the same for 86 percent of the students.[15] To those in the testing world, the similarity of the results obtained using the SAT I and the SAT II is not a big surprise: Students who earn the highest college GPAs are those who can translate their abilities into academic achievements; these students are likely to do well on either curriculum-based admissions tests or assessments that aim to be purer measures of "ability."

Although the degree to which a college admissions test relies on specific course material may have little influence on the resulting admissions decisions, an argument can be made in favor of tests like the ACT or the SAT II: Subject Tests from the perspective of public acceptance. Curriculum-based exams—the Advanced Placement tests, for example—

are generally perceived to be less esoteric and more fair than the SAT. It's hard to object to exams that are based on material that test-takers have—or at least should have—studied. The SAT I's antonyms (no longer included) and verbal analogies make a much easier target for test critics than questions based on course content, and a test that followed Snow's suggestion to include "imaginary sciences" like "Martian fauna"[16] would be even more susceptible to condemnation. So until there's strong evidence that the proposed "broader and deeper" measures help colleges to pick better entering classes, exams that have demonstrable ties to school learning may have an advantage, at least from a public-relations standpoint. Some have argued that the use of admissions tests that are linked to high school courses could also encourage universities to undertake a more active role in improving K–12 education.

The downside of moving to a more curriculum-based form of admissions testing is that exams that rely heavily on course content can also be viewed as unfair. Protests would certainly arise if the assessments relied on narrow and specific material that was covered in some schools but not others. As previous efforts have demonstrated, it is unlikely that a national consensus on curriculum requirements could be attained, and even if it were, teaching quality would still vary widely over our nation's schools. This means that students from weaker high schools could be substantially disadvantaged by tests that focus on what is—or should be—taught in class.

Reasoning Tasks in Graduate and Professional School Admissions Tests

Although the appropriateness of including highly complex reasoning tasks in college admissions tests is debatable, it is widely recognized that more advanced and specialized assessments are needed for graduate and professional school admissions. In his discussion of admissions testing, Snow claimed that "there is good evidence that [visual, spatial, and perceptual] ability relates to specialized achievements in such fields as architecture, dentistry, engineering, and medicine."[17] And in their critique of the GRE, Sternberg and Williams recommended incorporating mathematical problems that involve novel number operators, tasks that require the use of maps to plan out errands, and "scientific problems such as how one might be able to tell whether someone has been on the moon within the last month."[18] While test questions of this kind might run into public relations problems at the undergraduate level (too fanciful, too far removed from the curriculum), they may be appropriate for screening prospective graduate students in psychology—the purpose for which Sternberg and Williams recommended them. In general, it seems worthwhile to consider including more innovative and creative test items in admissions tests for graduate and professional school.

The Role of Writing Ability in Admissions Decisions

There is one possible area of common ground between the cognitive camp and the champions of curriculum mastery: Both sides agree that an assessment of writing ability should have a key role in admissions tests. Writing assessments have a double advantage: They can incorporate cognitively complex tasks, but are unlikely to be accused of measuring esoteric skills devoid of real-world applications. Currently, the GMAT, MCAT, and LSAT include writing samples. The ACT, SAT I, and GRE do not, although the SAT and GRE programs have "subject tests" in writing as separate options. (The GRE program has announced that in October 2002, the GRE Writing Assessment will be incorporated into the General Test, replacing the Analytical section of the GRE.)

Requiring a writing sample as part of the college and graduate school admissions process makes sense for two reasons. First, it is undeniable that writing plays a key role in college- and graduate-level work. Second, there is reason to believe that many students do not possess the writing abilities they need to be successful in higher education. For example, only 22 percent of America's 12th graders attained the "proficient" level in writing in the 1998 National Assessment of Educational Progress, and only 1 percent were judged to be "advanced."[19] Using a writing sample as an admissions criterion could help to identify students who need to further develop their writing skills before entering degree programs. And a greater emphasis on writing in admissions could eventually lead to improved writing instruction in high schools and colleges.

A writing sample requirement could have yet another advantage: It could improve the fairness of the admissions process to women. Research at the college level has shown that the underprediction of women's grades tends to be reduced when writing measures are included in the prediction equation (chapter 6), and the recent College Board study of competing admissions criteria showed that including the SAT II writing test as an admissions criterion along with the SAT I boosted the percentage of women in the entering class by 2.5 points.[20] These results alone would not be a sufficient justification for making a change in admissions criteria. But because writing is important to success in college and graduate school, its incorporation in admissions tests can be supported from a validity perspective as well.

One prominent concern about giving writing tests a more central role is the effect this would have on the admissions prospects for students who aren't native English speakers. It is often assumed that including verbal tests in admissions decisions penalizes these students. But a different picture emerged from my analyses of data on 1997 and 1998 freshmen at UC Santa Barbara, which showed that SAT verbal score played an important role in accurately predicting freshman GPAs. For students who said English wasn't their best language, using SAT math score alone to predict GPA tended to yield predicted grades that were higher than the ones these students actually attained, sometimes by a large margin.[21] It seems likely that freshman grades depend heavily on English proficiency, so it makes sense that including a verbal test improves prediction. As Hunter M. Breland, an expert in writing assessment, has noted, "the work of most students is heavily verbal and it can be argued that admissions tests should reflect the nature of the work a student will be expected to do."[22]

Exploiting Computers to Improve Tests

Whether the goal is to tie tests more closely to course work or to increase their focus on higher-level cognitive abilities, it's indisputable that advances in computer technology can permit standardized tests to assess a much fuller range of capabilities than the typical multiple-choice tests of past decades. Some new tests that have been developed outside the admissions sphere may point to fruitful directions for admissions tests:

- A multimedia testing system for selecting manufacturing plant employees uses computer-controlled video to present realistic workplace situations. Applicants are asked questions based on the video that are intended to assess their judgment, troubleshooting skills, and on-the-job learning ability.[23]
- A music listening test plays musical segments to test-takers, who listen through earphones connected to the computer. The test, which is used to assess the ability to remember melodies or tonal sequences, requires the test-taker to determine whether a pair of segments is alike and, if not, which tones are different.[24]
- A computer-administered test of the ability to interpret research results presents candidates with a situation and then asks them to formulate as

many explanations as possible. One item, for example, points out that the death rate for police officers dropped dramatically between 1970 and 1989. Test-takers key in their hypotheses—better bulletproof vests, better training, better medical care, and so on. A computerized scoring tool counts and evaluates the hypotheses.[25]

- A test of architectural site-design proficiency requires candidates to produce on-screen architectural drawings using computer-assisted design technology. An automated scoring procedure uses criteria established by a panel of expert architects to rate the drawings on key features like adherence to site boundaries, convenience of parking, and accessibility to the handicapped.[26]

In addition to allowing the development of innovative test questions, computer technology can also be used to improve the accommodations offered to test-takers with disabilities (see chapter 4). Computer administration facilitates the modification of both the input and output of information. Head-mounted mouse emulators and speech recognition tools are just two of the alternative ways for test-takers to enter their responses. Computer displays can be used to present sign-language interpretations of instructions for deaf candidates, and speech synthesizers can be used to administer tests to blind candidates.

Obviously, a lot has changed in the century that has elapsed since the College Board was founded. But while technology can make admissions tests broader in scope, there are dangers too. In the development of some of the more futuristic testing systems, measurement principles have taken a back seat. We shouldn't be so dazzled with computer capabilities that we abandon quality standards for admissions tests, nor should we incorporate high-tech features just to make tests flashier. The goal must always be improved measurement of the qualities considered desirable for students entering higher education.

Accountability and Information in the Testing World

Expanding test content and enhancing administration technology can improve the measurement properties of tests and also make them more interesting—perhaps even educational—for test-takers. But improving the tests themselves can only go so far. What can be done about the ongoing controversies about test fairness, the rampant misinformation about testing, and the complaints from test-takers who say they have been treated unreasonably by test makers or test users?

Today, various government entities and private organizations are involved in monitoring standardized tests and their uses in admissions (chapter 2). The federal government commissions studies through the National Academy of Sciences and the Congressional Office of Technology Assessment; the Office for Civil Rights of the U.S. Department of Education deals with testing complaints that involve discrimination; advocacy groups like FairTest keep a constant critical watch, and the National Board on Educational Testing and Public Policy and other university-based centers devote themselves to testing research. Judicial decisions and state and federal legislation play a role as well.

But this curious array of mechanisms and organizations provides at best a piecemeal approach to testing oversight. And there's still a substantial void: Where can a journalist go to read a balanced overview of the research on the effects of coaching on professional school admissions? Where can a test-taker go to complain about his unexpectedly low score if he failed to get a satisfactory answer from the testing company, but doesn't want to file a lawsuit? Where can an admissions counselor go if she wants to read about the tendency of women to earn higher freshman grades than their ACT or SAT scores predict? She won't find any mention of this phenomenon in the *ACT User Handbook* or the *Admission Staff Handbook for the SAT Program*.[27]

What's still needed is a consumer-oriented body dedicated specifically to issues of admissions testing. This organization needs to have a hotline that consumers can use to ask questions or initiate arbitration procedures. Jargon-free information briefs offering balanced perspectives on key testing issues should be available on a website and by telephone request.

Some of these functions may seem redundant. Testing companies already offer arbitration of test-taker complaints, for example, but this process is not generally perceived as impartial by test-takers. Testing companies and FairTest also publish information briefs on testing issues, but neither of these sources can be considered disinterested parties. Testing companies aren't likely to feature researchers who "despair" about the effects of the SAT on women[28] or claim that coaching schools work wonders, and FairTest probably won't include any information that's at odds with its portrayal of standardized testing as a malignant influence on our society.

What about the enforcement of arbitration decisions and testing standards? The establishment of a heavy-handed regulatory agency does not seem desirable, yet the current situation, in which professional testing standards are essentially unenforceable without a legal challenge, isn't acceptable either. (The National Board on Educational Testing and Public

Policy, which evidently contemplated serving such a function at one time, does not address individual consumer complaints.) One possible strategy for the future is to arrange for misuses of tests to lead to a well-publicized censure of the offending test user or testing company. This would be consistent with the approach used by the American Association of University Professors to censure institutions that treat faculty members in ways that are considered unfair. (Censured universities are listed in the *Chronicle of Higher Education* and on the AAUP's website.) An oversight agency of this kind could cut down on litigation, which is costly and time-consuming and is not even guaranteed to produce outcomes that are in keeping with professional testing standards (see chapter 2).

At the millennium, educational testing is expanding at an unparalleled rate, and public interest is intense. It is more important than ever that testing consumers have somewhere to turn for information and resolution of complaints. What's needed is neither a cadre of testing company officials spouting the party line nor a group of wild-eyed testing adversaries determined to rid the world of the evils of the standardized test. We need an agency that will foster a thoughtful public conversation about testing—a discussion that is sane, balanced, and informed.

A Final Thought

Why does the controversy about standardized admissions testing continue to simmer endlessly, ready to break into a full boil at any moment? To some degree, it's inevitable that any mechanism for allocating scarce resources will be a lightning rod for criticism. And if admissions criteria that don't include test scores are eventually instituted, these too will draw objections, claims of unfairness, and lawsuits. The current move, in several states, toward admissions based solely on class rank (see chapter 5) provides a perfect illustration of this phenomenon. Although these admissions policies were originally touted as a more equitable alternative to a reliance on standardized test scores, critics on both the left and the right now point out that "students who rank high in mediocre schools will win out over academically strong students who can't crack the top 20 percent at their elite schools—including minority students whom the policies are supposed to aid."[29]

And if there were an admissions lottery, that would also be condemned—for failing to recognize hard work and special talents. This highlights another reason for the never-ending national argument about tests—our ambivalence about being selective. We like the idea of opening wide the gates to our universities and squeezing in as many people as possible. But we're just as determined that preference be given to the most deserving, though we don't all agree on what that means.

Should standardized tests continue to influence decisions about who gets to enter the halls of academe? To some, admissions testing is a way of identifying the diamond in the rough—the "late bloomer . . . who . . . did not put forth great effort in high school but who has developed high levels of verbal and mathematical reasoning."[30] To more extreme test boosters, an admissions test is an all-purpose yardstick, accepted as an infallible index of everything from native intelligence to neighborhood quality. According to detractors, though, SATs and the like are "wealth tests" that are unrelated to subsequent school performance and serve primarily as barriers to academically talented minority and low-income test-takers. But differences in test performance among ethnic and socio-economic groups are proof of bias only if we believe that test-takers in all groups have equal educational opportunities, or that tests are solely measures of innate abilities. Neither of these beliefs is reasonable or defensible. We also need to keep in mind that the fairness of a test must always be evaluated against the fairness of alternative procedures. "In all societies individuals are evaluated in some manner," says testing expert Warren Willingham. "If not with this test or a better test, then real-life decisions will get made in other ways."[31]

In a 1989 essay, Michigan State professor William Mehrens gave an exceptionally clear explanation of the need for differentiating between tests and policies:

> A distinction should be drawn between opposition to policies regarding decisions being made and opposition to the data used to make a decision. For example, some individuals are opposed to selection decisions regarding who should be admitted to colleges of education. They believe everyone who wishes to should be given the chance to attend. Others may believe it is more appropriate to select applicants who have the best predicted chances to succeed in college. Either position may be defended on philosophical grounds. If one believes, however, in open admissions, the philosophical stance should be argued directly. It is inappropriate to argue that tests are not useful for selecting those most likely to succeed (too much evidence opposes such an argument). . . . Decisions are not always pleasant or in keeping with our philosophical stance, but we should not blame the unpleasantness on the tests. . . . Unfortunately some individuals seem to assume that if we do away with tests we can avoid making decisions. That is not likely to be the case.[32]

None of this lets tests off the hook. They can and must continue to improve, both in their content and in the technologies through which they are administered. But standardized testing is not intrinsically good or bad, neither boon nor bane. Some tests are of high quality; others are not. Some test uses are reasonable; others are clearly inappropriate. Sometimes test scores are interpreted responsibly; on other occasions, they are weighted far too heavily in admissions decisions. We will probably never stop talking about tests. But if we can make the debate more informed, we can also make it much more enlightening.

NOTES

Preface

1. Rooney, 1998, p. 76.
2. Weissglass, Apr. 15, 1998.
3. Sacks, June 8, 2001.
4. Atkinson, Feb. 18, 2001.
5. Clegg & Ostrowsky, July 2, 1999.
6. Bowen & Bok, 1998, p. 262.
7. Schwartz, Jan. 10, 1999, p. 30.
8. Educational Testing Service annual report (1949–50), p. 11.

CHAPTER 1: Today's Standardized Admissions Tests

1. This account is based on Webber, 1989, and Miyazaki, 1976. As the preface to his book notes (p. 9), Miyazaki chose to ignore the testing that took place in the Han dynasty and instead placed the beginning of the Chinese examination system in 589 A.D. Wainer (1990), on the other hand, says that formal testing procedures for candidates for office began in China in 1115 B.C. The last test given under the "old system" of Imperial exams took place in 1904 (Miyazaki, p. 138).
2. Webber, 1989, p. 38.
3. Office of Technology Assessment, 1992
4. Stewart, Jan. 25, 1998.
5. Computations based on tables 99 and 244 in Snyder, Hoffman & Geddes, 1997.
6. Brigham, 1923, p. 9.
7. Sellman & Arabian, 1997, page xv.
8. Snyder, Hoffman, & Geddes, 1997, table 244.
9. Nardi, 1992, pp. 21–22.
10. ETS annual report 1949–50, pages 9–10.
11. ETS annual report 1949–50, p. 14.
12. Saretzky, Feb. 6, 1991. ETS held the SSCQT contract intermittently during the next sixteen years. In 1967, President Lyndon Johnson ordered automatic deferments for all college students.
13. Brigham, 1923, p. 190.
14. Brigham, 1923, p. xxi.
15. Brigham, 1923, p. xix.
16. Gould, 1996, p. 135.
17. A recent controversial contribution to the debate on cognitive testing is *The Bell Curve*, by Richard J. Herrnstein and Charles Murray, which encourages the very beliefs criticized by Gould. The publication of this book in 1994 produced a cottage industry of critiques and rebuttals which is still flourishing. *The Bell Curve*'s pronouncement on affirmative action gives the flavor of the book: "Affirmative action . . . has been based on the explicit assumption that ethnic groups do not differ in the abilities that contribute to success in school and the workplace—or, at any rate, there are no differences that cannot be made up

with a few remedial courses or a few months on the job. Much of this book has been given over to the many ways in which that assumption is wrong" (p. 449).

18. Gould, 1996, p. 418–419.
19. Weissglass, 1998.
20. Office of Technology Assessment, 1992, p. 111.
21. Jencks, 1998, p. 65.
22. Gould, 1996, pp. 176–184.
23. The first to suggest the merger was evidently Ben D. Wood, the director of an organization called the Educational Records Bureau. Wood was an early proponent of multiple-choice testing and one of the developers of the first test-scoring machine.
24. Lemann, Aug. 1995.
25. Conant, 1964.
26. Brigham, 1930, p. 165.
27. Reviews of the material at the end of chapter 1 (as well as other basic information about the tests in this book) were solicited from each testing program. All programs except GMAT provided such reviews and offered supplementary information. Representatives from the GMAT program at ETS and from the Graduate Management Admission Council were given the materials, but did not provide a review.
28. This section draws on material in the ETS 1949–50 annual report and in Briel, O'Neill & Scheuneman, 1993; Saretzky, 1992; and Winterbottom, 1995.
29. Historical material is based on Hecht & Schrader, 1986 and Schmotter, 1993.
30. Historical material is based on ACT, Inc., 1999b; Brennan, 1999; Haney, Madaus & Lyons, 1993; and Peterson, 1983.
31. Peterson, 1983, pp. 111, 114.
32. Peterson, 1983, p. 164.
33. Beatty, Greenwood & Linn, 1999, p. 5.

CHAPTER 2: The Big Picture

1. Sacks, 1997, p. 25.
2. Toch & Walthall, Sept. 1, 1997.
3. Breland, 1998, pp. 3, 7. The watchdog organization FairTest claims that this percentage has declined in recent years ("Critics of SAT and ACT hail decline in colleges that use them," *Chronicle of Higher Education*, Aug. 8, 1997).
4. More recently, lottery admissions have been discussed by Sturm & Guinier, 2000/2001.
5. I use "IQ test" and "intelligence test" synonymously. Originally, an IQ (intelligence quotient) score was computed by dividing a measure of the test-taker's "mental age" by his or her chronological age and then multiplying by 100. Although modern intelligence tests are not scored this way, the term "IQ" has survived.
6. President emeritus talks about *The Big Test* and other timely subjects. *ETS Access*, Oct. 14, 1999.
7. Jencks, 1998, p. 56.
8. The SAT II: Subject Tests, and GRE Subject tests *are* based on specific knowledge, as described in chapter 1.
9. Wightman & Jaeger, 1998, p. 39.
10. A recent large-scale study showed that the correlation between the SAT I (verbal score plus math score) and the ACT (composite score) was .92 (Dorans, 1999). A correlation is a measure of association between two

characteristics which ranges from -1 to 1. A correlation of 1 would mean that ACT and SAT scores ordered candidates in exactly the same way. A correlation of 0 would, essentially, indicate no relationship between the scores.

11. Rigol & Kimmel, Nov., 1997, p. 5
12. Rigol & Kimmel, Nov., 1997, p. 8. The other two factors labeled "very important" by at least 10 percent of the colleges were recommendation letters and the personal essay component of the application.
13. California Postsecondary Education Commission, 1997, pp. 50–61. Students who are declared UC-eligible still must meet the admissions requirements of the UC campus of their choice.
14. Weiss, July 17, 1998. The regents voted in 2001 to reverse the affirmative action ban, but because of the passage of Proposition 209, which bans affirmative action statewide, the reversal was purely symbolic.
15. Chapa & Lazaro, 1998, p. 60.
16. Carnevale, Sept. 3, 1999.
17. National Center for Education Statistics, 2000, table 173.
18. Brownstein, Oct. 9, 2000.
19. Rigol & Kimmel, Nov., 1997, p. 6.
20. Mitchell, May 27, 1998.
21. Hernández, 1997, p. 6.
22. Hernández, 1997, p. 117.
23. Hernández, 1997, p. 222–223.
24. Hernández, 1997, pp. 190–191.
25. Kabaservice, Jan. 26, 2000, among other articles.
26. The description of San Diego's admissions process was obtained from Richard Backer, assistant vice chancellor, UCSD (May 9, 2001) and also draws from Kleiner, Aug. 30, 1999, p. 71; the description of Berkeley's process comes from Kell & Mena, spring 1998, from Pamela L. Burnett, director, office of undergraduate admissions (July 10, 2001), and from university materials. The Berkeley description applies to the College of Letters and Sciences; the College of Engineering has a separate admissions process. For all UC campuses, applicants must also meet UC-wide eligibility criteria. (A small number of exceptions is allowed.) The UC criteria specify that the applicant must have completed certain college preparatory courses and must have either a high school GPA of at least 3.3 or a combined GPA–test score index that exceeds a criterion level.
27. Although unadjusted GPAs ordinarily range from 0 to 4.0, with 4.0 representing an A, GPAs over 4.0 can be achieved because extra points are assigned for honors and Advanced Placement courses.
28. Kell & Mena, spring 1998, p. 22.
29. "UC's freshmen," *Los Angeles Times*, July 21, 1999.
30. ACT, 2001.
31. Smyth, 1995.
32. Dorans et al., 1997.
33. The general information in this section is based primarily on Skager, 1982, and Rigol & Kimmel, Nov., 1997, as well as materials from the testing programs themselves.
34. Rigol & Kimmel, Nov., 1997, p. 13.
35. Attiyeh & Attiyeh, 1997, p. 528.
36. Attiyeh & Attiyeh, 1997, p. 547.
37. Rigol & Kimmel, Nov., 1997, p. 12.
38. Johnson & Edwards, 1991.
39. Jolly, 1992, p. 566.

40. Nix, spring/summer 1996; Wightman, Apr. 1997.
41. Nix, spring/summer 1996; Wightman, Apr. 1997. William C. Kidder, a researcher for a Berkeley organization called "Testing for the Public" arrived at an entirely different conclusion, asserting that women and minorities are disadvantaged in the law school admissions process (Kidder, 2000). Although Kidder's analysis obviously represents a serious and intensive research effort, his reasoning is often questionable. For example, many of his arguments rest on an *a priori* assumption that differences among groups on LSAT scores are "artificial," while differences in undergraduate grades (e.g., the typical edge of women over men) are "real." His claim that the LSAT is discriminatory rests in part on a demonstration that, for a given level of undergraduate grades, Whites are admitted at a higher rate than minorities, and men are admitted at a slightly higher rate than women. This finding is suggestive of test bias only if one is willing to assume that undergraduate grades are entirely equitable across colleges, are free of any of the contaminating influences that can affect test scores, and are a sufficient basis on which to evaluate applicants' qualifications. When it comes to *law school* grades, Kidder takes a different view, arguing that the reason the law school grades of minorities tend to be lower than test scores predict (see chapter 5) is because of the bias in these grades.
42. Graduate Management Admission Council, 1998.
43. Dugan, Baydar, Grady, & Johnson, 1996, p. 18.
44. Langfitt, July 11, 2000.
45. National Commission on Testing and Public Policy, 1990, p. 21.
46. Ruch, 1925; see Madaus, 2001.
47. Heubert & Hauser, 1998, p. 8.
48. Beatty, Greenwood, & Linn, 1999, p. 2.
49. Office for Civil Rights, 1999, pp. 2–3. See chapter 5 for more discussion of disparate impact.
50. The College Board, June 21, 1999, pp. 1–2.
51. Office for Civil Rights, 2000, chapter 2, p. 3.
52. Office for Civil Rights, 2000, chapter 1, p. 1.
53. Schemo, June 27, 2001; see also www.ed.gov/offices/OCR/testing.
54. Rebell, 1989, p. 135.
55. Heubert & Hauser, 1998, p. 252.
56. Madaus, Sept. 5, 1990.
57. Rebell, 1989, p. 137.
58. Although the initial decision came earlier, it is the 1996 Fifth Circuit Court of Appeals decision that is typically labeled "the Hopwood decision."
59. Mangan, Heller & Wheeler, Oct. 15, 1999.
60. McAllister, 1991, p. 20.
61. The information on the AAMC was supplied by Robert Burgoyne, an attorney involved in the case on behalf of the AAMC, and was relayed to me by AAMC assistant vice president Ellen Julian, Aug. 14, 2001. Other details on the test disclosure litigation were provided by an ETS attorney and relayed to me by Patricia McAllister, executive director of the State and Federal Relations Office of ETS, Aug. 2, 2001.
62. Peer Review, Nov. 12, 1999.
63. Schaeffer, Feb. 19, 2000.
64. Olson, Oct. 30, 1985; see also Crouse & Trusheim, 1988, p. 38.
65. "Critics of SAT and ACT hail decline in colleges that use them," *Chronicle of Higher Education*, Aug. 8, 1997.
66. Rooney, 1998, p. 19. I estimated the acceptance rate for submitters based on the rates provided for nonsubmitters and for applicants as a whole.

67. An interview with William Hiss, September/October, 1993, p. 7.
68. An interview with William Hiss, September/October, 1993, p. 8.
69. An interview with William Hiss, September/October, 1993, p. 11.
70. Yablon, Oct. 30, 2000.

CHAPTER 3: Conventional and Computerized Admissions Tests

1. Cronbach, 1949, p. 212.
2. McBride, 1997. An early "computerized branching test," not cited by McBride, was developed by the U.S. Army Behavioral Science Research Laboratory (Bayroff & Seeley, 1967).
3. However, as discussed in chapter 7, certain test security problems may be exacerbated.
4. Hambleton, Jones & Rogers, 1993, pp. 145, 147; Mills & Steffen, 2000, p. 78; Martha Stocking, personal communication, May 31, 2001.
5. Guernsey, Feb. 12, 1999.
6. Gray, Nettles, and Millett, 1999.
7. Legg & Buhr, 1992, p. 26.
8. See Legg & Buhr, 1992; Powers & O'Neill, 1993.
9. Schaeffer et al., 1993, table F.1.
10. Bridgeman, 1998.
11. Legg & Buhr, 1992, p. 25. More discussion of these fairness issues appears in Zwick, 2000.
12. ETS, 1999, pp. 3–5.
13. Stocking, Swanson & Pearlman, 1991.
14. Bond, 1995. This discussion also draws on Zwick, Donoghue & Grima, 1993; Dunbar, Koretz & Hoover, 1991; Madaus, Raczek & Thomas, 1999; Ryan & Greguras, 1998, and Sackett, Schmitt, Ellingson & Kabin, 2001.
15. Linn, 1999, p. 83–84.
16. Specifically, the formula score is $R - W/(C - 1)$, where R is the number of right answers, W is the number of wrong answers, and C is the number of response choices. See Gulliksen, 1987, pp. 246–249 for a rationale.
17. Other properties of the item are also considered in the scoring formula: How precise is the item? How likely is it that the item would have been answered correctly through guessing? These characteristics of the item, as well as the difficulty, are estimated statistically during the item calibration phase.
18. Enbar, 1999.
19. Burstein, Kukich, Wolff, Lu & Chodorow, Apr. 1998.
20. Weissglass, Apr. 15, 1998.
21. A reliability coefficient can be interpreted as the percent of variation in test scores that is associated with variation in true scores (in this case, the true algebra abilities). Ideally, a test score would vary only when the underlying ability varied; in that case, the reliability would be 1.
22. Specifically, the standard deviation is the average distance between an individual score and the average score. The claims about two-thirds and 95 percent of testings require an assumption that scores have a normal distribution.
23. The SAT II: Subject Tests and the PSAT were affected as well, since their score scales are linked to those of the SAT I.
24. Ravitch, Aug. 28, 1996.
25. "How the recentered SAT sugarcoats the racial scoring gap," winter 1996/1997, p. 53.

26. The standard deviation was set to 100.
27. Computations based on table 104 in Snyder & Hoffman, 2000.
28. Turnbull, 1985.
29. Weinig, June 14, 2000.

CHAPTER 4: Test Validity

1. Gulliksen, 1987, p. 1.
2. Correlations ranged from .35 to .60; see Crouse & Trusheim, 1988, pp. 21–22.
3. Crouse & Trusheim, 1988, p. 6.
4. *The American Heritage Dictionary*, 1992, p. 1427.
5. Mehrens, 1989, p. 110.
6. Strictly speaking, this statement requires some qualification: If the true relationship between GPA and SAT is linear, and if the "best weighting" is defined as that which minimizes the sum of the squared differences between actual and predicted grades, the statement is true. Further detail can be found in references on least squares regression, such as Neter et al., 1996. Note also that the size of the weights depends in part on how spreadout the predictor values are: High school GPA, which ranges from 0 to 4, has a much larger weight than SAT verbal and math scores, which range from 200 to 800.
7. See Johnson, 1997; Stricker et al., 1994; and Willingham et al., 2000, for reviews.
8. This overview is based primarily on multi-institution studies or reviews published in 1985 or later, including the following: ACT, Inc., 1997; Anthony, Harris & Pashley, 1999; Beran, 1997; Briel, O'Neill & Scheuneman, 1993; Burton & Ramist, 2001; Camara & Echternacht, July 2000; The College Board and ETS, 1998; ETS, 1998; E. Julian, personal communication, Mar. 13, 2001; Linn, 1990; Noble, 1991, Ramist et al., 1994, 1999; Rigol, June 1997; Schneider & Briel, 1990; Wightman & Leary, 1985; Wightman & Muller, 1990; Willingham, 1998; Zwick, 1990, 1993.
9. SAT's better freshman predictor than grades, Jan. 16, 1991.
10. Burton & Ramist, 2001.
11. Hezlett, Kuncel, Vey, Ahart, Ones, Campbell & Camara, 2001.
12. E. Julian, personal communication, Mar. 13, 2001.
13. Huff et al., 1999.
14. Chambers, Lempert & Adams, summer 1999.
15. Zwick, 1993.
16. Burton & Turner, 1983; Kuncel, Hezlett & Ones, 1998; Schneider & Briel, 1990; Willingham, 1974.
17. Sternberg & Williams, 1997.
18. Study finds that GRE doesn't predict success in psychology, Aug. 15, 1997.
19. For example, see Kuncel, Campbell & Ones, 1998; Thayer & Kalat, 1998.
20. Willingham, 1974, p. 275.
21. Astin, et al., 1996, p. 14.
22. Hezlett, Kuncel, Vey, Ahart, Ones, Campbell & Camara, 2001.
23. Adelman, 1999, p. 15.
24. Manski & Wise, 1983, p. 15.
25. See the summary in Burton & Ramist, 2001, pp. 16–19.
26. Willingham, 1974; see also Rock, 1974.
27. Attiyeh, 1999.
28. Zwick, 1991.
29. Zwick, 1990.

30. This phenomenon was noted by Willingham, 1985, p. 105.
31. See Klitgaard, 1985, Appendix 2; Wiley & Koenig, 1996; Hezlett, Kuncel, Vey, Ahart, Ones, Campbell & Camara, 2001.
32. McClelland, 1973, p. 3.
33. McClelland, 1973, p. 4.
34. Barrett & Depinet, 1991; Barrett, 1994; Boyatzis, 1994; Cowen, 1994; McClelland, 1994.
35. Berkowitz, 1998, p. 84.
36. Chambers, Lempert & Adams, summer 1999, p. 19.
37. Schrader, 1978.
38. Schrader, 1980, p. 13.
39. Klitgaard, 1985, p. 130.
40. Sarbin, 1942; see Gough, 1962, p. 556.
41. Dawes, 1971; Wiggins & Kohen, 1971; see Dawes & Corrigan, 1974, p. 98.
42. Gough, 1962, p. 527.
43. Messick, 1988, p. 33. Italics in original.
44. Mandinach, Cahalan & Camara, 2001, p. 5.
45. Bennett, 1999 p. 185.
46. Willingham et al., 1988, p. 156.
47. Wightman, 1993; Ziomek & Andrews, 1996.
48. Camara et al., 1998, p. 3.
49. Weiss, Jan. 9, 2000.
50. Leatherman, Dec. 4, 2000; see also California State Auditor, Nov. 2000.
51. Mandinach, 2000.
52. American Educational Research Association, American Psychological Association, and National Council on Measurement in Education, 1999, p. 105.
53. Bennett, 1999; Geisinger, 1998; Willingham et al., 1988.
54. See the critique by Wainer, 1993.
55. Beginning in 1992, the state assessment component of the National Assessment of Educational Progress, conducted by the U.S. Department of Education, partially replaced admissions test scores as the basis for media comparisons of states' educational performance.
56. The College Board, 1988.
57. Wainer, 1989.
58. Powell & Steelman, 1996.
59. Marks, Mar. 18, 2000.
60. Sedlacek, winter 1998, p. 11; Sedlacek, 1999.
61. Tracey & Sedlacek, 1984.
62. Pulley, June 23, 2000, p. A42.
63. Willingham, 1985, p. 184.
64. Gose, Dec. 3, 1999.

CHAPTER 5: Are Standardized Admissions Tests Fair to People of Color?

1. Snyder & Hoffman, 2000, table 45, p. 60 and table 275, p. 318. For the doctoral data, percentages were recalculated using the total number of doctorates, rather than the number of doctorates granted to U.S. citizens, as a base. A quarter of U.S. doctorates were earned by foreign students.
2. Lemann, 1999, p. 110.
3. The cases cited are *Plessy v. Ferguson,* 163 U.S. 537 (1896); *Missouri ex rel. Gaines v. Canada,* 305 U.S. 337 (1938); *Sweatt v. Painter,* 339 U.S. 629 (1950); *Brown v. Board of Education,* 347 U.S. 483 (1954).

4. Hebel, Jan. 5, 2001.
5. Freedman, 2000, p. B7; Klitgaard, 1985.
6. Nakanishi, November/December, 1989; Sun, 1997.
7. For example, Weissglass, Apr. 15, 1998.
8. For example, Linn, 1990, pp. 307–308.
9. Cole, 1999, p. 217; Sacks, 1997; Steinberg, Sept. 15, 1999.
10. The Princeton Review, Apr. 1997.
11. For example, see Bowen & Bok, 1998, p. 262.
12. Nettles & Nettles, 1999, p. 2.
13. Donahue, Finnegan, Lutkus, Allen & Campbell, 2001; Braswell, Lutkus, Grigg, Santapau, Tay-Lim & Johnson, 2001. In the 2000 math assessment, grade 4 results for Asian Americans were not reported.
14. Hughes, Feb. 18, 1998.
15. Office for Civil Rights, Apr. 1999, p. 3. The language of the final version of the guide (OCR, 2000) was considerably more moderate.
16. Ramist et al., 1994, p. 9.
17. Technically, the index of association between a *set* of predictors and another variable (e.g., the efficiency with which SAT scores, together with high school grades, can predict college grades) is called a *multiple* correlation; see chapter 4. Note that Ramist et al. obtained separate ethnic group prediction equations for each college and then averaged them to obtain the reported ethnic group results.
18. Ramist et al., 1994, p. 31. Among the numerous studies that have demonstrated this result was a statewide study conducted by the University of California (Kowarsky, 1997, p. 25).
19. Vars & Bowen, 1998, p. 458. In his extensive literature review, Young (July 2000) reported that this finding was typical. On the other hand, Noble (Oct. 16, 2000) recently found ACT scores and high school grades to be more predictive of college performance for African Americans than for Whites.
20. Cleary, 1968, p. 115. This definition was proposed earlier by Humphreys, 1952.
21. More specifically, in least squares linear regression, the residuals sum to zero.
22. Ramist et al., 1994, p. 32.
23. Braun & Jones, 1981; Braun & Jones, 1985; Koenig, Sireci & Wiley, 1998; Noble, Oct. 16, 2000; Wightman & Muller, 1990.
24. Klitgaard, 1985, p. 163.
25. Sacks, 1997, p. 26.
26. Raspberry, Aug. 31, 1999. Italics in original.
27. For example, Cleary, 1968. A new review of the test validity literature (Young, July 2000) has reaffirmed the prevalence of this finding.
28. Linn, 1983, p. 33.
29. Linn, 1983.
30. The effect is simplest to understand in the case of one predictor. Here, under typical assumptions about the nature of measurement errors in test scores, the effect of the measurement error on the regression analysis is to produce a regression line that is flatter (less steep) than the line that would theoretically be obtained with an error-free predictor.
31. Noble, Oct. 16, 2000; Wightman & Muller, 1990; see Vars & Bowen, 1998, for additional SAT results.
32. See Crouse & Trusheim, 1988, p. 199, note 18.
33. Fordham & Ogbu, 1986.
34. McWhorter, 2000.
35. C. M. Steele, Aug. 1999, pp. 4, 5.
36. C. M. Steele & Aronson, 1998, pp. 425–426.

37. Vars & Bowen, 1998, p. 475; Bowen & Bok, 1998, p. 81.
38. C. M. Steele & Aronson, 1998; C. M. Steele, 1997.
39. Shih, Pittinsky & Ambady, 1999.
40. Stricker, 1998; Stricker & Ward, 1998.
41. Loveless, 2000.
42. A troublesome aspect of the Steele and Aronson stereotype threat research is that they use SAT verbal scores to statistically adjust for initial differences in academic skills among their experimental groups (C.M. Steele & Aronson, 1995, p. 799). The essential purpose of this type of adjustment is to ask, "How would the performance of these groups in the experimental situation compare if their average skill levels had been equal?" Using SAT scores to make this adjustment seems awkward at best in the context of a research program that seeks to demonstrate that "stereotype threat is an underappreciated source of classic deficits in standardized test performance . . . suffered by Blacks" (p. 810). If this is so, then the statistical adjustment based on SAT scores is invalid, and the overall results of the research are in question. Steele and Aronson acknowledge that their use of SAT-based adjustments may be viewed as problematic, but argue that it is unlikely to have compromised the interpretation of their results (p. 810).
43. Pennock-Román, 1990, pp. 129–130.
44. Ramist et al., 1994, p. 15.
45. Zwick & Schlemer, 2000.
46. Marco, 1988, pp. 109–110; Olson, Oct. 30, 1985.
47. Anrig, 1987.
48. Rebell, 1989, p. 158.
49. Marco, 1988, pp. 117–118.
50. Hackett, Holland, Pearlman & Thayer, 1987, pp. 17–18.
51. Angoff, 1993, p. 15.
52. Linn & Drasgow, 1987, p. 13. Italics in original.
53. Of course, a certain circularity is involved in using the overall test score as a basis for identifying biased test items. The analysis can detect test questions that are measuring something different from the skill that is being assessed by the test as a whole, but cannot detect whether the test as a whole is biased. It is sometimes possible to match test-takers on the basis of some independent measure, rather than the total score on the test that is being investigated. See Camilli & Shepard (1994) and Holland & Wainer (1993) for more on the history, theory, and practice of item bias analyses.
54. The following distinction is sometimes made between the two terms: Differential item functioning is said to occur if the item shows statistical evidence of performance differences for the matched members of two groups. Bias is said to occur if this difference is subsequently judged to result from unfairness (as opposed to, say, differences in interests).
55. Bleistein & Wright, 1987; Rogers & Kulick, 1987; Schmitt, 1987.
56. Schmitt & Dorans, 1988; O'Neill & McPeek, 1993.
57. Schmitt, 1987, p. 22.
58. O'Neill & McPeek, 1993, p. 266. Antonym items are no longer included on the SAT.
59. O'Neill and McPeek, 1993, p. 270.
60. Zwick & Ercikan, 1989.
61. Rogers & Kulick, 1987, p. 7. See also O'Neill & McPeek, 1993, pp. 262–263.
62. Burton & Burton, 1993.
63. This section draws in part from Zwick, Feb. 10, 1999; Zwick, Dec. 1999; Zwick, Sept. 3, 2000; Zwick, Mar./Apr. 2001; and Zwick, summer 2001.

64. Atkinson, Feb. 18, 2001.
65. California Postsecondary Education Commission, 1997, pp. 50–61. See also Zwick, Dec. 1999.
66. Legum et al., 1998, tables 56 and 63.
67. Owings, McMillen & Burkett, 1995.
68. U of California Weighs Optional S.A.T.'s, Sept. 21, 1997.
69. Sacks, 1997, p. 27; see also Sacks, 1999.
70. See Camara & Schmidt, 1999, p. 9. The findings are based on College Board data on 1997 college-bound seniors.
71. An admissions plan approved in 1999 by Oklahoma regents also involved class rank, but it imposed minimum levels for high school GPA as well.
72. S. Steele, Feb. 7, 2000, p. 24.
73. These data were provided by the UCSB institutional research office, May 30, 2001.
74. Selingo, July 21, 2000.
75. Klein & Hegarty, Sept. 3, 2000.
76. Marcus, Aug. 31, 1999, p. B1.
77. The Princeton Review, Sept. 1, 1999.
78. Thernstrom, Sept. 27, 1999, pp. 27, 29.
79. Bakst, 1998, p. 6.
80. Carnevale & Haghighat, 1998, p. 123.
81. Only candidates with combined SAT scores between 1000 and 1200 were considered as potential strivers, apparently on the grounds that students with higher scores don't need any help and students with lower scores may have difficulty with college work.
82. Table 1 (p. 125) in Carnevale and Haghighat may contain an error. The percentages of Asian, Hispanic, Black, and White students add to only 95 percent for the "applicant" pool, but add to 100 percent for the "admits" for each of two versions of the Strivers method.
83. Orlofsky & Olson, Jan. 11, 2001, pp. 102, 105.
84. Bakst, 1998, p. 80.
85. Bakst, 1998, p. 81.
86. Jencks, 1989, p. 117.

CHAPTER 6: Are Standardized Admissions Tests Fair to Women?

1. Mann, Mar. 26, 1997.
2. Sommers, May 2000.
3. Ramist et al., 1994.
4. See Clark & Grandy, 1984.
5. Sources are Bridgeman & McHale, 1996; Wightman, 1994; Willingham, Cole, Lewis & Leung, 1997, pages 84–85; testing program documents; and the Digest of Education Statistics 1998. Men's scores on educational tests tend to be more variable (i.e., more spread out) than women's. Therefore, even when men and women have similar average scores, men are often found to outnumber women among high scorers. See Hedges & Nowell, July 7, 1995.
6. In fact, the College Board ultimately stuck by an earlier decision not to add a writing section to the main part of the SAT. That decision was made at least partly because one of the largest SAT customers, the University of California, argued that the change would be unfair to Asian Americans and other minorities (Evangelauf, Nov. 7, 1990). A writing test is available as part of the SAT II tests, formerly the Achievement Tests.

7. Reisberg, Jan. 23, 1998.
8. Also, average test score differences between males and females who have been "selected" on the basis of academic criteria are likely to be larger than the differences that exist before the selection criteria are applied. See Hoover & Han, 1995; Lewis & Willingham, 1995. Similar phenomena may apply in the case of ethnic group differences.
9. The College Board, Feb. 1998.
10. The College Board, 2000; ACT, Inc., 2000b; also see Coley, 2001.
11. C. M. Steele, 1997, p. 613.
12. C. M. Steele, 1997, p. 619.
13. An extensive review by Young (July 2000) confirmed the tendency for validity coefficients to be higher for women. In more selective colleges, where both men and women are presumably more dedicated to their academic work, validities for men and women tend to be more similar to each other. See also Bridgeman et al., 2000, table 4, page 5; Ramist et al., 1994, table 18, p. 25.
14. Willingham & Cole, 1997, Leonard & Jiang, 1999, and Young (July 2000) provide reviews. See also Ramist et al., 1999.
15. Instead of first-year GPA, Leonard and Jiang chose to use the cumulative GPA as of graduation, transfer, or departure from the university. They focused on the students who were admitted solely on the basis of the academic index score.
16. The one substantial exception is engineering: Here, men's college grades were slightly better than those of women with the same academic index scores.
17. The College Board, Feb. 1998, p. 2.
18. Pennock-Román, 1994.
19. Stricker et al., 1993. For related discussions, see Dwyer & Johnson, 1997; Willingham, Pollack & Lewis, 2000.
20. The College Board test formerly called the English Composition Achievement Test is now called the SAT II Writing test.
21. Koenig, Sireci & Wiley, 1998; Ramist et al., 1994, p. 27; see also Young, 1991, July 2000.
22. The main purpose of this study was to determine whether changes in the content and score scale of the SAT affected validity conclusions. The results included here are for the new version of the SAT; these proved to be nearly indistinguishable from those for the old version.
23. To complicate things further, the same degree of underprediction for White women was evident when high school GPA alone was used as a predictor—a departure from the results that were obtained when all women were considered together.
24. Brigham, 1923, p. 30.
25. Dorans & Holland, 1993, p. 46.
26. Educational Testing Service, 1999.
27. Bridgeman & Schmitt, 1997, p. 194.
28. O'Neill & McPeek, 1993, p. 262.
29. Rosser, 1989, pp. 6–7.
30. O'Neill & McPeek, 1993, p. 269.
31. Gallagher, Morley & Levin, 1999.
32. Zwick & Ercikan, 1989.
33. Willingham, Cole, Lewis & Leung, 1997, table 3.3, p. 89.
34. Burton & Burton, 1993.
35. Preliminary evidence indicates that the SAT II Writing Test is a good predictor of college English grades (Breland et al., 1999).
36. Leonard & Jiang, 1999, p. 402.

CHAPTER 7: **Gaming the Tests**

1. Miyazaki, 1976, p. 17.
2. Haney et al., 1993, p. 174.
3. Office of Technology Assessment, 1992, p. 153.
4. Hammer, Apr. 24, 1989, pp. 15–18.
5. Lemann, 1999, p. 397.
6. Schwartz, Jan. 10, 1999, p. 32.
7. Lemann, 1999, p. 227; Haney et al., 1993, p. 180.
8. Federal Trade Commission, 1978. The May 1979 cover memo from the U.S. Department of Health, Education, and Welfare is titled, "Notice to recipients of the Boston Regional Office report on the effects of coaching on standardized admission exam."
9. Federal Trade Commission, 1979; see also Messick, 1980.
10. Gose, Nov. 25, 1998.
11. The Princeton Review, Nov. 30, 1998.
12. In fact, some studies involving random assignment have been attempted, with variable results; see Bond, 1989, pp. 436–438.
13. Powers & Rock, 1999.
14. This may be especially true for computerized tests: A practice opportunity may be particularly helpful by familiarizing students with this form of test administration. As noted in chapter 3, the SAT is not computerized, but several standardized admissions tests are.
15. Perry, Aug. 30, 1999.
16. FairTest, winter 1999.
17. Becker, 1990.
18. Briggs, 2001. The editor's note appears on p. 18.
19. Haney et al., 1993, p. 241.
20. The Princeton Review, Nov. 30, 1998.
21. The PSAT, or Preliminary SAT, was used as the initial test for some of the students in the Powers-Rock study as well.
22. Scholes & McCoy, 1998.
23. Powers, 2001, p. 21.
24. Walfish, Feb. 2001; letter from ETS officials P. Swan, K. Forte, T. Rochon & M. Rymniak to graduate deans and undergraduate deans of admission, dated Jan. 2001.
25. Powers, 1983.
26. Swinton & Powers, 1983; Powers & Swinton, 1984; Powers, 1986a; 1986b. As noted in chapter 1, ETS has announced that in 2002, the Analytical section of the GRE will be replaced with a Writing Assessment.
27. Koenig & Leger, 1997; Jones, Apr. 1986.
28. Berkowitz, 1998, p. 6.
29. Leary & Wightman, 1983.
30. The Princeton Review, 1999.
31. Brownstein, Jan. 12, 2001.
32. Schwartz, Jan. 10, 1999, p. 51.
33. Mangan, May 11, 1998.
34. Wightman & Muller, 1990, p. 5.
35. Leary & Wightman, 1983, p. 5.
36. The College Board, Nov. 23, 1998.
37. The Princeton Review, Jan. 31, 2000.
38. Weissert, Dec. 17, 1999.
39. Haney et al., 1993, p. 222.

40. Strosnider, Nov. 8, 1996; Hamilton, July 5, 1998; Richardson, Oct. 29, 1996.
41. Kim, Jan. 27, 2000.
42. Goodnough, Dec. 8, 1999.
43. Clines, June 12, 2000; Hoff, June 21, 2000; Kleiner, June 12, 2000; Sandham, Apr. 7, 1999; Wilgoren, Feb. 25, 2000.
44. These accounts are based on Miyazaki, 1976, pp. 21, 27, 44; Cizek, 1999, p. 75; Dunn, Feb. 7, 1999; Riots in Bangladesh follow English tests, Jan. 13, 2001.
45. Saretzky, 1984.
46. Dunn, Feb. 7, 1999.
47. Frantz & Nordheimer, Sept. 28, 1997.
48. Haney, Sept. 29, 1993.
49. Haney et al., 1993, p. 275.
50. Haney, Sept. 29, 1993, p. B3.
51. Holland, 1996.
52. More specifically, suppose a particular "subject" is suspected of copying from a particular "source." We could determine what proportion of test-takers "with the same number of incorrect responses as the Subject agree as much or more on the Source's incorrect responses as the Subject does" (Holland, 1996, p. 14). This is the proportion that is approximated by the K-index. Recent analyses suggest that the K-index is not very good at detecting even substantial amounts of copying; see Lewis & Thayer, 1998.
53. Haney, Sept. 29, 1993, p. B3.

CHAPTER 8: **New Directions for Admissions Testing**

1. Sternberg, 1991, p. 388.
2. Sternberg, 1991, p. 385.
3. Sternberg & Williams, 1997.
4. Leonhardt, May 24, 2000, p. C9.
5. Snow, 1999, p. 134.
6. Mariantes, Nov. 2, 1999.
7. Atkinson, Feb. 18, 2001.
8. Kirst, 1998, p. 10.
9. Lemann, 1999, p. 349.
10. Bejar, Embretson & Mayer, 1987, p. 46.
11. Snow, 1999, p. 136.
12. Neeff, Dec. 5, 1986; Bejar, Embretson & Mayer, 1987, p. 7.
13. All correlations given in this section are "uncorrected"; corrected correlations would be higher. See chapter 4. UCSB results are from Zwick & Schlemer, 2000; UC Berkeley results are from Berkeley's own institutional analyses. Preliminary results of an analysis of combined data from the campuses of the University of California showed that scores on an SAT II "composite" (consisting of the SAT II Writing and Math tests, as well as a third SAT II test of the candidate's choice) were slightly more predictive of freshman GPA than were SAT I scores (Geiser & Studley, Mar. 12, 2001). See Geiser & Studley, Oct. 24, 2001 and Kobrin & Camara, 2001 for more recent analysis.
14. This analysis by the UC Office of the President (Geiser & Studley, July 11, 2001), was based on 63,462 students who were admitted to UC between 1996 and 1999. The analyses has some limitations: First, combining data across institutions can lead to misleading results, as described in chapter 4. Second, both the SAT I and SAT II scores in the analysis were actually "composites"— averages of multiple scores. In the case of the SAT I, the composite was an

average of the math and verbal sections. The case of the SAT II is even more complex. All UC applicants are required to take the SAT II Mathematics and Writing tests, plus a third SAT II test of their own choice. The composite is the average score on the three tests; the components therefore vary across students.

15. Bridgeman, Burton & Cline, 2001, p. 3. The authors found that one factor that did affect the composition of the hypothetical entering class was whether scores on SAT II language tests were considered. In most analyses, a student's "SAT II score" was, in fact, the average score for all SAT II tests taken by that student. When SAT II language test scores were included in the average, the percentage of Mexican-American and "other Latino" students who were admitted was much higher than when language test scores were excluded from consideration. A drawback of this study is that the admissions criteria were applied to data from students who had, in fact, already been admitted to college, rather than to data from applicants.

16. Snow (1999) cites Pask & Scott (1972) in this connection.

17. Snow, 1999, p. 136.

18. Sternberg & Williams, 1997, p. 640.

19. Results retrieved July 9, 2001, from www.nces.ed.gov.nationsreportcard/tables.

20. Bridgeman, Burton & Cline, 2001, p. 3.

21. Zwick & Schlemer, 2000.

22. Breland, 1999, p. 106.

23. McBride, 1998, p. 28.

24. Vispoel et al., 1997.

25. Kaplan & Bennett, 1994.

26. Bejar, 1991; Oltman, Bejar & Kim, 1993.

27. I checked the 2000–2001 edition of the ACT handbook (ACT, Inc., 2000a) and the 1998–1999 edition of the SAT handbook (College Board/ETS, 1998).

28. Leonard & Jiang, 1999.

29. Selingo, June 2, 2000, p. A31.

30. Linn, 1994, p. 30.

31. Willingham, 1999, p. 227.

32. Mehrens, 1989, pp. 96–97.

BIBLIOGRAPHY

The American Heritage dictionary of the English language (3rd ed.). (1992). Boston: Houghton Mifflin.

Critics of SAT and ACT hail decline in colleges that use them. (1997, Aug. 8). *Chronicle of Higher Education*, A41.

A dialogue on race with President Clinton (Transcript from the Newshour with Jim Lehrer). (1998, July 9). Public Broadcasting Service. Retrieved Nov. 12, 1999 from the World Wide Web: http://www.pbs.org.

How the recentered SAT sugarcoats the racial scoring gap. (1996/97). *Journal of Blacks in Higher Education, 14,* 52–53.

An interview with William Hiss. (1993, September/October). *Long-Term View,* 5–13.

Peer review. (1999, Nov. 12). *Chronicle of Higher Education,* A14

President emeritus talks about the big test and other timely subjects. (1999, Oct. 14). *ETS Access, 10,* 2.

Riots in Bangladesh follow English tests. (2001, Jan. 13). *Chronicle of Higher Education,* A45.

SAT's better freshman predictor than grades. (1991, Jan.). *Chronicle of Higher Education,* A35.

Study finds that GRE doesn't predict success in psychology. (1997, Aug. 15). *Chronicle of Higher Education,* A33.

U of California weighs optional S.A.T.'s. (1997, Sept. 21). *New York Times,* p. 32.

UC's freshmen (1999, July 21). *Los Angeles Times,* p. B2.

ACT, Inc. (1997). *ACT Assessment technical manual.* Iowa City, IA: Author.

ACT, Inc. (1999a). *Preparing for the ACT Assessment 1999–2000.* Iowa City, IA: Author.

ACT, Inc. (1999b). *ACT Assessment user handbook 1999.* Iowa City, IA: Author.

ACT, Inc. (2000a). *ACT Assessment user handbook 2000–2001.* Iowa City, IA: Author.

ACT, Inc. (2000b). *The high school profile report: Normative data.* Iowa City, IA: Author.

ACT, Inc. (2001). *Facts about the ACT Assessment* (ACT Newsroom). Author. Retrieved July 25, 2001, from the World Wide Web: http://www.act.org.

ACT, Inc. (2001). *2001 ACT National and State Scores: Selections from the 2001* National Score Report. Author. Retrieved Oct. 15, 2001, from the World Wide Web: http://www.act.org.

Adelman, C. (1999). *Answers in the tool box: Academic intensity, attendance patterns, and bachelor's degree attainment.* Washington, DC: U. S. Department of Education.

American Educational Research Association, American Psychological Association, and National Council on Measurement in Education (1999). *Standards for educational and psychological testing.* Washington, DC: Author.

Angoff, W. H. (1993). Perspectives on differential item functioning methodology. In P. W. Holland & H. Wainer (Ed.), *Differential Item Functioning* (pp. 3–23). Hillsdale, NJ: Lawrence Erlbaum Associates.

Anrig, G. R. (1987). "Golden Rule." Second thoughts. *APA Monitor,* p. 3.

Anthony, L. C., Harris, V. F., & Pashley, P. J. (1999). *Predictive validity of the LSAT: A national summary of the 1995–1996 correlation studies.* (LSAT Technical Report 97–01). Newtown, PA: Law School Admission Council.

Association of American Medical Colleges (1999). *MCAT 1999 announcement.* Washington, DC: Author.

Astin, A., Tsui, A., & Avalos, J. (1996). *Degree attainment rates at American colleges and universities: Effects of race, gender, and institutional type.* Los Angeles: University of California, Los Angeles, Higher Education Research Institute.

Atkinson, R. (2001, Feb. 18). *Standardized tests and access to American universities.* The 2001 Robert H. Atwell Distinguished Lecture, delivered at the 83rd annual meeting of the American Council on Education, Washington, DC.

Attiyeh, G. M. (1999). *Determinants of persistence of graduate students in Ph.D. programs.* (ETS Research Report 99–4). Princeton, NJ: Educational Testing Service.

Attiyeh, G. & Attiyeh, P. (1997). Testing for bias in graduate school admissions. *Journal of Human Resources, 32,* 524–548.

Bakst, D. (Ed.). (1998). *Hopwood, Bakke, and beyond: Diversity on our nation's campuses.* (Excerpts from the Hopwood, Bakke and Beyond Summit held by the American Association of Collegiate Registrars and Admissions Officers in Oct. 1997). Washington, DC: AACRAO.

Barrett, G. V. (1994). Empirical data says it all. *American Psychologist, 49,* 69–71.

Barrett, G. V., & Depinet, R. L. (1991). A reconsideration of testing for competence rather than for intelligence. *American Psychologist, 46,* 1012–1024.

Bayroff, A. G., & Seeley, L. C. (1967, June). *An exploratory study of branching testing* (Technical Research Note 188). Washington, DC: U.S. Army Behavioral Science Research Laboratory.

Beatty, A., Greenwood, M. R., & Linn, R. (Ed.). (1999). *Myths and tradeoffs: The role of testing in undergraduate admissions.* Washington, DC: National Academy Press.

Becker, B. J. (1990). Coaching for the Scholastic Aptitude Test: Further synthesis and appraisal. *Review of Educational Research, 60,* 373–417.

Bejar, I. I. (1991). A methodology for scoring open-ended architectural design problems. *Journal of Applied Psychology, 76* (4), 522–532.

Bejar, I. I., Embretson, S., & Mayer, R. (1987). *Cognitive psychology and the SAT: A review of some implications* (ETS Research Report 87–28). Princeton, NJ: Educational Testing Service.

Bennett, R.E. (1999). Computer-based testing for examinees with disabilities: On the road to generalized accommodation. In S. J. Messick (Ed.), *Assessment in higher education: Issues of access, quality, student development, and public policy* (pp. 181–191). Mahwah, NJ: Lawrence Erlbaum Associates.

Beran, R. (1997). *Evolution of the MCAT* (AAMC internal document). Washington, DC: American Association of Medical Colleges.

Berkowitz, R. (1998). One point on the LSAT: How much is it worth? Standardized tests as a determinant of earnings. *American Economist, 42* (2), 80–89.

Bird, C. (1927). The detection of cheating on objective examinations. *School and Society, 25,* 261–262.

Bleistein, C. A., & Wright, D. J. (1987). Assessment of unexpected differential item difficulty for Asian-American examinees on the Scholastic Aptitude Test. In A. P. Schmitt & N. J. Dorans (Ed.), *Differential item functioning on the Scholastic Aptitude Test* (ETS Research Memorandum No. 87–1). Princeton, NJ: Educational Testing Service.

Bond, L. (1989). The effects of special preparation on measures of scholastic ability. In R. L. Linn (Ed.), *Educational measurement.* New York: American Council on Education/ Macmillan.

Bond, L. (1995). Unintended consequences of performance assessment: Issues of bias and fairness. *Educational Measurement: Issues and Practice, 14* (4), 21–24.

Bowen, W. G., & Bok, D. (1998). *The shape of the river: Long-term consequences of considering race in college and university admissions.* Princeton, NJ: Princeton University Press.

Boyatzis, R. E. (1994). Rendering unto competence the things that are competent. *American Psychologist, 49,* 64–66.

Braswell, J. S., Lutkus, A., Grigg, W. S., Santapau, S. L., Tay-Lim, B., & Johnson, M. (2001). *The nation's report card: Mathematics 2000.* (NCES 2001517). National Center for Education Statistics. Retrieved Aug. 7, 2001, from the World Wide Web: http://www.neces.ed.gov.

Braun, H. I., & Jones, D. H. (1981). *The Graduate Management Admission Test prediction bias study* (GMAC Report 81–4). Princeton, NJ: Educational Testing Service.

Braun, H. I., & Jones, D. H. (1985). *Use of empirical Bayes methods in the study of the validity of academic predictors of graduate school performance.* (ETS Research Report 84–34). Princeton, NJ: Educational Testing Service.

Breland, H. M. (1978). *Population validity and college entrance measures* (College Board Research Bulletin). New York: College Entrance Examination Board.

Breland, H. M. (1998). *National trends in the use of test scores in college admissions.* Paper presented at the National Academy of Sciences Workshop on the Role of Tests in Higher Education Admissions, Washington, DC.

Breland, H. M. (1999). From 2 to 3 R's: The expanding use of writing in admissions. In S. J. Messick (Ed.), *Assessment in higher education: Issues of access, quality, student development, and public policy* (pp. 91–112). Mahwah, NJ: Lawrence Erlbaum Associates.

Breland, H. M., Kubota, M. Y., & Bonner, M. W. (1999). *The performance assessment study in writing: Analysis of the SAT II: Writing Subject Test* (College Board Report 99–4). New York: College Entrance Examination Board.

Brennan, R. L. (1999, July). *A perspective on educational testing: The Iowa testing programs and the legacy of E. F. Lindquist.* Paper presented to the National Institute for Testing and Evaluation, Jerusalem.

Bridgeman, B. (1998). *Fairness in computer-based testing: What we know and what we need to know.* (The GRE FAME Report Series Vol. 2) (pp.4–11). Princeton, NJ: Educational Testing Service.

Bridgeman, B., Burton, N., & Cline, F. (2001). *Substituting SAT II: Subject Tests for SAT I: Reasoning Tests: Impact on admitted class composition and quality* (Research Report 2001–3). New York: College Entrance Examination Board.

Bridgeman, B., McCamley-Jenkins, L., & Ervin, N. (2000). *Prediction of freshman grade-point average from the revised and recentered SAT I: Reasoning Test* (College Board Report 2000–1). New York: College Entrance Examination Board.

Bridgeman, B., & McHale, F. (1996). *Gender and ethnic group differences on the GMAT Analytical Writing Assessment* (ETS Research Report 96–2). Princeton, NJ: Educational Testing Service.

Bridgeman, B., & Schmitt, A. (1997). Fairness issues in test development and administration. In W. W. Willingham & N. Cole, *Gender and fair assessment* (pp. 185–226). Mahwah, NJ: Lawrence Erlbaum Associates.

Briel, J. B., O'Neill, K. A., & Scheuneman, J. D. (1993). *GRE technical manual.* Princeton, NJ: Educational Testing Service.

Briggs, D. (2001). The effect of admissions test preparation: Evidence from NELS: 88. *Chance, 14* (1), 10–18.

Brigham, C. C. (1923). *A study of American intelligence.* Princeton, NJ: Princeton University Press.

Brigham, C. C. (1930). Intelligence tests of immigrant groups. *Psychological Review, 37,* 158–165.

Brown v. Board of Education, 347 U. S. 483 (1954).

Brownstein, A. (2000, Oct. 9). Admissions officers weigh a heretical idea: Affirmative action for men. *Chronicle of Higher Education.* Retrieved Mar. 7, 2001, from the World Wide Web: http://www.chronicle.com.

Brownstein, A. (2001, Jan. 12). Testing service embraces College Board web site with $15 million investment. *Chronicle of Higher Education.* Retrieved Jan. 12, 2001, from the World Wide Web: http://www.chronicle.com.

Burstein, J., Kukich, K., Wolff, S., Lu, C., & Chodorow, M. (1998, Apr.). *Computer analysis of essays* (NCME Symposium on Automated Scoring). Educational Testing Service. Retrieved July 3, 2000 from the World Wide Web: http://www.ets.org.

Burton, E., & Burton, N. W. (1993). The effect of item screening on test scores and test characteristics. In P. W. Holland & H. Wainer (Ed.), *Differential item functioning* (pp. 321–336). Hillsdale, NJ: Lawrence Erlbaum Associates.

Burton, N. W., & Ramist, L. (2001). *Predicting success in college: SAT studies of classes graduating since 1980* (Research Report 2001–2). New York: College Entrance Examination Board.

Burton, N. W., & Turner, N. (1983). *Effectiveness of Graduate Record Examinations for predicting first year grades: 1981–82 summary report of the Graduate Record Examinations Validity Study Service.* Princeton, NJ: Educational Testing Service.

California Civil Rights Initiative (Proposition 209). Cal Const, Art I § 31 (1996).

California Postsecondary Education Commission (1997, Nov.). *Eligibility of California's 1996 high school graduates for admission to the state's public universities.* (CPEC Report 97–9). Sacramento, CA: Author.

California State Auditor (2000, Nov.). *Standardized tests: Although some students may receive extra time on standardized tests that is not deserved, others may not be getting the assistance they need* (Summary of Report 2000–108). Sacramento, CA: Bureau of State Audits.

Camara, W. J., & Echternacht, G. (2000, July). *The SAT and high school grades: Utility in predicting success in college* (College Board Research Note RN-10). New York: College Entrance Examination Board.

Camara, W. J., & Schmidt, A. E. (1999). *Group differences in standardized testing and social stratification* (College Board Report 99–5). New York: College Entrance Examination Board.

Camara, W. J., Copeland, T., & Rothchild, B. (1998). *Effects of extended time on the SAT I: Reasoning Test score growth for students with learning disabilities* (College Board Report 98–7). New York: College Entrance Examination Board.

Camilli, G., & Shepard, L. A. (1994). *Methods for identifying biased test items*. Thousand Oaks, CA: Sage.

Carnevale, D. (1999, Sept. 3). Lawsuit prompts U. of Georgia to end admissions preferences for male applicants. *Chronicle of Higher Education*, A68.

Carnevale, A. P., & Haghighat, E. (1998). Selecting the strivers: A report on the preliminary results of the ETS 'educational strivers' study. In D. Bakst (Ed.), *Hopwood, Bakke, and beyond: Diversity on our nation's campuses* (pp. 122–128). Washington, DC: AACRAO.

Chambers, D. L., Lempert, R. O., & Adams, T. K. (1999, summer). *Doing well and doing good: the careers of minority and white graduates of the University of Michigan Law School 1970–1996*. University of Michigan Law School. Retrieved July 20, 1999, from the World Wide Web: http://www.law.umich.edu.

Chapa, J., & Lazaro, V. A. (1998). Hopwood in Texas: The untimely end of affirmative action. In G. Orfield & E. Miller (Ed.), *Chilling admissions: The affirmative action crisis and the search for alternatives* (pp. 51–70). Cambridge, MA: Harvard Education Publishing Group.

Cizek, G. J. (1999). *Cheating on tests: How to do it, detect it, and prevent it*. Mahwah, NJ: Lawrence Erlbaum Associates.

Clark, M. J., & Centra, J. A. (1982). *Conditions influencing the career accomplishments of Ph.D.s* (GRE Board Report 76–2R). Princeton, NJ: Graduate Record Examinations Board.

Clark, M. J., & Grandy, J. (1984). *Sex differences in the academic performance of Scholastic Aptitude Test-takers* (College Board Report 84–8). New York: College Entrance Examination Board.

Cleary, T. A. (1968). Test bias: Prediction of Negro and White students in integrated colleges. *Journal of Educational Measurement, 5* (2), 115–124.

Clegg, R., & Ostrowsky, L. (1999, July 2). Test guidelines will coerce colleges and cheat students. *Chronicle of Higher Education*, B8.

Clines, F. X. (2000, June 12). Cheating report renews debate over use of tests to evaluate schools. *New York Times*, p. A16.

Cole, N. S. (1999). Merit and opportunity: Testing and higher education at the vortex. In A. L. Netttles & M. T. Nettles (Ed.), *Measuring up: Challenges minorities face in educational assessment* (pp. 215–224). Boston: Kluwer Academic.

Coley, R. J. (2001). *Differences in the gender gap: Comparisons across racial/ethnic groups in education and work* (ETS Policy Information Report). Princeton, NJ: Educational Testing Service.

The College Board (1988). *Guidelines on the uses of College Board test scores and related data*. New York: Author.

The College Board (1998). *1998 College-bound seniors: A profile of SAT program test takers*. New York: Author.

The College Board (1998, Feb.). *SAT and gender differences* (College Board Research Summary RS-4). New York: The College Board, Office of Research and Development.

The College Board. (1998, Nov. 23). *New studies document limited value of coaching on SAT scores: Strong academic preparation key to success*. Author. Retrieved May 8, 1999, from the World Wide Web: http://www.collegeboard.org.

The College Board (1999, June 21). *Technical and psychometric comments on the draft resource guide for nondiscrimination in high stakes testing*. Author. Retrieved Oct. 16, 1999 from the World Wide Web: http://www.collegeboard.org.

The College Board (2000). *College-bound seniors 2000*. Author. Retrieved Sept. 1, 2000, from the World Wide Web: http://www.collegeboard.org.

The College Board (2001). *2001 College-bound seniors.* Author. Retrieved Oct. 15, 2001, from the World Wide Web: http://www.collegeboard.org.

The College Board and the Educational Testing Service (1998). *Admission staff handbook for the SAT program 1998–1999.* Princeton, NJ: Authors.

The College Board and the Educational Testing Service (1999). *Taking the SAT I: Reasoning Test 1999–2000.* Princeton, NJ: Authors.

Colvin, R. L. (1997, Oct. 1). Q & A: Should UC do away with the SAT? *Los Angeles Times,* B2.

Conant, J. B. (1964). *Shaping educational policy.* New York: McGraw-Hill.

Cowen, J. J. (1994). Barret and Depinet versus McClelland. *American Psychologist, 49,* 64.

Cronbach, L. J. (1970). *Essentials of psychological testing* (3rd ed.). New York: Harper.

Crouse, J., & Trusheim, D. (1988). *The case against the SAT.* Chicago: University of Chicago Press.

Curley, W. E., & Schmitt, A. P. (1992, Apr.). *Revising SAT-Verbal items to eliminate DIF: Does it work? When? How?* Paper presented at the American Educational Research Association/ National Council on Measurement in Education, San Francisco.

Dalessandro, S. P., Anthony, L. C., & Reese, L. M. (2001). *LSAT performance with regional, gender, and ethnic breakdowns: 1993–1994 through 1999–2000 testing years.* (LSAT Technical Report 00–01). Law School Admission Council.

Dalton v. Educational Testing Service, 206 AD2d 402, 614 N.Y.S.2d 742, modified.

Dawes, R. M. (1971). A case study of graduate admissions: Application of three principles of human decision making. *American Psychologist, 26,* 180–188.

Dawes, R. M., & Corrigan, B. (1974). Linear models in decision making. *Psychological Bulletin, 81* (2), 95–106.

Donahue, P. L., Finnegan, R. J., Lutkus, A. D., Allen, N. L., & Campbell, J. R. (2001, Apr.). *The nation's report card: Fourth-grade reading 2000* (NCES 2001499). National Center for Education Statistics. Retrieved June 25, 2001, from the World Wide Web: http://www.nces.ed.gov.

Dorans, N. J. (1999). *Correspondences between ACT and SAT I scores* (College Board Report 99–1). New York: College Entrance Examination Board.

Dorans, N. J., & Holland, P. W. (1993). DIF detection and description: Mantel–Haenszel and standardization. In P. W. Holland & H. Wainer (Ed.), *Differential item functioning* (pp. 35–66). Hillsdale, NJ: Lawrence Erlbaum Associates.

Dorans, N. J., Lyu, C. F., Pommerich, M., & Houston, W. M. (1997). Concordance between ACT assessment and recentered SAT I sum scores. *College and University, 73* (2), 24–32.

Dugan, M. K., Baydar, N., Grady, W. R., & Johnson, T. R. (1996). Affirmative action: Does it exist in graduate business schools? *Selections,* 11–18.

Dunbar, S. B., Koretz, D. M., & Hoover, H. D. (1991). Quality control in the development and use of performance assessments. *Applied Measurement in Education, 4,* 289–303.

Dunn, A. (1999, Feb. 7). Welcome to the evil house of cheat. *Los Angeles Times Magazine.* Retrieved Nov. 7, 1999, from the World Wide Web: http://www.latimes.com.

Dwyer, C. A., & Johnson, L. M. (1997). Grades, accomplishments, and correlates. In W. W. Willingham & N. Cole, *Gender and Fair Assessment* (pp. 127–156). Mahwah, NJ: Lawrence Erlbaum Associates.

Educational Testing Service (1949–1950). *Educational Testing Service annual report to the Board of Trustees.* Princeton, NJ: Author.

Educational Testing Service (1995). *Appeals court upholds ETS's system of investigating suspicious SAT scores.* Author. Retrieved July 31, 1999, from the World Wide Web: http://www.ets.org.

Educational Testing Service (1996). *New York students win with testing bill.* Author. Retrieved Apr. 10, 1999, from the World Wide Web: http://www.ets.org.

Educational Testing Service (1998). *GRE 1998–1999 guide to the use of scores.* Princeton, NJ: Author.

Educational Testing Service (1999). *Overview: ETS fairness review.* Author. Retrieved Aug. 30, 1999, from the World Wide Web: http://www.ets.org.

Educational Testing Service (1999). *Preparing for the GRE General Test.* Princeton, NJ: Author.

Educational Testing Service (2001). *Sex, race, ethnicity, and performance on the GRE General Test 2001–2002.* Princeton, NJ: Author.

Enbar, N. (1999, Jan. 21). This is e-rater. It'll be scoring your essay today. *Business Week*. Retrieved Oct. 15, 1999, from the World Wide Web: http://www.business week.com.

Evangelauf, J. (1990, Nov. 7). College Board to introduce new version of entrance exam. *Chronicle of Higher Education*. Retrieved Feb. 18, 2001, from the World Wide Web: http://www.chronicle.com.

FairTest. (1999, winter). *SAT coaching coverup continues*. Author. Retrieved May 21, 1999, from the World Wide Web: http://www.fairtest.org.

Federal Trade Commission. (1978). *The effects of coaching on standardized admission examinations* (Staff memorandum of the Boston Regional Office of the Federal Trade Commission). Washington, DC: Author.

Federal Trade Commission. (1979). *Effects of coaching on standardized admission examinations* (Revised statistical analyses of data gathered by Boston Regional Office of the Federal Trade Commission). Washington, DC: Author.

Fordham, S., & Ogbu, J. U. (1986). Black students' school success: Coping with the burden of "Acting White." *Urban Review, 18* (3), 176–206.

Frantz, D., & Nordheimer, J. (1997, Sept. 28). Giant of exam business keeps quiet on cheating. *New York Times*, pp. 1, 14.

Freedman, J. O. (2000, Dec. 1). Ghosts of the past: Anti-Semitism at elite colleges. *Chronicle of Higher Education*, B7.

Gallagher, A., Morley, M. E., & Levin, J. (1999). *Cognitive patterns of gender differences on mathematics admissions tests* (The GRE, FAME Report Series 3) (pp. 4–11). Princeton, NJ: Educational Testing Service.

Geiser, S., & Studley, R. (2001, Mar. 12). *Relative contribution of high school grades, SAT I and SAT II scores in predicting success at UC: Preliminary findings* (internal report). Oakland, CA: University of California Office of the President.

Geiser, S., & Studley, R. (2001, July 11). *Preliminary findings on the relationship between SAT scores, socioeconomic status, and UC freshman GPA* (memorandum). Oakland, CA: University of California Office of the President.

Geiser, S., & Studley, R. (2001, October 24). *UC and the SAT: Predictive validity and differential impact of the SAT I and SAT II at the University of California*. Oakland, CA: University of California Office of the President.

Geisinger, K. F. (1998). *Testing accommodations for the new millennium: Computer-administered testing in a changing society* (The GRE FAME Report Series Vol. 2, pp.12–20). Princeton, NJ: Educational Testing Service.

Goodnough, A. (1999, Dec. 8). Investigator says teachers in city aid cheating. *New York Times*, pp. A1, A24.

Gose, B. (1998, Nov. 25). Coaching for SAT improves students' scores only slightly, College Board study finds. *Chronicle of Higher Education*. Retrieved Nov. 23, 1999 from the World Wide Web: http://www.chronicle.com.

Gose, B. (1999, Dec. 3). Seeking diversity, 9 colleges try alternative to standardized tests. *Chronicle of Higher Education*, A50.

Gough, H. G. (1962). Clinical versus statistical prediction in psychology. In L. Postman (Ed.) *Psychology in the making: Histories of selected research problems* (pp. 526–584). New York: Alfred A. Knopf.

Gould, S. J. (1996). *The mismeasure of man* (Revised & expanded edition). New York: Norton.

Graduate Management Admission Council (1998). *MBA Q. & A*. McLean, VA: GMAC and Design Partners, Inc.

Graduate Management Admission Council (2000). *Profile of Graduate Management Admission Test candidates*. McLean, VA: Author.

Gray, W. H., III, Nettles, M. T., & Millett, C. M. (1999). Tests as barriers to access. In A. L. Nettles & M. T. Nettles (Ed.), *Measuring up: Challenges minorities face in educational assessment* (pp. 197–207). Boston: Kluwer Academic.

Gross, J. (1999, Aug. 9). Multiple choice and margaritas. *New York Times Magazine*. Retrieved Aug. 15, 1999, from the World Wide Web: http://www.nytimes.com.

Guernsey, L. (1999, Feb. 12). Bowing to criticism, ETS suspends computerized tests in 20 African nations. *Chronicle of Higher Education*, A47.

Gulliksen, H. (1987). *Theory of mental tests*. Hillsdale, NJ: Lawrence Erlbaum Associates.

Hackett, R. K., Holland, P. W., Pearlman, M., & Thayer, D. T. (1987). *Test construction manip-*

ulating score differences between Black and White examinees: Properties of the resulting tests (ETS Research Report 87–30). Princeton, NJ: Educational Testing Service.

Hambleton, R. K., & Jones, R. W. (1994). Comparison of empirical and judgmental procedures for detecting differential item functioning. *Educational Research Quarterly, 18,* 21–36.

Hambleton, R. K., Jones, R. W., & Rogers, H. J. (1993). Influence of item parameter estimation errors in test development. *Journal of Educational Measurement, 30* (2), 143–155.

Hamilton, D. (1998, July 5). The big cheat. *Los Angeles New Times.* Retrieved July 4, 1999, from the World Wide Web: http://www.newtimesla.com.

Hammer, J. (1989, Apr. 24). Cram scam. *New Republic,* pp. 15–18.

Haney, W. (1993, Sept. 29). Preventing cheating on standardized tests. *Chronicle of Higher Education,* B3.

Haney, W. M., Madaus, G. F., & Lyons, R. (1993). *The fractured marketplace for standardized testing.* Boston: Kluwer Academic.

Hebel, S. (2001, Jan. 5). Desegregation pacts set in Maryland, Tennessee, and Louisiana. *Chronicle of Higher Education,* A35.

Hecht, L. W., & Schrader, W. B. (1986). *Graduate Management Admission Test: Technical report on test development and score interpretation for GMAT users.* Princeton, NJ: Graduate Management Admission Council.

Hedges, L. V., & Nowell, A. (1995). Sex differences in mental test scores, variability, and numbers of high-scoring individuals. *Science, 269,* 41–45.

Hernandez, M. (1997). *"A" is for admission: The insider's guide to getting into the ivy league and other top colleges.* New York: Warner Books.

Herrnstein, R. J., & Murray, C. A. (1994). *The bell curve: Intelligence and class structure in American life.* New York: Free Press.

Heubert, J. P. & Hauser, R. M. (Ed.). (1998). *High stakes: Testing for tracking promotion, and graduation.* Washington, DC: National Research Council.

Hezlett, S. A., Kuncel, N. R., Vey, M., Ahart, A. M., Ones, D. S., Campbell, J. P., & Camara, W. (2001, Apr.). *The effectiveness of the SAT in predicting success early and late in college: A meta-analysis.* Paper presented at the 2001 AERA/NCME annual meeting, Seattle, WA.

Hoff, D. J. (2000, June 21). As stakes rise, definition of cheating blurs. *Education Week,* p. 1.

Holland, P. W. (1996). *Assessing unusual agreement between the incorrect answers of two examinees using the K-index* (Program Statistics Research Technical Report 96–4). Princeton, NJ: Educational Testing Service.

Holland, P. W., & Wainer, H. (Ed.). (1993). *Differential item functioning.* Hillsdale, NJ: Lawrence Erlbaum Associates.

Hoover, H. D., & Han, L (1995, Apr.). *The effect of differential selection on gender differences in college admission test scores.* Paper presented at the annual meeting of the American Educational Research Association, San Francisco, CA.

Hopwood v. Texas 78 F.3d 932 (5th Cir. 1996), *reh'g en banc denied,* 84 F.3d 720, *cert. denied,* 518 U.S. 1033 (1996), *remanded for further proceedings,* 999 F. Supp. 872 (W.D. Tex. 1998), *aff'd in part and rev'd and remanded in part,* 236 F.3d 256,272 (5th Cir. 2000), *reh'g and reh'g en banc denied* 2001 U. S. App. Lexis 1492 (Jan. 17, 2001).

Huff, K. L., Koenig, J., Treptau, M., & Sireci, S. G. (1999). Validity of MCAT scores for predicting clerkship performance of medical students grouped by sex and ethnicity. *Academic Medicine, 74* (10), 41S-44S.

Hughes, T. (1998, Feb. 18). *Admissions criteria: Standardized testing* (California State Senate Bill 1807). Legislative Counsel's Digest. Retrieved June 27, 2001, from the World Wide Web: http://www.sen.ca.gov.

Humphreys, L. G. (1952). Individual differences. *Annual Review of Psychology, 3,* 131–150.

Jencks, C. (1989). If not tests, then what? In B. R. Gifford (Ed.), *Test policy and test performance: Education, language, and culture* (pp. 116–121). Boston: Kluwer Academic.

Jencks, C. (1998). Racial bias in testing. In C. Jencks & M. Phillips (Ed.), *The Black-White test score gap* (pp. 55–85). Washington, DC: Brookings Institution Press.

Johnson, V. E. (1997). An alternative to traditional GPA for evaluating student performance. *Statistical Science, 12* (4), 251–278.

Johnson, E. K., & Edwards, J. C. (1991). Current practices in admission interviews at U. S. medical schools. *Academic Medicine, 66* (7), 408–412.

Jolly, P. (1992). Academic achievement and acceptance rates of underrepresented-minority applicants to medical school. *Academic Medicine, 67* (11), 765–769.

Jones, R. F. (1986, Apr.). *The effect of commercial coaching courses on MCAT performance* (Medical College Admission Test Interpretive Studies Series 86–1). Washington, DC: Association of American Medical Colleges.

Kabaservice, G. (2000, Jan. 26). *Bill Bradley's SAT scores: When dumb things happen to smart people.* MSN Websites. Retrieved Jan. 31, 2000, from the World Wide Web: http://www.slate.msn.com

Kaplan, R. M., & Bennett, R. E. (1994). *Using the free-response scoring tool to automatically score the formulating-hypotheses item* (GRE Research Report 94–08). Princeton, NJ: Graduate Record Examinations Board.

Kell, G., & Mena, J. (1998, spring). New admissions process launched. *Berkeley Magazine,* pp. 21–23.

Kidder, W. G. (2000). The rise of the testocracy: An essay on the LSAT, conventional wisdom, and the dismantling of diversity. *Texas Journal of Women and the Law, 9,* 167–218.

Kim, A. L. (2000, Jan. 27). 2 sentenced in elaborate scheme to cheat on law school entry test. *Los Angeles Times,* B1.

Kirst, M. W. (1998). *Improving and aligning K–16 standards, admissions, and freshman placement policies* (NCPI-2–06). Menlo Park, CA: National Center for Postsecondary Improvement.

Klein, B., & Hegarty, S. (2000, Sept. 3). College program has little impact. *St. Petersburg Times.* p. 1A.

Kleiner, C. (1999, Aug. 30). A peek behind closed doors. *U. S. News & World Report,* pp. 70–72.

Kleiner, C. (2000, June 12). Test case: Now the principal's cheating. *U. S. News & World Report.* Retrieved Feb. 27, 2001, from the World Wide Web: http://www.usnews.com.

Klitgaard, R. E. (1985). *Choosing elites.* New York: Basic Books.

Kobrin, J. L. & Camara, W. J. (2001). The utility of the SAT I: Reasoning Test and SAT II: Subject Tests for admissions decisions in California and the nation. (College Board draft paper.)

Koenig, J. A., & Leger, K. F. (1997). Test-taking behaviors and their impact on performance: A comparison of retest performance and test-preparation methods for MCAT examinees grouped by gender and race-ethnicity. *Academic Medicine, 72* (10), S100-S102.

Koenig, J. A., Sireci, S. G., & Wiley, A. (1998). Evaluating the predictive validity of MCAT scores across diverse applicant groups. *Academic Medicine, 73* (10), 1095–1106.

Kowarsky, J. A. (1997). *University of California follow-up analyses of the 1996 CPEC eligibility study.* Oakland, CA: University of California Office of the President Student Academic Services.

Kuncel, N. R., Campbell, J. P., & Ones, D. S. (1998). Validity of the Graduate Record Examination: Estimated or tacitly known? [Comment on Sternberg & Williams]. *American Psychologist, 53* (5), 567–568.

Kuncel, N. R., Hezlett, S. A., & Ones, D. S. (1998). *The predictive validity of the Graduate Record Examinations: A meta-analysis.* Paper presented at the 13th annual conference of the society for Industrial and Organizational Psychology, Dallas, TX.

Langfitt, F. (2000, July 11). China's make or break exam. *The Baltimore Sun,* p. 2A.

Law School Admission Council (1999). *LSAT & LSDAS registration information book.* Newtown, PA: Author.

Leary, L. F., & Wightman, L. E. (1983). *Estimating the relationship between use of test-preparation methods and scores on the Graduate Management Admission Test* (ETS Research Report 83–22). Princeton, NJ: Educational Testing Service.

Leatherman, C. (2000, Dec. 4). California study finds racial disparities in granting of extra time on SAT. *Chronicle of Higher Education,* N5.

Legg, S. M., & Buhr, D. C. (1992). Computerized adaptive testing with different groups. *Educational Measurement: Issues and Practice, 11* (2), 23–27.

Legum, S., Caldwell, N., Davis, B., Haynes, J., Hill, T. J., Litavecz, S., Rizzo, L., Rust, K., & Vo, N. (1998). *The 1994 high school transcript study tabulation: Comparative data on credits earned and demographics for 1994, 1990, 1987, and 1982 high school graduates* (Revised, NCES 98–532). Washington, DC: National Center for Education Statistics.

Lemann, N. (1995, Aug.). The structure of success in America. *Atlantic Monthly,* pp. 41–60.

Lemann, N. (1999). *The big test: The secret history of the American meritocracy.* New York: Farrar, Strauss, and Giroux.

Lempert, R. O., & Adams, T. K. (1998). *Doing well and doing good: The careers of minority and white graduates of the University of Michigan Law School 1970–1996.* University of Michigan. Retrieved from the World Wide Web: http://www.law.umich.edu.

Leonard, D., & Jiang, J. (1999). Gender bias and the college prediction of the SATs: A cry of despair. *Research in Higher Education, 40* (4), 375–408.

Leonhardt, D. (2000, May 24). On testing for common sense. *New York Times,* C1, C9.

Lewis, C., & Thayer, D. T. (1998). *The power of the K–index (or PMIR) to detect copying* (ETS Research Report 98–49). Princeton, NJ: Educational Testing Service.

Lewis, C., & Willingham, W. W. (1995). *The effects of sample restriction on gender differences* (ETS Research Report 95–13). Princeton, NJ: Educational Testing Service.

Linn, R. L. (1983). Predictive bias as an artifact of selection procedures. In H. Wainer & S. Messick (Ed.), *Principals of modern psychological measurement: A Festschrift for Frederic M. Lord* (pp. 27–40). Hillsdale, NJ: Lawrence Erlbaum Associates.

Linn, R. L. (1990). Admissions testing: Recommended uses, validity, differential prediction, and coaching. *Applied Measurement in Education, 3* (4), 297–318.

Linn, R. L. (1994). The education reform agenda: Assessment, standards, and the SAT. *College Board Review,* pp. 22–25, 30.

Linn, R. L. (1999). Implications of standard-based reform for admissions testing. In S. J. Messick (Ed.), *Assessment in higher education: Issues of access, quality, student development, and public policy* (pp. 73–90). Mahwah, NJ: Lawrence Erlbaum Associates.

Linn, R. L., & Dragsow, F. (1987). Implications of the Golden Rule settlement for test construction. *Educational Measurement: Issues and Practice, 6 (2),* 13–17.

Loveless, P. (2000). *Does self-stereotyping affect performance on the ACT assessment?* (ACT Research Report 2000–6). Iowa city, IA: ACT, Inc.

Madaus, G. (1990, Sept. 5). Standardized testing needs a consumer-protection agency. *Chronicle of Higher Education.* Retrieved July 31, 1999, from the World Wide Web: http://www.chronicle.com.

Madaus, G. (2001). *A brief history of attempts to monitor testing* (NBETPP Statements, Vol. 1, No. 2). Boston: National Board of Educational Testing and Public Policy.

Madaus, G. F., Raczek, A. E., & Thomas, S. (1999). Performance assessment and issues of differential impact: The British experience—lessons for America. In A. L. Nettles & M. T. Nettles (Ed.), *Measuring up: Challenges minorities face in educational assessment* (pp. 137–165). Boston: Kluwer Academic.

Mandinach, E. B. (2000, Apr.). *Flagging: Policies, perceptions, and practices.* Paper presented at the annual meeting of the American Educational Research Association, New Orleans, LA.

Mandinach, E. B., Cahalan, C., & Camara, W. J. (2001, Apr.). *The impact of flagging on the admissions process: Policies, practices, and implications.* Paper presented at the annual meeting of the American Educational Research Association, Seattle, WA.

Mangan, K. S. (1998, May 11). Law-school council says access to LSAT courses is unrelated to racial disparity in scores. *Chronicle of Higher Education.* Retrieved May 23, 2000, from the World Wide Web: http://www.chronicle.com.

Mangan, K., Heller, S., & Wheeler, D. L. (1999, Oct. 15). Dean of Texas law school that was focus of Hopwood resigns. *Chronicle of Higher Education,* A14.

Mann, J. (1997, Mar. 26). *SAT fails the bias test again. Washington Post.* Retrieved June 2, 1999, from the World Wide Web: http://www.inform.umd.edu.

Manski, C. F., & Wise, S. A. (1983). *College choice in America.* Cambridge, MA: Harvard University Press.

Marco, G. L. (1988). Does the use of test assembly procedures proposed in legislation make any difference in test properties and in the test performance of Black and White test takers? *Applied Measurement in Education, 1* (2), 109–133.

Marcus, A. D. (1999, Aug. 31). New weights can alter SAT scores: Family is factor in determining who's a 'striver'. *Wall Street Journal,* pp. B1, B8.

Mariantes, L. (1999, Nov. 2). Exploring alternatives to the SAT. *Christian Science Monitor.* Retrieved Nov. 1, 1999 from the World Wide Web: http://www. csmonitor.com.

Marks, P. (2000, Mar. 18). Bush TV ad attacks Gore, who swiftly answers back. *New York Times,* p. A9.

McAllister, P. H. (1991). Overview of state legislation to regulate standardized testing. *Educational Measurement: Issues and Practice, 10* (4), 19–22.

McBride, J. R. (1997). Technical perspective. In W. A. Sands, B. K. Waters, & J. R. McBride (Ed.), *Computerized adaptive testing: From inquiry to operation* (pp. 29–44). Washington, DC: American Psychological Association.

McBride, J. R. (1998). Innovations in computer-based ability testing: Promise, problems, and perils. In M. D. Hakel (Ed.), *Beyond multiple choice: Evaluating alternatives to traditional testing for selection* (pp. 23–39). Mahwah, NJ: Lawrence Erlbaum Associates.

McClelland, D. C. (1973). Testing for competence rather than intelligence. *American Psychologist, 28,* 1–14.

McClelland, D. C. (1994). The knowledge-testing-educational complex strikes back. *American Psychologist, 49* (1), 66–69.

McWhorter, J. H. (2000). *Losing the race: Self sabotage in Black America.* New York: Free Press.

Meehl, P. E. (1954). *Clinical versus statistical prediction.* Minneapolis, MN: University of Minnesota Press.

Mehrens, W. A. (1989). Using test scores for decision making. In B. R. Gifford (Ed.), *Test policy and test performance: Education, language, and culture* (pp. 93–114). Boston: Kluwer Academic.

Messick, S. (1980). *The effectiveness of coaching for the SAT: Review and reanalysis of research from the fifties to the FTC.* Princeton, NJ: Educational Testing Service.

Messick, S. (1988). The once and future issues of validity: Assessing the meaning and consequence of measurement. In H. Wainer & H. I. Braun (Ed.), *Test Validity* (pp. 33–45). Hillsdale, NJ: Lawrence Erlbaum Associates.

Mills, C. N. & Steffen, M. (2000). The GRE computer adaptive test: Operational issues. In W. Van der Linden & C. A. W. Glas (Ed.), *Computerized adaptive testing: Theory and practice (pp. 75–99).* Dordrecht, The Netherlands: Kluwer Academic.

Missouri ex rel. Gaines v. Canada, 305 U. S. 337 (1938).

Mitchell, J. S. (1998, May 27). SAT's don't get you in. *Education Week,* 33–34.

Miyazaki, I. (1976). *China's examination hell: The civil service examinations of Imperial China* (1st ed.). New York: Weatherhill.

Nakanishi, D. T. (1989, Nov/Dec). A quota on excellence. *Change, 21,* 38–47.

Nardi, W. M. (1992). *The origins of Educational Testing Service.* Princeton, NJ: Educational Testing Service.

National Center for Education Statistics. (1998). *Digest of education statistics 1998.* U. S. Department of Education. Retrieved Dec. 1999, from the World Wide Web: http://nces.ed.gov.

National Center for Education Statistics (2000). *Digest of education statistics 1999* (NCES 2000–031). Washington, DC: U. S. Department of Education.

National Commission on Testing and Public Policy. (1990). *From gatekeeper to gateway: Transforming testing in America.* Chestnut Hill, MA: Author.

Neeff, A. S. (1986, Dec. 5). *Chronology of developmental changes in the SAT* (ETS internal document). Princeton, NJ: Educational Testing Service.

Neter, J., Kutner, M., Nachtsheim, C., & Wassermann, W. (1996). *Applied linear regression models* (3d ed.). Chicago: Richard D. Irwin.

Nettles, A. L., & Nettles, M. T. (1999). Introduction: Issuing the challenge. In A. L. Nettles & M. T. Nettles (Ed.), *Measuring up: Challenges minorities face in educational assessment* (pp. 1–11). Boston: Kluwer Academic.

Nix, D. (1996, spring/summer). The LSAT and affirmative action in U. S. law schools. *Mankind Quarterly, 21* (3,4), 335–361.

Noble, J. P. (2000, Oct. 16). *Non-race-based admissions decisions using ACT composite scores and/or high school grade averages.* (ACT draft report). Iowa City, IA: ACT, Inc.

Noble, J. P. (1991). *Predicting college grades from ACT assessment scores and high school course work and grade information* (ACT Research Report 91–3). Iowa City, IA: American College Testing Program.

Office for Civil Rights. (Apr., 1999). *Nondiscrimination in high-stakes testing: A resource guide* (draft). Washington, DC: U.S. Department of Education.

Office for Civil Rights. (Dec., 2000). *The use of tests when making high-stakes decisions for students: A resource guide for educators and policymakers.* Author. Retrieved July 1, 2001, from the World Wide Web: http://www.ed.gov/ocr.

Office of Technology Assessment. (1992). *Testing in American schools: Asking the right questions*. Washington, DC: U.S. Government Printing Office.

Olson, L. (1985, Oct. 30). Rights of test-takers will be monitored by 'FairTest' group. *Education Week*. Retrieved Nov. 6, 1999, from the World Wide Web: http://www.edweek.com.

Oltman, P. K., Bejar, I. I., & Kim, S. H. (1993). An approach to automated scoring of architectural designs. In U. Fleming & S. Van Wyk (Ed.), *CAAD Futures '93* (pp. 215–224). Elsevier Science Publishers B.V.

O'Neill, K. A., & McPeek, W. M. (1993). Item and test characteristics that are associated with differential item functioning. In P. W. Holland & H. Wainer (Ed.), *Differential item functioning* (pp. 255–276). Hillsdale, NJ: Lawrence Erlbaum Associates.

Orlofsky, G. F., & Olson, L. (2001, Jan. 11). The state of the states. (Special Issue: Quality Counts). *Education Week*, pp. 86–193.

Owings, J., McMillen, M., & Burkett, J. (1995). *Making the cut: Who meets highly selective college entrance criteria?* (NCES 95–732). National Center for Education Statistics. Retrieved Aug. 18, 1999, from the World Wide Web: http://www.nces.ed.gov.

Pask, G., & Scott, B. C. E. (1972). Learning strategies and individual competence. *International Journal of Man-Machine Studies, 4,* 217–253.

Pennock-Román, M. (1990). *Test validity and language background: A study of Hispanic American students at six universities*. New York: College Entrance Examination Board.

Pennock-Román, M. (1994). *College major and gender differences in the prediction of college grades* (College Board Report 94–2). New York: College Entrance Examination Board.

Perry, J. (1999, Aug. 30). Test-prep flap: Are costly cramming courses a waste of money? *U. S. News & World Report*. Retrieved Aug. 19, 1999, from the World Wide Web: http://www.usnews.com.

Peterson, J. J. (1983). *The Iowa testing programs*. Iowa City, IA: Iowa University Press.

Plessy v. Ferguson, 163 U. S. 537 (1896).

Ponessa, J. (1996, Jan. 10). Court backs test-taker in suit against ETS. *Education Week*. Retrieved June 12, 2001, from the World Wide Web://www.edweek.com.

Powell, B., & Steelman, L. C. (1996). Bewitched, bothered, and bewildering: The use and misuse of state SAT and ACT scores. *Harvard Educational Review, 66,* 27–55.

Powers, D. E. (1983). *Effects of coaching on GRE aptitude test scores* (GRE Board Report 83–7). Princeton, NJ: Graduate Record Examinations Board.

Powers, D. E. (1986a). *Effects of test preparation on the validity of GRE analytical scores* (ETS Research Report 86–22). Princeton, NJ: Educational Testing Service.

Powers, D. E. (1986b). *Test preparation for the GRE analytical ability measure: Differential effects for subgroups of GRE test takers* (ETS Research Report 86–40). Princeton, NJ: Educational Testing Service.

Powers, D. E. (2001). Comment: Using National Education Longitudinal Study (NELS) data to evaluate the effects of commercial test preparation. *Chance, 14* (1), 19–21.

Powers, D., & O'Neill, K. (1993). Inexperienced and anxious computer users: Coping with a computer-administered test of academic skills. *Educational Assessment, 1* (2), 153–173.

Powers, D. E., & Rock, D. A. (1999). Effects of coaching on SAT I: Reasoning Test scores. *Journal of Educational Measurement, 36* (2), 93–118.

Powers, D. L., & Swinton, S. S. (1984). Effects of self-study for coachable test item types. *Journal of Educational Psychology, 76* (2), 266–278.

The Princeton Review. (1997, Apr.). *The best college for you*. Time/The Princeton Review. Retrieved Apr. 1997, from the World Wide Web: www.review.com.

The Princeton Review. (1998, Nov. 30). *The Princeton Review responds to College Board's report on SAT coaching*. Author. Retrieved Sept. 21, 1999, from the World Wide Web: http://www.review.com.

The Princeton Review. (1999). *The Princeton Review GMAT course*. Author. Retrieved July 10, 1999, from the World Wide Web: http://www.review.com.

The Princeton Review. (1999, Sept. 1). *The Princeton Review says ETS' new "Striver" program confirms that SAT should be eliminated*. Author. Retrieved Oct. 27, 1999, from the World Wide Web: http://www.review.com.

The Princeton Review. (2000, Jan. 31). *President Clinton proposes government-funded SAT prep for low-income students*. Author. Retrieved May 22, 2000, from the World Wide Web: http://www.review.com.

Pulley, J. L. (2000, June 23). A $1-billion experiment seeks a new way to identify talented minority students. *Chronicle of Higher Education*, A42.

Ramist, L., Lewis, C., & McCamley–Jenkins, L. (1994). *Student group differences in predicting college grades: Sex, language, and ethnic groups* (College Board Report 93–1). New York: College Entrance Examination Board.

Ramist, L., Lewis, C., & McCamley–Jenkins, L. (1999). *Using Achievement Tests/SAT II Subject Tests to demonstrate achievement and predict college grades: Sex, language, ethnic, and parental education groups* (draft report). Princeton, NJ: Educational Testing Service.

Raspberry, W. (1999, Aug. 31). College admissions not a black-and-white issue. *Austin American-Statesman*, A9.

Ravitch, D. (1996. Aug. 28). *Defining literacy downward.* Thomas B. Fordham Foundation. Retrieved July 4, 1999, from the World Wide Web: http://www.edexcellence.net.

Rebell, M. A. (1986). Disparate impact of teacher competency testing on minorities: Don't blame the test-takers—or the tests. *Yale Law and Policy Review, 4*, 375.

Rebell, M. A. (1989). Testing, public policy, and the courts. In B. R. Gifford (Ed.), *Test policy and the politics of opportunity allocation: The workplace and the law* (pp. 135–162). Boston: Kluwer Academic.

Regents of the University of California v. Bakke, 438 U. S. 265 (1978).

Reisberg, L. (1998, Jan. 23). Girls' scores on PSAT rise slightly, but critics aren't appeased. *Chronicle of Higher Education*, pp. A42.

Richardson, L. (1996, Oct. 29). Time-zone caper: Suspect is arrested in testing scheme. *New York Times*. Retrieved July 25, 1999, from the World Wide Web: http://www.nytimes.com.

Rigol, G. W. (1997, June). *Common sense about SAT score differences and test validity* (College Board Research Notes RN–01). New York: College Entrance Examination Board.

Rigol, G. W., & Kimmel, E. W. (1997, Nov.). *A picture of admissions in the United States.* New York: The College Board and Educational Testing Service.

Rock, D. A. (1974). *The prediction of doctorate attainment in psychology, mathematics and chemistry.* (GRE Board Report 69–6aR). Princeton, NJ: Educational Testing Service.

Rogers, H. J., & Kulick, E. (1987). An investigation of unexpected differences in item performance between Blacks and Whites taking the SAT. In A. P. Schmitt & N. J. Dorans (Ed.), *Differential item functioning on the Scholastic Aptitude Test* (ETS Research Memorandum No. 87–1). Princeton, NJ: Educational Testing Service.

Rooney, C. (1998). *Test scores do not equal merit: Enhancing equity & excellence in college admissions by deemphasizing SAT and ACT results.* Cambridge, MA: FairTest.

Rosser, P. (1989). *The SAT gender gap: Identifying the causes.* Washington, DC: Center for Women Policy Studies.

Ruch, G. M. (1925). Minimum essentials in reporting data on standard tests. *Journal of Educational Research, 12*, 349–358.

Ryan, A. M., & Greguras, G. G. (1998). Life is not multiple-choice: Reactions to the alternatives. In M. D. Hakel (Ed.), *Beyond multiple-choice: Evaluating alternatives to traditional testing for selection* (pp. 183–202). Mahwah, NJ: Lawrence Erlbaum Associates.

Sacks, P. (1997). Standardized testing: Meritocracy's crooked yardstick. *Change, 29*, 25–31.

Sacks, P. (1999). *Standardized minds.* Cambridge, MA: Perseus Books.

Sacks, P. (2001, June 8). How admissions tests hinder access to professional and graduate school. *Chronicle of Higher Education*, pp. B11-B12.

Sackett, P. R., Schmitt, N., Ellingson, J. E., & Kabin, M. B. (2001). High-stakes testing in employment, credentialing, and higher education. *American Psychologist, 56* (4), 302–318.

Sandham, J. L. (1999, Apr. 7). Exam-testing breaches put focus on security. *Education Week*. Retrieved Apr. 7, 1999, from the World Wide Web: http://www.educationweek.com.

Sarbin, T. R. (1942). A contribution to the study of actuarial and individual methods of prediction. *American Journal of Sociology, 48*, 593–602.

Saretzky, G. (1984). *Treatment of scores of questionable validity: The origins and development of the ETS Board of Review* (ETS Occasional Paper). Princeton, NJ: Educational Testing Service.

Saretzky, G. (1991, Feb. 6). *40 Years ago–The SSCQT* (LAN Bulletin No. 13, ETS Archives). Princeton, NJ: Educational Testing Service.

Saretzky, G. (1992, Sept. 1). *Return of the MCAT* (Bulletin No. 57, ETS Archives). Princeton, NJ: Educational Testing Service

Schaeffer, R. (2000, Feb. 19). Who wants to be a contestant? *New York Times*, p. A29.

Schaeffer, G., Reese, C. M., Steffen, M., McKinley, R. L., & Mills, C. N. (1993, Apr.). *Field test of a computer-based GRE general test* (GRE Board Professional Report 88–08P). Princeton, NJ: Graduate Record Examinations Board.

Schemo, D. J. (2001, Feb. 17). Head of U. of California seeks to end SAT use in admissions. *New York Times*, pp. A1, A11.

Schemo, D. J. (2001, June 27). Foe of affirmative action is chosen for rights post. *New York Times*, p. A18.

Schmitt, A. P. (1987). Unexpected differential item performance of Hispanic examinees. In A. P. Schmitt & N. J. Dorans (Ed.), *Differential item functioning on the Scholastic Aptitude Test* (ETS Research Memorandum No. 87–1). Princeton, NJ: Educational Testing Service.

Schmitt, A. P. & Dorans, N. J. (1988). Differential item functioning for minority examinees on the SAT (ETS Research Report 88–32). Princeton, NJ: Educational Testing Service.

Schmotter, J. W. (1993). The Graduate Management Admission Council: A brief history 1953–1992. *Selections*, *9* (2), 1–11.

Scholes, R. J., & McCoy, T. R. (1998, Apr.). *The effects of type, length, and content of test preparation activities on ACT assessment scores.* Paper presented at the annual meeting of the American Educational Research Association, San Diego, CA.

Schneider, L. M., & Briel, J. B. (1990). *Validity of the GRE: 1988–89 summary report.* Princeton, NJ: Educational Testing Service.

Schrader, W. B. (1978). *Admissions test scores as predictors of career achievement in psychology* (GRE Board Report 76–1R). Graduate Record Examinations Board.

Schrader, W. B. (1980). *GRE scores as predictors of career achievement in history* (GRE Board Report 76–1bR). Princeton, NJ: Graduate Record Examinations Board.

Schwartz, T. (1999, Jan. 10). The test under stress. *New York Times Magazine*, pp. 30–35, 51, 56, 63.

Sedlacek, W. E. (1998, Winter). Multiple choices for standardized tests. *Priorities, 10,* 1–15.

Sedlacek, W. E. (1999). *An alternative to standardized tests in postsecondary admissions.* University of Maryland. Retrieved Aug. 31, 1999, from the World Wide Web: http://www.inform.umd.edu.

Selingo, J. (2000, June 2). What states aren't saying about the 'X-Percent' solution. *Chronicle of Higher Education*, A31–A34.

Selingo, J. (2000, July 21). Judge clears Fla. plan on affirmative action. *Chronicle of Higher Education*, A23.

Sellman, W. S. & Arabian, J. M. (1997). Foreword. In W. A. Sands, B. K. Waters, & J. R. McBride (Ed.), *Computerized adaptive testing: From inquiry to operation* (pp. xv–xvii). Washington, DC: American Psychological Association.

Shih, M., Pittinsky, T. L., & Ambady, N. (1999). Identity salience and shifts in quantitative performance. *Psychological Science, 10,* 80–83.

Skager, R. (1982). On the use and importance of tests of ability in admission to postsecondary education. In A. K. Wigdor & W. R. Garner (Ed.), *Ability testing: Uses, consequences, and controversies* (pp. 286–314). Washington, DC: National Academy Press.

Smyth, F. L. (1995). Standardized testing in college admission: How the ACT and the SAT are used and compared. *Journal of College Admission, 148,* 24–31.

Snow, R. E. (1999). Commentary: Expanding the breadth and depth of admissions testing. In S. J. Messick (Ed.), *Assessment in higher education: Issues of access, quality, student development, and public policy* (pp. 133–140). Mahwah, NJ: Lawrence Erlbaum Associates.

Snyder, T. D., & Hoffman, C. M. (2000). *Digest of education statistics 1999* (NCES 2000–031). Washington, DC: National Center for Education Statistics.

Snyder, T. D., Hoffman, C. M., & Geddes, C. M. (1997). *Digest of education statistics, 1997* (NCES 98–015). Washington, DC: National Center for Education Statistics.

Sommers, C. H. (2000, May). The war against boys. *Atlantic Monthly*, pp.59–74.

Steele, C. M. (1997). A threat in thin air: How stereotypes shape intellectual identity and performance. *American Psychologist, 52* (6), 613–629.

Steele, C. M. (1999, Aug.). Thin ice: "Stereotype threat" and Black college students. *Atlantic Monthly*. Retrieved Sept. 19, 1999, from the World Wide Web: http://www.theatlantic.com

Steele, C. M., & Aronson, J. (1995). Stereotype threat and the intellectual performance of African Americans. *Journal of Personality and Social Psychology, 69,* 797–811.

Steele, C. M., & Aronson, J. (1998). Stereotype threat and the test performance of academically successful African Americans. In C. Jencks & M. Phillips (Ed.), *The Black–White test score gap* (pp. 401–427). Washington, DC: Brookings Institution Press.

Steele, S. (2001, Feb. 7). X-percent plans: After preferences, more race games. *National Review,* pp. 22, 24.

Steinberg, J. (1999, Sept. 15). Idea of rewarding 'strivers' is opposed by College Board. *New York Times,* p. B10.

Sternberg, R. J. (1991). Cognitive theory and psychometrics. In R. K. Hambleton & J. N. Zaal (Ed.), *Advances in educational and psychological testing* (pp. 367–394). Boston: Kluwer Academic.

Sternberg, R. J., & Williams, W. M. (1997). Does the Graduate Record Examination predict meaningful success in the graduate training of psychologists? *American Psychologist, 52* (6), 630–641.

Stewart, D. M. (1998, Jan. 25). *Why Hispanic students need to take the SAT.* The College Board. Retrieved Apr. 4, 1999, from the World Wide Web: http://www.collegeboard.org

Stocking, M. L., Swanson, L., & Pearlman, M. (1991). *Automatic item selection (AIS) methods in the ETS testing environment* (ETS Research Memorandum 91–5). Princeton, NJ: Educational Testing Service.

Stricker, L. J. (1998). *Inquiring about examinees' ethnicity and sex: Effects on AP Calculus AB examination performance* (College Board Report 98–1). New York: College Entrance Examination Board.

Stricker, L. J., & Ward, W. C. (1998). *Inquiring about examinees' ethnicity and sex: Effects on Computerized Placement Tests performance* (College Board Report 98–2). New York: College Entrance Examination Board.

Stricker, L. J., Rock, D. A., & Burton, N. W. (1993). Sex differences in predictions of college grades from Scholastic Aptitude Test scores. *Journal of Educational Psychology, 85* (4), 710–718.

Stricker, L. J., Rock, D. A., Burton, N. W., Muraki, E., & Jirele, T. J. (1994). Adjusting college grade point average criteria for variations in grading standards: A comparison of methods. *Journal of Applied Psychology, 79* (2), 178–183.

Strosnider, K. (1996, Nov. 8). Man charged with putting answers to tests on pencils. *Chronicle of Higher Education,* A38.

Sturm, S., & Guinier, L. (2000, Dec./2001, Jan.). The future of affirmative action. *Boston Review.* Retrieved May 21, 2001, from the World Wide Web: http://www.bostonreview.mit.edu.

Sun, T. C.-C. (1997). *The admission dispute: Asian Americans versus University of California at Berkeley.* Lanham, MD: University Press of America.

Sweatt v. Painter, 339 U. S. 629 (1950).

Swinton, S. S., & Powers, D. E. (1983). A study of the effects of special preparation on GRE analytical scores and item types. *Journal of Educational Psychology, 75* 104–115.

Thayer, P. W., & Kalat, J. K. (1998). Questionable criteria [Comment on Sternberg and Williams]. *American Psychologist, 53* (5), 566–567.

Thernstrom, A. (1999, Sept. 27). The end of meritocracy: Should the SAT account for race? No. *The New Republic,* pp. 27, 29.

Toch, T., & Walthall, M. (1997, Sept. 1). The test of merit fails that standard. *U.S. News & World Report.* Retrieved May 27, 1999 from the World Wide Web: http://www.usnews.com.

Tracey, T. J., & Sedlacek, W. E. (1984). Noncognitive variables in predicting academic success by race. *Measurement and Evaluation in Guidance, 16* (4), 171–178.

Turnbull, W. W. (1985). *Student change, program change: Why SAT scores kept falling* (College Board Report 85–2). Princeton, NJ: Educational Testing Service.

Vars, F. E., & Bowen, W. G. (1998). Scholastic Aptitude Test scores, race, and academic performance in selective colleges and universities. In C. Jencks & M. Phillips (Ed.), *The Black–White test score gap* (pp. 457–479). Washington, DC: Brookings Institution Press.

Vispoel, W. P., Wang, T., & Bleiler, T. (1997). Computerized adaptive and fixed-item testing of music listening skill: A comparison of efficiency, precision, and concurrent validity. *Journal of Educational Measurement, 34,* 43–63.

Wainer, H. (1989). Eelworms, bullet holes, and Geraldine Ferraro: Some problems with statistical adjustment and some solutions. *Journal of Educational Statistics, 14* (2), 121–140.

Wainer, H. (1990). Introduction and history. In H. Wainer (Ed.), *Computerized adaptive testing: A primer* (pp. 1–21). Hillsdale, NJ: Lawrence Erlbaum Associates.

Wainer, H. (1993). Does spending money on education help? A reaction to the Heritage Foundation and the Wall Street Journal. *Educational Researcher, 22* (9) 22–24.

Walfish, D. (2001, Feb. 4). ETS sues exam-coaching school in China, charging theft of test questions. *Chronicle of Higher Education.* Retrieved Feb. 6, 2001, from the World Wide Web: http://www.chronicle.com.

Washington Initiative Measure 200, Wash. Rev. Code § 49.60.400(1).

Webber, C. (1989). The mandarin mentality: University admissions testing in Europe and Asia. In B. R. Gifford (Ed.), *Test policy and the politics of opportunity allocation: The workplace and the law* (pp. 33–57). Boston: Kluwer Academic.

Weinig, K. M. (2000, June 14). The 10 worst educational disasters of the 20th Century: A traditionalist's list. *Education Week,* pp. 31, 34.

Weiss, K. R. (1998, July 17). UC regents decry but keep entrance favors. *Los Angeles Times,* pp. A3, A23.

Weiss, K. R. (2000, Jan. 9). New test-taking skill: Working the system. *Los Angeles Times.* Retrieved Dec. 20, 2000, from the World Wide Web: http://www.latimes. com

Weissert, W. (1999, Dec. 17). NAACP urges support for test-prep courses for minority students. *Chronicle of Higher Education,* A34.

Weissglass, J. (1998, Apr. 15). The SAT: Public-spirited or preserving privilege? *Education Week.* Retrieved Aug. 15, 1999 from the World Wide Web: http://www.edweek.com.

Wiggins, N., & Kohen, E. S. (1971). Man vs. model of man revisited: The forecasting of graduate school success. *Journal of Personality and Social Psychology, 19,* 100–106.

Wightman, L. F. (1993). *Test takers with disabilities: A summary of data from special administrations of the LSAT* (LSAC Research Report 93–03). Newtown, PA: Law School Admission Council.

Wightman, L. F. (1994). *Analysis of LSAT performance and patterns of application for male and female law applicants* (LSAC Research Report 94–02). Newtown, PA: Law School Admission Council.

Wightman, L. F. (1997, Apr.). The threat to diversity in legal education: An empirical analysis of the consequences of abandoning race as a factor in law school admission decisions. *New York University Law Review, 72,* 1–53.

Wightman, L. F., & Jaeger, R. M. (1998). *High stakes and ubiquitous presence: An overview and comparison of the ACT assessment program and the SAT program.* Paper presented at the National Academy of Sciences Workshop on the Role of Tests in Higher Education Admissions, Washington, DC.

Wightman, L. E., & Leary, L. F. (1985). *GMAC validity study service: A three-year summary.* Princeton, NJ: Graduate Management Admission Council.

Wightman, L. F., & Muller, D. G. (1990). *Comparison of LSAT performance among selected subgroups* (Law School Admission Council Statistical Report 90–01). Newtown, PA: Law School Admission Council.

Wiley, A., & Koenig, J. A. (1996). Undergraduate performance assessment and prediction: The validity of the Medical College Admission Test for predicting performance in the first two years of medical school. *Academic Medicine, 71* (10), S83-S85.

Wilgoren, J. (2000, Feb. 25). Cheating on statewide tests is reported in Massachusetts. *New York Times,* A14.

Willingham, W. W. (1974). Predicting success in graduate education. *Science, 183,* 273–278.

Willingham, W. W. (1985). *Success in college: The role of personal qualities and academic ability.* New York: College Entrance Examination Board.

Willingham, W. W. (1989). Standard testing conditions and standard score meaning for handicapped examinees. *Applied Measurement in Education, 2* (2), 97–103.

Willingham, W. W. (1998). *Validity in college selection: Context and evidence.* Paper presented at the National Academy of Sciences Workshop on the Role of Tests in Higher Education Admissions, Washington, DC.

Willingham, W. W. (1999). A systemic view of test fairness. In S. J. Messick (Ed.), *Assessment in higher education: Issues of access, quality, student development, and public policy* (pp. 213–242). Mahwah, NJ: Lawrence Erlbaum Associates.

Willingham, W., & Cole, N. (1997). *Gender and fair assessment.* Mahwah, NJ: Lawrence Erlbaum Associates.

Willingham, W. W., Cole, N. S., Lewis, C. & Leung, S. W. (1997). Test performance. In W. W. Willingham & N. Cole (Ed.), *Gender and Fair Assessment* (pp. 55–126). Mahwah, NJ: Lawrence Erlbaum Associates.

Willingham, W. W., Pollack, J. M., & Lewis, C. (2000). *Grades and test scores: Accounting for observed differences* (ETS Research Report 00–15). Princeton, NJ: Educational Testing Service.

Willingham, W. W., Ragosta, M., Bennett, R. E., Braun, H., Rock, D. A., & Powers, D. E. (1988). *Testing handicapped people.* Boston: Allyn and Bacon, Inc.

Winterbottom, J. A. (1995). *A historical survey of test development in the Law School Admission Test program 1947–1978* (Report in ETS Archives). Princeton, NJ: Educational Testing Service.

Yablon, M. (2000, Oct. 30). Test flight: The real reason colleges are abandoning the SAT. *The New Republic,* pp. 24–25.

Young, J. W. (1991). Improving the prediction of college performance of ethnic minorities using the IRT-based GPA. *Applied Measurement in Education,* 4 (3), 229–239.

Young, J. W. (2000, July). *Differential validity, differential prediction, and college admissions testing: A comprehensive review and analysis* (draft, College Board Research Monograph No. 12). New York: The College Board.

Ziomek, R. L., & Andrews, K. M. (1996). *Predicting the college grade point averages of special-tested students from their ACT assessment scores and high school grades.* (ACT Research Report 96–7). Iowa City, IA: ACT, Inc.

Zwick, R. (1990). *The validity of the GMAT for the prediction of success in doctoral study in business and management* (ETS Research Report 90–24). Princeton, NJ: Educational Testing Service.

Zwick, R. (1991). *An analysis of graduate school careers in three universities: Differences in attainment patterns across academic programs and demographic groups.* (ETS Research Report 91–17). Princeton, NJ: Educational Testing Service.

Zwick, R. (1993). The validity of the GMAT for the prediction of grades in doctoral study in business and management: An empirical Bayes approach. *Journal of Educational Statistics,* *18* (1), 91–107.

Zwick, R. (1999, Dec.). Eliminating standardized tests in college admissions: The new affirmative action? *Phi Delta Kappan,* pp. 320–324.

Zwick, R. (1999, Feb. 10). Backdoor affirmative action. *Education Week,* pp. 56, 35.

Zwick, R. (2000). An assessment of differential item functioning in computer adaptive tests. In W. Van der Linden & C. A. W. Glas (Ed.) *Computerized adaptive testing: Theory and practice* (pp. 221–244). Dordrecht, The Netherlands: Kluwer Academic.

Zwick, R. (2000, Sept. 3). College admissions: Moving the bar (Commentary). *Santa Barbara News-Press,* pp. G1-G2.

Zwick, R. (2001, March/April). What causes the test-score gap in higher education? Perspectives on the Office for Civil Rights resource guide on high-stakes testing. *Change,* pp.33–37.

Zwick, R. (2001, Summer). Making the grade: The SAT versus the GPA. *National CrossTalk,* p. 10.

Zwick, R., Donoghue, J. R. & Grima, A. (1993). Assessment of differential item functioning for performance tasks. *Journal of Educational Measurement,* 30, 233–251.

Zwick, R., & Ercikan, K. (1989). Analysis of differential item functioning in the NAEP history assessment. *Journal of Educational Measurement,* 26, 55–66.

Zwick, R., & Schlemer, L. (2000). *SAT validity for linguistic minorities* (draft report). Santa Barbara, CA: University of California, Santa Barbara.

AUTHOR INDEX

SUBJECT INDEX